Sensitive Trade

The Perspective of European States

P.I.E. Peter Lang

Bruxelles · Bern · Berlin · Frankfurt am Main · New York · Oxford · Wien

Quentin MICHEL (ed.)

Sensitive Trade

The Perspective of European States

NON-PROLIFERATION
n° 5

Support of the Federal Ministry of Foreign Affairs of the Kingdom of Belgium and Wallonie-Bruxelles International for the funding and organisation of the conference held in Chaudfontaine (September 2010) under the aegis of the Belgian Presidency of the Council of the European Union.

ÉDITIONS SCIENTIFIQUES INTERNATIONALES
Brussels, 2011
1 avenue Maurice, 1050 Brussels, Belgium
info@peterlang.com; www.peterlang.com

Printed in Germany

ISSN 1377-0608
ISBN 978-90-5201-775-4
D/2011/5678/53

Sensitive trade : the perspective of European states / Quentin Michel (ed.).
p. cm. -- (Non-proliferation ; no. 5)
Includes bibliographical references. ISBN 978-90-5201-775-4
1. Nuclear nonproliferation--Government policy--European Union countries.
2. Nuclear industry--Government policy--European Union countries.
3. Export controls--European Union countries. I. Michel, Quentin.
JZ5675.S49 2011 327.1'747094--dc23 2011032235

CIP also available from the British Library, GB

Bibliographic information published by "Die Deutsche Nationalbibliothek"
"Die Deutsche Nationalbibliothek" lists this publication in the "Deutsche Nationalbibliografie"; detailed bibliographic data is available in the Internet at <http://dnb.de>.

Disclaimer

The views and opinions expressed in this book do not represent those of the institutions the authors may be working for. The authors hereby present, discuss and express their views on the legislations and practices of European States only in their scientific capacities.

Acknowledgement

The director would like to express his gratitude to the Federal Ministry of Foreign Affairs of the Kingdom of Belgium and Wallonie-Bruxelles International for their support in the funding and organisation of the seminar held in Chaudfontaine under the aegis of the Belgian Presidency of the Council of the European Union, second semester 2010.

His gratitude goes also to the European Commission, to the services of the Personal Representative on Non-Proliferation of WMD and the European Parliament for their active contribution to the debates held during the seminar.

To the persons who have contributed to the success of the seminar and the realisation of this book, notably Virginie and Emily.

And the participants and authors of the following contributions, as well as Sandro Zero for sharing his experience.

May this only be the beginning.

Contents

Introduction

Quentin MICHEL

Professor, European Studies Unit, Université de Liège

Since the beginning of the 1990s, the fight against the proliferation of weapons of mass destruction has become one of the most widely discussed topics by the international community. Different attempts to breach the non-proliferation commitments have shown, on one hand, that the threat has not decreased and, on the other hand, that the strengthening of the trade controls was a necessity. Numerous efforts developed by the UN Security Council, in particular the adoption in 2004 of the Resolution 1540 enhancing the necessity for the States to establish effective domestic export and trans-shipment control regimes, have without a doubt amplified the obligation of the States to review their national trade control regimes.

In this respect, in the last ten years each of the five export control regimes has conducted a revision of its guidelines. One of the common elements of these reviews was to reconsider the proliferation responsibility of non-State actors. If terrorist groups have already been the focus of the debate, the role of industrial operators has been also raised. It was considered that the effectiveness of the fight against the proliferation of weapons of mass destruction (WMD) could no longer be provided only by national authorities. It should be therefore shared with industrial operators. Being at the frontline of information due to their contacts with customers, industrial operators are those who might be the first to appraise the potential risk of diversion of their exports. An unexpected requirement from an unusual industrial sector or an unusual end-use are the examples of elements that operators might be the first and the most accurate to detect.

Therefore, the *catch-all* provisions have been progressively introduced in different trade control regimes such as the Nuclear Supplier Group (NSG), the Missile Technology Control Regime (MTCR), the Wassenaar Arrangement (WA) and the Australia Group (AG). However only the AG and the WA have included principles extending the non-proliferation responsibility to the industrial operators. This trend is illustrated by so-called catch-all level 2 and 3 that require operators to inform their authorities in case they are aware or have grounds for suspecting that the items they intend to export might contribute to the elaboration of weapons of mass destruction. In order to face such new responsibility industrial operators have started to develop internal compliance programmes by establishing a network for information exchange between the different actors interfering with customers and deciding on the transactions (commercial, research and development, production).

The European Union was at the origin of the initiative to strengthen the responsibility of industrial operators. Since 1994 catch-all provisions have been included in the EU legislation and they have been regularly reviewed to extend their scope to transit and brokering activities and to encourage the role of operators in the fight against the proliferation of WMD. In the last revision of the Regulation adopted in 2009, the possibility for Member States to require exporters to establish an internal compliance program before applying for a global authorisation has been introduced.

Currently the EU has without exaggeration the most comprehensive system with regards to the responsibility of operators. Nevertheless, if European legislation appears to be quite advanced, it essentially focuses on the defining of the main principles to be implemented by Member States. For instance the possibility to constrain an exporter to inform the national authorities in case of suspicion of WMD-related activity remains optional and was actually put in practice by only a few Member States. Therefore, in order to have an entire picture of the EU approach, it is necessary to analyse each Member State's export control regime.

Considering that the full review of 27 legal systems risks being too lengthy and may not have much interest due to the fact that the EU legislation does not offer 27 possibilities to implement its provisions, a limited number of 14 countries have been selected to illustrate the range of possibilities.

Each contributor to this book was asked to describe his or her Member State's approach towards the implementation of the EU legal provisions, and therefore increasing the industrial operators' non-proliferation responsibility. Such Member State implementation can only be understood by considering it as one part of a national system, therefore, each contribution includes a comprehensive analysis of the Member States trade control regime.

This book is the first outcome of the Chaudfontaine Group, which convenes young researchers from 27 Member States to discuss and compare experiences related to strategic trade control issues. Different chapters constitute the written adaptations of presentations delivered during a two-day seminar organised in October 2010. Each contribution has been widely discussed by the group and does not reflect the official policies of Member States. It tends to present an independent and objective analysis of Member States' trade control regimes.

A New Role of Industrial Operators in Trade in an Evolving Nuclear Export Control[1] Regime

Beyond Legal Responsibilities?

Odette JANKOWITSCH-PREVOR

Independent Expert

Background

Industry has always been a principal actor – though not necessarily a visible one – in the development of the corpus of nuclear law in all its components. Industry was notably at the origin of the international instruments on civil liability for third party nuclear damage and of the development of international safety and security norms regulating the transport and physical protection of all nuclear material. The industrial operator is also the main addressee of nuclear safety related instruments and, as analysed in this paper, both a stakeholder, and an invisible and silent player in the international nuclear export control regime.

The non-proliferation norm since adoption of the Treaty on the Non-Proliferation of Nuclear Weapons in 1970 was always addressed exclusively to States. The NPT and its spin offs name only the sovereign State, Party to the Treaty and sole legislator of norms that are binding upon all physical and legal persons operating within its jurisdiction. The industrial operator, like any other stakeholder, is legally bound to comply with the legal regime set up by the State. This ground rule fully applies to trade in the nuclear field.

This paper attempts to look at an essential particularity of nuclear trade, namely the international export control regimes in the context of a rapidly changing industrial and non-proliferation environment. The approach is that of an issue paper focussing on questions that have

1 For a comprehensive analysis of the nuclear export control mechanism, see: Quentin Michel, "The Control of International Nuclear Trade – Difficult Balance between Trade Development and Non-proliferation of Nuclear Weapons", in *International Nuclear Law: History, Evolution and Outlook*, Nuclear Energy Agency, OECD 2010, p. 271-306.

recently been raised or that might be raised, however without any pretence to provide answers. The review may lead to tentative conclusions and more questions as to the possible emergence of a new role of industry, which may need to go beyond compliance with national laws and regulations as would be required of any other industrial operator. The analysis will focus briefly on the historical background and functioning of the nuclear export control regime(s) and its recent evolution, as a key to understanding present developments, and see to what extent new dimensions created by the globalization of the nuclear industry in the framework of the so-called nuclear renaissance may have direct consequences on the national export control regimes. The background to the globalisation is given by the unprecedented challenges to the non-proliferation regime. One of the underlying questions is how far can the scope of industry involvement change, and can it go beyond the frame of its legal obligations in light of a trade control approach that is essentially driven by non-proliferation concerns.

One aspect of this discussion is the growing disparity between the long-term trend of general expansion of trade and industry, the abolition of trade barriers and other obstacles, the liberalization rounds etc. for manufactured products, general industrial goods and services and, on the other hand, the increasing controls and other impediments to the free trade of the items, processes or technology directly or indirectly related to nuclear material, production of nuclear energy and even isotopes for industrial and medical uses. The global trade deregulation objective is opposed here to the concept of increasingly strict substantive and geopolitical trade regulation. In this context, the manufacturing industry is the clear beneficiary of the GATT's global achievements, whereas nuclear industry is more and more regulated by strengthened binding export control mechanisms and regimes. At the same time, it is more and more difficult to determine whether a given industrial item will belong for its end-user to the first or to the second category.

To characterize export control provisions that apply to nuclear trade as being essentially obstacles[2] to world trade would provide a much

---

[2] INFCIRC/539/Rev.3, 30 May 2005 including a paper entitled "The Nuclear Suppliers Group: Its Origins, Role and Activities": "The aim of the NSG Guidelines is to ensure that nuclear trade for peaceful purposes does not contribute to the proliferation of nuclear weapons or other nuclear explosive devices, and that international trade and cooperation in the nuclear field is not hindered unjustly in the process. The NSG Guidelines facilitate the development of trade in this area by providing the means whereby obligations to facilitate peaceful nuclear cooperation can be implemented in a manner consistent with international nuclear Non-proliferation norms"... Also INFCIRC/254/Rev.8/ Part 2 of July 2010 "The Guidelines are not designed to impede international co-operations as long as such co-operation will not contribute to a

more simplified but basically incorrect picture: in fact, the exporting State hosting the industrial operator undertakes a number of obligations based on the State's international non-proliferation commitments that are not aimed at hampering, but rather at facilitating this specific international trade and protecting the industrial operators' decision making. The desired effect of the export control law is to contribute to limiting political risks in addition to the general commercial risks. The State takes the prime responsibility for compliance with the binding international non-proliferation norm.

Whereas manufacturing industry has in general expanded and "globalized" in an almost linear manner over the last decades, overcoming nationalisation and privatisations alike, nuclear industry has rather unexpectedly "jump started" recently after several decades of stagnation, or even "lull". In a generous overview of "Emerging Nuclear Energy Countries", the World Nuclear Organisation[3] states that over 45 countries ranging from sophisticated economies to developing nations are actively considering embarking upon nuclear power programs. The IAEA in its Annual Report for 2009,[4] states that more than 60 countries – mostly in the developing world – have informed the Agency of their interest in considering or actively planning nuclear power programmes. The numerous and diverse factors that led to this, now termed "nuclear renaissance" are beyond the scope of this paper, but there is no doubt that their combined effects will bring about consequences that are of immediate relevance to the subject of export controls. This includes notably an expanded number, size and origin of industrial actors, state, private or mixed companies acting in the nuclear and other renewable energy sectors, a plurality of host and home States with their respective differing legal regimes and, an exponential expansion of trade in non-nuclear, nuclear, and dual-use items.

The Nuclear Export Control Regime: The Initial Construct

The concept and the adoption of an international nuclear export control regime followed the entry into force of the Treaty on the Non-Proliferation of Nuclear Weapons (NPT), 1970, thereby responding to the obligation created by the Treaty to devise means of implementing

---

nuclear explosive activity, an unsafeguarded nuclear fuel-cycle activity or acts of nuclear terrorism".

3 http://www.world-nuclear.org/info/inf192.html of 29 November 2010.

4 "2009 in Perspective". IAEA, Annual Report 2009 GC(54)/4 issued 2010, p. 1.

the provisions of Articles I[5] and III.2.[6] As of 1971, a group of fifteen States, Parties to the Treaty at that time, met in their capacity of suppliers or potential suppliers of nuclear material and equipment in order to reach an understanding on two essential matters: namely, the definition of the material and equipment described, but not further defined in Article III.2 of the NPT, and on the conditions and related procedures that would govern exports of such material and equipment, in order to meet the obligations of the Treaty on the basis of fair commercial competition.

It should be recalled here that the status of that group, known as the Zangger Committee[7] was and remains informal.

The Committee reached its first major consensus on basic rules to be applied to the supply of material. Two memoranda were issued on the export of source and special fissionable materials, and on exports of equipment and of non-nuclear material, respectively. The members of the Committee exchanged formal notes among themselves for declaring that the Committee's Undertakings would take effect by way of respective domestic control legislation. The members also individually notified the Director General of the IAEA of their decision to act in conformity with the provisions set out in the Undertaking and asking him to communicate this decision to all Member States of the IAEA.[8] The memorandum dealing with equipment became known as the "Trigger List": meaning that the export items enumerated on it triggered requirements for IAEA safeguards. Moreover, an Annex was attached to the Trigger List for further defining or clarifying the items described on it. Over time, several further clarifications[9] were added in light of technological developments and need for detail and precision. That Understanding also established three distinct conditions for the supply of nuclear

---

5 NPT Article I: "Each nuclear-weapon State Party to the Treaty undertakes not to transfer to any recipient whatsoever nuclear weapons or other nuclear explosive devices or control over such weapons or explosive devices directly, or indirectly; and not in any way to assist, encourage, or induce any non-nuclear weapon State to manufacture or otherwise acquire nuclear weapons or other nuclear explosive devices, or control over such weapons or explosive devices".

6 NPT Article III 2. "Each State Party to the Treaty undertakes not to provide: (a) source or special fissionable material, or (b) equipment or material especially designed or prepared for the processing, use or production of special fissionable material, to any non-nuclear weapon State for peaceful purposes, unless the source or special fissionable material shall be subject to the safeguards required in this Article".

7 The Committee was called by the name of its chairman Professor Claude Zangger of Switzerland.

8 The letters and memoranda were accordingly published as IAEA Document INFCIRC/209, of 3. September 1974.

9 INCIRC/209/Mod 1 and following.

material to non-nuclear weapon states: a non-explosive-use assurance, an IAEA safeguards requirement and a re-transfer provision that requires the receiving state to apply the same conditions when re-exporting these items.

For further reference, it is also relevant to clarify the legal status of the documents that were and continue to be officially circulated by the IAEA to all its Member States, reflecting the Understandings reached by the members of the Committee. As decided from the onset, the Zangger Committee's decisions would not be legally binding on its members, equally not on other States and thus *per se* have no legal status under international law. They constitute a political obligation of each State member of the Committee to give effect to the content of the Understanding by enacting it in their respective national export control legislation or as appropriate in other relevant laws.

As analysed below, the export control regime established by groups of likeminded suppliers, evolved dramatically in the course of the following decades primarily as a result of unforeseen events: 1974, the same year as the Trigger List was first published by the IAEA, the "peaceful explosion" conducted by India, a non NPT State, indeed triggered a major international concern as to whether existing export controls were sufficient to prevent trade in items that could serve such "nuclear explosions".

The need to strengthen export controls by *inter alia* including suppliers that are – or were – not Party to the NPT led to the establishment of a further informal export control group, the Nuclear Suppliers Group, formerly known as the London Club (NSG)[10] which notably invited France non-NPT Party at that time.

The NSG developed two discrete sets of guidelines: the first to govern the export of items that are exclusively for nuclear use, the second set of guidelines to govern the export of nuclear-related dual-use items and technologies, which, for example, also have non-nuclear use in the industry. Thus, the NSG achieved *ab initio* a more comprehensive and at the same time flexible approach to export controls.[11] It took into account the work done by the Zangger Committee and added further specific procedures and conditions. This included notably the requirement for

---

10 "The Nuclear Suppliers Group: Its Origins, Role and Activities", in INFCIRC/539/Rev.3 30 May 2005. The original version of the paper circulated on behalf of the Member States of the Nuclear Suppliers Group was issues under the same code in 1997, further revised 2000 and 2003.

11 INFCIRC/254 of 1978: Part 1 "Guidelines for Nuclear Transfers". Part 2 "Guidelines for Transfers of Nuclear-Related Dual-Use Equipment, Software (…) and Related Technology", (subsequently amended).

formal government assurances to be given by recipients to the effect that transfers would not be diverted to unsafeguarded nuclear fuel cycle or nuclear explosive activities, as well as to adopt physical protection measures and strengthened re-transfer provisions. In 2004, the NSG decided *inter alia* to establish a *catch-all* mechanism in the frame of the guidelines to control the export of nuclear related items that are not on the control lists, when such items may be intended for use with a nuclear weapons program thereby going beyond a common approach of the control regime by allowing the individual supplier State to set up a domestic legal basis and exert a more direct discretionary powers over and above standardized trigger lists.

Further "globalisation" of the control regime was achieved by ensuring consistency of the guidelines with the regional non-proliferation treaties.[12]

Landmarks, Learning Lessons and Adjusting Responses[13]

Soon after the establishment of the second group of nuclear suppliers, the export control regime began to change rapidly and incrementally under the impact of international events of direct relevance to the non-proliferation norms challenging the adequacy, nature and content of the Understandings and of the Guidelines prescribed so far for implementing the commitments of the NPT.

The Review Conferences of the NPT that from 1975 onwards took place routinely every five years was then predominantly concerned with issues of disarmament, negotiation of a Comprehensive Test Ban Treaty, and security assurances from the nuclear weapon States. Much before the general liberalisation of international trade in industrial goods, matters of export control were not centre stage. They became an open controversial issue in 1980 between the Eastern and the Western Group of States and the Non Aligned Movement (NAM). Another matter was the absence of an agreement as to whether IAEA safeguards (INFCIRC/153) should be a condition of supply to non-NPT States.

The 1990 Review Conference took place just before the international community became aware of Iraq's clandestine non-peaceful nuclear

---

12 Initially: Treaty of Taltelolco; Treaty of Rarotonga, Treaty of Pelindaba; Treaty of Bangkok.

13 *Op. cit.*, supra Quentin Michel, "The Control of International Nuclear Trade"; Chapter L – *NPT Briefing Book*, April 2005 Edition, issued by Mountbatten Centre for international studies, University of Southampton, and Centre for Non-proliferation Studies, Monterrey Institute of International Studies. IAEA Information Circulars (INFIRC) grouped under the title "Nuclear Material, Import and Export Provisions", see: www.iaea.org/Publiations/Documents/Infcircs in chronological and substantive order.

weapon programme. As was later discovered, the weapons programme was based extensively on imported, dual-use items, not covered by NSG lists.

The 1995 Review and Extension Conference, though primarily concerned with the issue of the Treaty's extension – *i.e.* indefinite duration – decided on a set of principles that were further strengthened by recommendations formulated by the 2000 Review Conference also stressing that "transparency in nuclear related export controls should be promoted within the framework of dialogue and cooperation among all interested States".

In the following years, both nuclear and non-nuclear international events influenced and redirected the further evolution of the export control norms: these events include notably: 1998 India and Pakistan in short intervals carried out and openly declared testing nuclear non-peaceful devices; 2001, following the "9/11" attacks on the US the threat of terrorist acts involving nuclear material could no longer be excluded. 2002, the NSG in an Extraordinary Plenary Meeting adopted strengthened Guidelines[14] aimed at preventing and countering the threat of possible diversion of nuclear exports to nuclear terrorist purposes.

The preparatory meetings for the 2005 NPT Review Conference devoted much more attention than ever before to the subject of export controls. The Preparatory Committee meeting in 2004[15] though welcoming Libya's abandonment of its nuclear weapon program, at the same time expressed serious concern about the existence of covert international proliferation trafficking networks that might have been used for Libyan procurement. As a consequence, the NSG again reviewed and strengthened the Guidelines[16] for transfers of nuclear related and dual-use equipment, material and technology and introduced a notification obligation for the transfer of a given dual-use item, material, software or related technology.

The NPT Review Conferences had thus become a large new open forum, which played an increasing role in the development, understanding and acceptance of the export control mechanisms and objectives. In fact, at the same time as added export control mechanisms came into force, non-members of the NSG in particular criticised the lack of transparency of that process. Increasingly, this concern was well understood by the NSG as transparency was indeed in the Group's best interest in order to reach out to States that had not been involved in the decision making process, but that were equally bound to implementing

[14] INFCIRC/254/Rev.5/Part 1, 16 January 2002.

[15] NPT Briefing Book, *op. cit.*, Part I Section 5, p. 29.

[16] INFCIRC/254/Rev.8/Part 2.

the Guidelines. Initiatives to promote openness and transparency were first launched in the framework of the 1995 NPT Review Conference in a document entitled "Principles and Objectives for Nuclear Non-Proliferation and Disarmament" The effect of that new policy led to a cautious opening to other stakeholders including the industrial operator.

Today's Nuclear Export Control Regime

As the evolution of the international export control regimes shows, the original approach was limited to one list of specific items circulated by the IAEA to its Member States, which gave way five years later to two distinct Groups of Supplier States and soon thereafter to two distinct lists. Another decade later, the two control lists had been amended and expanded several times, other conditions added and catch-all provisions allowed.

Modifications and adjustments of the regime however, had evolved so far essentially within the NSG/Zangger approach: the NPT norm was to be implemented faithfully and adjusted as needed within its original Treaty context by agreement of the supplier States, members of these Groups. In the 1990s, the NPT Review Conference first opened the discussions on export control to all NPT Parties with different agendas in the unchartered waters of multi-subject conferences.

The most recent change of the export control norm making resulted in a fundamental transformation of its scope of application. Embedded in a legally binding resolution of the UN Security Council,[17] addressed to all UN Member States, *i.e.* to nuclear weapon and non-nuclear weapon States, to States members or not of the Zangger or NSG, the nuclear export control regime became part of a broader international strategy context.

The landmark resolution 1540 (2004) by the Security Council[18] declaring the proliferation of weapons of mass destruction "a threat to

---

17 Charter of the United Nations, Chapter VII, Article 41.

18 United Nations Security Council Resolution 1540(2004) in S/Res/1540 (2004) dated 28 April 2004: "*The Security Council [...] Determined to facilitate henceforth an effective response to global threats in the area of Non-proliferation, Acting under Chapter VII of the Charter of the United Nations: [1.]... [2.]...*

3. Decides also that all States shall take and enforce measures to establish domestic controls to prevent the proliferation of nuclear, chemical or biological weapons... and to this end shall: [(a)], [(b)][(c)]...

(d) Establish, develop, review and maintain appropriate effective national export and trans-shipment controls over such items, including appropriate laws and regulations to control exports, transit, trans-shipment and re-export and controls... as well as establishing end-user controls... and establishing and enforcing appropriate criminal or civil penalties for violations of such export control laws and regulations;

international peace and security" achieved two milestone changes to the nuclear export control regime as it existed before:

First, it elevated the national export control measures agreed by the consensus in the NSG and Zangger groups to the status of a specific international binding obligation to be adopted by all States. In particular, operative paragraph 3 (d) of the Resolution requires States in *expressis verbis* not only to enact appropriate laws including penal laws, but also to enforce them.

Second, by expressing the Council's wish for the participation of industry in the implementation of the resolution[19] it strongly encouraged the flow of information and the possibility of cooperation of stakeholders directly concerned by the export control regime.

The 2010 Review Conference, devoted much attention to this subject. As recorded in its Final Document[20] "The Conference recognizes that national rules and regulations of States parties are necessary to ensure that the States parties are able to give effect to their commitments with respect to the transfer of nuclear and nuclear-related dual-use items to all States taking into account articles I, II and III of the Treaty, and, for States Parties, also fully respecting article IV".

The Conference further noted[21] that in the view of many States "effective and transparent export control are important to facilitating the fullest possible exchange of equipment, material and scientific and technological information for the peaceful uses of nuclear energy, which, in the view of those States, depends on the existence of a climate of confidence about non-proliferation". In its Conclusions and recommendations for follow-on actions,[22] the Conference urged all States Parties "to ensure that their nuclear-related exports do not directly or indirectly assist the development of nuclear weapons or other nuclear

---

The Security Council also [...] *Calls upon all States:*

[(a)], [(b)], [(c)]

(d) To develop appropriate ways to work with and inform industry and the public regarding their obligations under such laws[...]".

19 UNSC Resolution 1540(2004) Paragraph.8 (d), "To develop appropriate ways to work with and inform industry and the public regarding their obligations under the laws".

20 Final Document: 2010 Review Conference of the Parties to the Treaty on the Non-proliferation of Nuclear Weapons. 27 May 2010 last draft version as adopted in Doc.NPT/CONF.2010/L.2 Part I, "Review of the operation of the Treaty..." Paragraph 27.

21 *Ibid.*, paragraph 27, 2010 Review Conference: Final Document, *op. cit.*, "Review of the operation of the Treaty..."

22 2010 Review Conference, *op. cit.*, Chapter II, Nuclear Non-proliferation, "Action 35".

explosive devices [...]", and in an indirect reference to the NSG and Zangger lists,[23] that States Parties make "use of multilaterally negotiated and agreed guidelines and undertakings in developing their own national export controls".

It is worth noting that cooperation with or among industry is not mentioned in the context of non-proliferation, whereas specific "actions" are recommended regarding the "Peaceful uses of Nuclear Energy"[24] notably the nuclear power development. Action 60 calls upon States Parties to "promote the sharing of best practices in the area of nuclear safety and security, including through dialogue with the nuclear industry and the private sector, as appropriate".

A new Role of Industry: Back- or Front- Stage?

The industrial nuclear operator did not and still does not sit at intergovernmental table. There are a number of reasons that such participation was not considered necessary by either industry or Government: Such reasons include: (i) the fact that in most countries the nuclear industry was predominantly or even exclusively in the domain of the sovereign State; (ii) rights and obligations of the nuclear weapon States and the non-nuclear weapon States respectively as set out in the NPT are addressed to States only in terms of binding obligations under international law; (iii) the export control regimes established by the Zangger Committee and by the NSG are agreed by consensus among States, and understood as binding the individual State to implement these agreed guidelines and enforce them in the area of their jurisdiction; this applies equally unless otherwise specified to UN Security Council resolutions; (iv) the supplier State takes the legal responsibility to enact domestic legislation binding the industrial operator; (v) moreover, the establishment of trade rules in any field and their domestic implementation are a sovereign prerogative.

However, a number of relevant developments have occurred during the last years both concerning the industrial operator and the State. Industry has emerged today as the dominant global actor in nuclear trade and investment. Nuclear industry much like other international industrial sectors expanded by way of foreign investment, international mergers and acquisitions. This emerging picture now includes newly created multinational companies with potentially a plurality of "host" or "installation States" in addition to their original headquarters. End-users are global as are intermediate users.

---

[23] 2010 Review Conference, *op. cit.*, Chapter II, "Action 36".

[24] 2010 Review Conference, *op. cit.*, Chapter III.

As in the past, industry has the legal responsibility to comply with domestic laws, regulations and procedures. However, in light of new challenges to the non-proliferation regime, domestic laws and regulations are subject more than ever before to sudden revisions and amendments. Internationally expanded industry also has to seek the cooperation of its host State and through it of foreign States in elaborating inter-industry contracts and in ascertaining possible existing international procedures that apply in addition to domestic law. In this changing environment nuclear industry different from other *e.g.* renewable energy or manufacturing sectors, has to make well-informed decisions long in advance with little room for flexibility.

From the State's perspective, the legal and political responsibility to fully comply with its non-proliferation commitments, has become stricter, more controlled and under constant evolution.[25] Possibly more than in previous years, the State has an international responsibility to ensure compliance by national industrial actors with domestic law, which in turn must give effect to NSG Guidelines, agreed procedures, UNSC decisions, national embargoes etc. In fact, the sovereign State is continuously called upon by the international community to abide by its non-proliferation commitments.

The question is how far will these developments influence the direct relationship of the State with its industrial operators beyond that of legislator and law enforcer, and beyond, at the European and international levels. Some recent international decisions may lead to new approaches.

The wider question of government/industry relations has also entered the agenda of other *fora* as published in recent IAEA Symposium on International Safeguards.[26] In discussing Safeguards in a "Changing and Transnational World", the authors argue that "while the State actors try to drive their ambitious nuclear projects forward towards completion, it is the private companies" responsibility to undertake to procure "what is required for the nuclear activities […] on the other side of the supply chain are also private entities, either middle men or the manufacturer".

---

[25] September 2010: The US President unveils plans to alter the Federal governments system for controlling sensitive exports by consolidating listings of regulated materials and creating new offices for carrying out certain enforcement actions. No list but three tiers approach: The purpose is "to build higher walls around the export of the most sensitive items while allowing the export of less critical ones under less restrictive conditions", Source: NTI, 7 September 2010.

[26] In Book of Abstracts, p. 86, "Industry Contribution to Thwart Illicit Nuclear Trade", R. Wirtz; W. Beck. Oerlikon Leybold Vacuum, Cologne. Symposium on International Safeguards: "Preparing for Future Verification Challenges", 1-5 November 2010, Vienna, IAEA.

A conclusion of this analysis is that data available to companies, usually shared with the individual State in their view, should also be made available to the IAEA in order to assist stakeholders. Done on a large scale, this data would lead to an ad hoc improvement of the verification efforts and help establish a unique warning system.

Realistic or not – which is beyond this author's judgment – this proposal describes the need for intermediaries to overcome the difficulties that may be encountered by the smaller industrial operators and the smaller State to gain awareness and knowledge of attempted, intercepted and seized export shipments of sensitive or dual-use items. It is also a plea for further transparency measures.

The Broader Context: Scope for a more Active Transparency

The fragments of advice addressed both to governments and to industrial operators for increasing transparency and proactive cooperation as regards export control measures are not readily translated into practice.

Thus, some issues may need to be further investigated:

Is dialogue on a regular, institutionalized level between the NSG and industrial operators conceivable?

Considering that communication between the NSG and the governments, rather than with the industrial operator, is channelled through the IAEA by way of INFCIRCs and, at the domestic level through the participating States according to their own respective rules and procedures and required levels of transparency.

Would encouraged participation of industrial operators in such dialogue raise more problems than offer solutions?

Is it exclusively within the realm of established governmental procedures to provide industry with structured, reliable and accessible information?

Are standard channels of communication from governments through official gazettes and similar published special advice sufficient in providing reliable up to date information for industry's export decision making?

How can export-oriented industry satisfy its need to seek actively relevant information from government, beyond knowledge of the domestic laws and regulations, and its need to understand the reasons or origin of such measures?

Looking specifically at the wider context of non-proliferation and the nuclear renaissance, a recent study[27] based on a broad survey of (US) nuclear companies researched and evaluated the opinions, possible contribution, and responsibilities of the nuclear industry. Industry's predominant view was that "the current non-proliferation regime is functioning well, and that any steps to strengthen it are primarily the responsibility of governments and international institutions".[28]

The authors of the Study on the other hand, reach somewhat different, even diametrically opposed conclusions: notably that "industry must be more proactive in working with governments to find mechanisms that maximize commercial efficiency within a comprehensive proliferation resistant framework that addresses new concerns that will arise from increased movement of sensitive nuclear materials, the spread of sensitive fuel cycle technologies, and the diffusion of technical knowledge". Starting from the generally accepted premise of a changing dynamic of the international nuclear landscape, industry must, in their opinion, recognize that it is "on the frontlines of defence" against threats to the non-proliferation regime. The authors conclude that industry must be more proactive in working with governments... And play a bigger role as it carries responsibility as a corporate global citizen. In their view, the opportunities for constructive collaboration are numerous, and "a stronger relationship between the nuclear industry, governments and international institutions will result in a more secure nuclear industry".

The purpose of an issue paper is to raise questions rather than reach conclusions. In this authors view, a new debate – a discussion conducted from new angles – needs to be started without necessarily aiming at instant concrete results or implementation measures. It may be simply encouraging a new readiness to open new avenues and reconsider the validity of old patterns.

---

27 "Non-proliferation and the Nuclear 'Renaissance': the contribution and responsibilities of the Nuclear Industry", Energy Security Initiative at The Brookings Institution Washington, DC. May 2010.

28 Brookings study, *op. cit.*, p. 37.

Germany
Administrative Efforts Paired with Company's Responsibility

Claudia TOPP

PhD Student, Université de Liège

Introduction: Germany's Economical Landscape

Germany is widely known as the home country for high technology, automobile industry and precision engineering. Its products are in demand all over the world and German enterprises are in many branches, world market leaders. Thus Germany's economy is strongly export-oriented and is therefore depending on exports. For many years Germany has been the world export champion. Recently, it lost its pole position to China but remains one of the worlds leading exporters.[1] With an export volume of Euros 951.9 billion in 2010,[2] the main exported goods in the first half of 2010 encompass motor vehicles and parts, machines, chemical products, data processing, electronic and optical products as well as technical equipment.[3] Together they represent more than the half of the German foreign trade. Hence it is not surprising, that exports form more than one third of Germany's GDP.[4]

On the other hand, the value of granted single-transaction export licences on military equipment reached approximately Euros 5.04 billion

---

1 *Statistisches Bundesamt Deutschland* (www.destatis.de) press release No. 045, 9 February 2010.

2 *Ibid.*, press release, No. 052, 9 February 2011.

3 *Ibid.*, press release, No. 318, 10 September 2010.

4 Federal Ministry of Economics and Technology of Germany, *External Economic Policy*, February 2011 (http://www.bmwi.de/English).

in 2009.[5] Also in this area Germany is in a leading position according to different statistics on international level.[6]

Taking these numbers into consideration, export controls are of paramount importance for Germany. At the latest as German companies got involved in international export scandals in the late 1980s, *i.e.* by the supply of a poison gas factory to Libya "Rabta",[7] the German economy felt the destroying force of such scandals. These events lead to an amplification and intensification of export controls in Germany.

From an Export Control Department to a Central Licensing Authority

Hence, in 1992 the department of "Export control" within the German Federal Office of Economics (BAW)[8] became a separate federal office, namely the Federal Office of Exports (BAFA).[9][10] However, its history dates back until the end of the Second World War. Starting from the Central Office of Economics as the central economic administration of the British sector in 1946, to the Administrative Office of Economics in the Bizone, over the Economic Administration of the united economic territory until the official foundation of the Federal Office of Economics on 9 October 1954.[11]

With regards to export controls, today the BAFA is Germany's central licensing authority subordinated to the Federal Ministry of Economics and Technology and executing the export control policy of the Federal Government.[12] In 2009 approximately 3000 companies applied

5 Ministry of Economics and Technology, *2009 Military Equipment Report*, Berlin, January 2011, p. 7; www.bmwi.de.

6 Baumann, N., "*Rüstungsexporte: Warum Deutschland Europameister ist*", *Focus-online*, 15 March 2010 (www.focus.de); Holtom, P., Bromley, M., Wezeman, P.D., and Wezeman, S.T., "*Trends in international arms transfers*", in SIPRI Fact Sheet, 2009, March 2010, p. 1.

7 BAFA (ed.), *Praxis der Exportkontrolle*, Köln, 2006, p. 24.

8 *Bundesamt für gewerbliche Wirtschaft.*

9 Since 21 December 2000 named *Bundesamt für Wirtschaft und Ausfuhrkontrolle* (Federal Office of Economics and Export Control).

10 "*Das BAFA, Ein halbes Jahrhundert Begleitung wirthschaftspolitischer Entwicklung*", Festschrift, Köln, 2004, Preface of President of the Federal Office of Economics and Export Control, Dr. Heizer, B., p. 5 and Greetings of the Minister of Economics and Labour, Clement, W., p. 8 and President of the Federal Office of Economics and Export Control retired, Dr. Danner, W., "Das Bundesausfuhramt – Entstehungsgeschichte", p. 23.

11 *Ibid.*, Dr. Heizer, B., p. 5; www.bafa.bund.de/en/the_office/history.

12 *Ibid.*, Minister of Economics and Labour, Clement, W., p. 7; www.bafa.bund.de/bafa/en.

for more than 31,000 licences at BAFA and more than 3,500 companies consulted its technical or administrative experts. Given that export control is based on interagency cooperation, BAFA reported approximately 500 cases to control and investigation offices.[13] Compared to these numbers 1.6 percent encompassing export controls of the German export volume of commercial goods in 2009[14] sounds few but recovers a lot of effort and complexity.

Being by far Europe's largest licensing authority[15] the German BAFA disposes on its own technical department.[16] For more than five years BAFA has been the implementing agent for EU-Outreach projects in the field of export controls in thirty countries outside the EU. In the framework of these activities, BAFA, in cooperation with the experts of other EU Member States, advises and supports third countries in establishing or enhancing effective export control systems.[17]

The Legal Foundation: European Framework and National Accentuation

The international regulations and commitments, such as the export control regimes[18] as well as the European regulations, are the main foundations of the German export control system. Regarding its history and taking into account that export controls in our present understanding were established after the events of the Second World War, Germany somehow naturally became part of all international binding commitments and export control regimes since their foundation.[19]

---

13 BAFA, *Bericht 2009/2010*, April 2010, p. 9; www.bafa.bund.de.

14 *Id.*

15 See speech of the President of BAFA, Dr. Wallraff, A., on the "Day of Export Control" on 24 February 2011 in Münster, p. 4; BAFA has approximately 850 employees including all – also "not export control" – departments. See: www.bafa.de.

16 Weith, N., Wegner, Ch., Ehrlich, W. (eds.), "*Grundzüge der Exportkontrolle*", Köln, 2006, p. 57; BAFA, *Brief Outline Export Controls*, Edition 25 July 2009, p. 164; See organisation chart on: www.bafa.de.

17 See speech of Dr. Arnold Wallraff, *op. cit.*, and Irina Albrecht, Claudia Topp, "*Exportkontrollkooperation, Osteuropa* 57", February-March 2007, p. 311, as well as Natascha Wessel, "*Nonproliferationskooperation*, Osteuropa 57", February-March 2007, p. 305.

18 In particular Wassenaar Arrangement, Missile Technology Regime, Australia Group, Nuclear Suppliers Group.

19 *I.e.* the former CoCom, Wassenaar Arrangement, Missile Technology Regime, Australia Group, Nuclear Suppliers Group.

Germany adheres to and implements all international commitments, agreements and decisions of International Organisations, such as the Chemical Weapons Convention or the Nuclear Proliferation Treaty.[20]

From the European point of view, as in all EU Member States, the European Dual-Use Regulation (Dual-Use Regulation) sets up the Community regime for the control of exports, transfer, brokering and transit of dual-use items including a harmonised list of dual-use items.[21] This regulation is directly enforceable.

After in-depth consultations under significant German participation the European "Anti-Torture Regulation"[22] was adopted on 30 July 2005, regulating prohibitions and licensing requirements of goods that could be used for the purpose of capital punishment or for the purpose of torture and other cruel, degrading or inhuman treatment or punishment. Before the enactment of this EU-wide regulation, the export of these goods was already subject to licensing requirements at the national level. The German example is leading the way towards a regulation on EU level.[23]

The sanctions regulations of the European Union that mainly implement resolutions of the United Nations Security Council, *e.g.* the Iran sanctions Regulation (EU) No. 961/2010 or the EU Regulation (EC) No. 881/2002 stipulate restrictive measures to combat terrorism, and are *lex specialis* provisions to the general export control provisions. That means, that within their scope of application, the provisions in the sanctions regulations supersede the EU Dual-Use Regulation and national export control provisions.

The national regulations were subject to various changes in the last decades. Initially formed by the occupying forces after the Second World War the national export control was mainly limited to prohibitions and the obstruction of foreign trade. Little by little the direction on foreign trade was conferred to the German Ministry of Economy who progressively transferred the general principle of interdiction of exports into the freedom of foreign trade limited by restrictions.[24] On the contrary, Article 26(2) of the German Basic Law and the War Weapons Con-

---

20 Weith, N., Wegner, Ch., Ehrlich, W. (eds.), "*Grundzüge der Exportkontrolle*", Köln, 2006, p. 56.

21 Council Regulation (EC) 428/2009 of 5 May 2009 *setting up a Community regime for the control of exports, transfer, brokering and transit of dual-use items.*

22 Council Regulation (EC) 1236/2005 of 27 June 2005.

23 http://www.auswaertiges-amt.de/DE/Aussenpolitik/Friedenspolitik/Abruestung/Exportkontrolle/Dual-use-Wassenaar.html/

24 Weith, Wegner, Ehrlich, *op. cit.*, p. 39.

trol Act (KWKG)[25] makes clear that war weapons remain exempt from this principle.

On the assumption of the principle of freedom of external economic transactions the exporter has the legal claim of the issuance of an export licence exempt in the case of restriction.[26] The legal basis for restrictions in the framework of foreign trade in German national law can be found in the provisions of the German Foreign Trade and Payments Act (AWG)[27] in conjunction with the German Trade and Payments Ordinance (AWV)[28] as well as in the KWKG.

The key provision in this matter presents Section 7 paragraph 1(1-3) of the AWG, which gives the authorisation for restrictions concerning military and dual-use goods[29] in order to:

– "Guarantee the vital security interests of the Federal Republic of Germany,

– Prevent a disturbance of the peaceful coexistence between nations, or

– Prevent a major disruption of the foreign relations of the Federal Republic of Germany".

On national level the AWG, in conjunction with the AWV as well as the KWKG stipulate such restrictions, namely prohibitions, licensing requirements and specific enactment.[30] In the following the most significant regulations are presented.

While the AWG provides definitions and penal provisions, the AWV comprises licensing requirements and specific prohibitions. Licensing requirements for exports, transfer, trafficking and brokering transactions as well as provisions concerning technical assistance may result – besides the EU Dual-Use Regulation – from the AWG and the AWV, irrespective of embargoes.

---

[25] Act to implement Article 26(2) of the German Basic Law (War Weapons Control Act – KWKG) in the version promulgated on 22 November 1990, *Federal Law Gazette I*, p. 2506 (as last amended by Article 2 of the Law of 6 June 2009, *Federal Law Gazette II*, p. 502).

[26] See Section 1 in conjunction with Section 3 of the AWG.

[27] *Aussenwirtschaftsgesetz* – AWG, Revised by notification on 27 May 2009, *Federal Law Gazette I*, p. 1150.

[28] *Aussenwirtschaftsverordnung* – AWV in the version promulgated on 22 November 1993 (*Federal Law Gazette I*, p. 2493), last amended by the Ninetieth Ordinance Amending the AWV of 18 August 2010 (*Federal Law Gazette*, No. 126, p. 2891).

[29] With detailed background information see Wolffgang/Simonsen (ed.), *Kommentar zum Außenwirtschaftsrecht*, loose-leaf-collection, Köln, 2002, volume 2, § 7 margin number 7 pp.; Weith, Wegner, Ehrlich, *op. cit.*, p. 64.

[30] See the systematic of restrictions in BAFA (ed.), *Praxis der Exportkontrolle*, Köln, 2006, p. 41.

In application of Article 8 of Dual-Use Regulation Germany exercises further export controls with a regards to dual-use goods, *nota bene*, outside the scope of the Dual-Use Regulation.

Therefore the German exporter needs to respect not only the listed goods within the Annex's of the Dual-Use Regulation but as well those listed within the so-called German Export List.[31] This export list represents one core element within German export control and is divided into two parts, Part I contains two sections A and C.

Section A covers the military equipment. Comparable to the EU Common Military List, Part I Section A of the German Export List emanated mainly from the Munitions List of the Wassenaar Arrangement to meet the political obligations arising from this export control Regime. However, concerning military equipment the German export control system distinguishes between war weapons and "other military equipment". War weapons are listed within 62 positions in the War Weapons List,[32] which is part of the military equipment listed entirely in Section A.[33]

Section C lists the dual-use goods. In order to be clear and user-friendly, this section reflects the entire Annex I of the Dual-Use Regulation, extended by some nationally listed dual-use goods.[34] These items concern certain industrial goods, *e.g.* land vehicles, helicopters or transmitters. Although exports of all goods covered by the Export List require a licence, this holds for nationally controlled dual-use items for certain countries only.[35]

With regards to non-listed dual-use items Germany disposes two further national "catch-all" clauses regarding cases, which are of course outside of the scope of the European Dual-Use Regulation.

On the one hand the German AWV stipulates a licensing requirement, which concerns non-listed goods related to (conventional) military end-use for destinations part of the Country List K. While the term of military end-use[36] is equivalent to the definition given in Article 4(2) EU Dual-Use Regulation, Country List K contains at present two coun-

---

[31] Annexed to the AWV.

[32] Annexed to the KWKG.

[33] Federal Ministry of Economics and Technology, *2009 Military Equipment Report*, January 2011, p. 8.

[34] See Weith, Wegner, Ehrlich, *op. cit.*, p. 73, and BAFA, *Praxis der Exportkontrolle*, Köln, 2006, p. 47.

[35] See Section 5 (2) AWV in conjunction with Section 7 (1) AWG, further information BAFA, *Brief Outline: Export Controls*, edition 25 July 2009, p. 9 (www.ausfuhrkontrolle.info).

[36] See Section 5c (1), No. 1-3 AWV.

tries.[37] On the other hand Section 5d requires an export licence, which concerns non-listed goods related to civil nuclear use for specific countries listed there. Anyway BAFA may establish the licensing requirement in both cases, equivalent to the information mechanism given in Article 4 of the Dual-Use Regulation.[38]

Taking a closer look at the German export control policy concerning the licensing of military equipment listed in the Export List Part I A, it has to be stated that the German Government follows a very restrictive policy, especially for small arms and light weapons.

This policy is concretized by the "Political Principles Adopted by the Government of the Federal Republic of Germany for the Export of War Weapons and Other Military Equipment",[39] it implements the EU Common Position on Arms Exports,[40] which guide the execution of discretionary by the Federal Government when deciding about an export. It refers especially to human rights. Subsequently, exports of war weapons, other military equipment as well as dual-use goods with an intended military end-use are not licensed, if misuse is suspected for human rights violations or internal repressions. In addition the principles specify that exports of military equipment to countries outside the EU, the NATO or NATO-equated members are restrictively administered as well. Moreover the destination country shall seize effective export controls.[41]

With regards to the control of military equipment it is necessary to consider war weapons separately. As outlined previously, the general principle of the freedom of external economic transactions does not apply to activities concerning war weapons. The KWKG deals with these items and identifies a war weapons list in its annex. It is interesting to note that the KWKG also defines the licensing requirement for the production, acquisition, transfer of actual control, and every type of transport or brokering transaction.[42] The export of war weapons is characterized first by a licensing obligation – "transport authorisation

---

37 BAFA, *Brief Outline: Export Controls*, edition 25 July 2009, p. 10; www.ausfuhrkontrolle.info.

38 For more detailed information, see Section 5c and 5d Foreign Trade and Payments Ordinance and BAFA, *ibid.*, p. 10; www.ausfuhrkontrolle.info.

39 *Political Principles Adopted by the Government of the Federal Republic of Germany for the Export of War Weapons and Other Military Equipment* of 19 January 2000.

40 Common Position 2008/944 CFSP of 8 December 2009 *defining common rules governing controls of exports of military equipments and technologies.*

41 See: www.auswaertigesamt.de/DE/Aussenpolitik/Aussenwirtschaftsförderung/Exportkontrollpol-national_node.html of 7 February 2008.

42 See sections 2-4a KWKG.

for the purpose of export" – according to the KWKG and thereafter a licence under the AWG and the AWV.

Even though the BAFA is the central licensing authority in the area of export control, the Federal Ministry of Economics and Technology is the licensing authority of all commercial transactions for war weapons. Moreover, the Federal Ministry of Finance, the Federal Ministry of Interior and the Ministry of Defence are all responsible licensing authorities with regards to interactions with war weapons within their competences.[43]

Furthermore the responsibility depends on the legal basis of the licensing requirement and the location of the respective good. The licensing requirement is based on the Dual-Use Regulation. BAFA is responsible if the exporter is established in Germany, irrespective of where the items are situated within the EU.[44] In the case that the licensing requirement originates from the German Foreign Trade and Payments Act, BAFA's responsibility arises if the items are located in Germany.[45]

Finally the AWG regulates the so-called "specific enactment", which authorises the Federal Ministry of Economics and Technology in agreement with the Foreign Office and the Federal Ministry of Finance to decree restriction on foreign trade transactions if Germany's security interests are in danger or to prevent a disturbance of the foreign relations.[46] This provision applies in extraordinary circumstances for any good without being limited to specific countries.[47]

Licensing Procedure and Decision-Making Process

The exporter initiates the licensing procedure by sending his application. The application form may be downloaded on BAFA's website or the online access for which an electronic application may be used. The exporter has to register electronically on BAFA's website. Nevertheless the printed and signed application form including all required original documents needs to be sent afterwards to BAFA.[48] The end-use certificate, technical data of the item, information literature and documents concerning the contract shall accompany the application form.[49]

---

[43] Section 11 of the KWKG; further information Federal Ministry of Economics and Technology, *2009 Military Equipment Report*, January 2011, p. 8.

[44] See Article 4 Dual-Use Regulation.

[45] See Weith, Wegner, Ehrlich, *op. cit.*, p. 175.

[46] See Section 2(2) AWG.

[47] See Haddex, volume 1, part 1 margin, No. 40 (34 supplemental set, December 2003).

[48] See BAFA, *Brief Outline: Export Controls*, Edition 25 July 2009, p. 17; www.ausfuhrkontrolle.info/ausfuhrkontrolle/de/antragstellung/index.html.

[49] See related Section 17 (2) AWV.

Recalling the above-mentioned number of German exports and its high amount of licensing applications, it does not surprise that the companies bear the responsibility to comply with export control regulations. In practice the granting of a licence depends mainly of the reliability of the applicant.[50] In conjunction with the internal directive for the German administration "Principles of the Federal Government to check the reliability of exporters"[51] establishes the basis for one of Germany's most important "institutions" within export controls: the person responsible for exports. Companies exporting listed dual-use items or military items[52] have to nominate such an "officer", who needs to be member of the board of directors or the executive management.

Against this background the exporter has to guarantee an appropriate organisation of its export control (division) and its integration in the processes of the company to meet the legal obligations within export controls. In this position the export control officer is incumbent to select the appropriate stuff and its continuous training. Moreover he has the duty to monitor the export control activities.

Within the licensing procedure the export control officer has to formally declare his personal responsibility concerning export activities *vis-à-vis* BAFA. BAFA on its side is assuming the reliability of the company and doesn't require a general certificate of the "existence" of an internal compliance programme (ICP). However a reliability check of the minimum standards is carried out by BAFA if there is the suspicion of violation of the foreign trade legislation.[53] Moreover, within the licensing procedure the exporter may face sanctions, such as the suspension or the denial of an application if there is a doubt on his reliability.[54]

Taking into account the high degree of responsibility and the amplitude of this "German institution" one could expect a further legal regulation besides the internal administrative directive.

The fundamental idea of the export control officer can be retrieved in a set of cases. For instance prior to granting a collective export licence BAFA reviews the company's ICP, demanding additional standards,

---

50 See Section 3 (2) AWG.

51 *Principles of the Federal Government to check the reliability of exporters* of 25 July 2001.

52 Export or transfer of items specified in Part I, Section A of the German Export List, including items subject to the War Weapons List, exports of items specified in Annex I of the EC Dual-Use Regulation except exports to countries listed in Annex II Part 3 EC Dual-Use Regulation, exports items specified in Part I Section C of the Export List except exports to countries listed in Annex II Part 3 EC Dual-Use Regulation.

53 Beutel, H., Richter, A.-K., "*Aktuelle Entwicklungen im Bereich der innerbetrieblichen Exportkontrollsysteme (ICP)*", AW-Prax, May 2010, p. 190.

54 Weith, Wegner, Ehrlich, *op. cit.*, p. 180.

such as appropriate IT-Systems, compared to the above mentioned reliability check in companies.[55] Even the proper usage of a national general licence demands the presence of an ICP, as BAFA can withdraw such a licence if compliance with the export control regulations is not guaranteed. The principles of the reliability of exporters under Section 3(2) AWG apply accordingly. A look back to the European level to Article 12 (2) EC Dual-Use Regulation, where this key idea is incorporated, the granting of a global licence may depend on an ICP.[56] Aside from that an analogy might be discovered in the defence area on the European level through integration of the certification procedure of the EC Directive on intra-EU transfers.[57]

To conclude the licensing procedure the issuance of an export licence is decided with the obliging administrative discretion. Nevertheless the decision whether to grant or deny an export licence concerning dual-use goods is much more complex due to the multiple use possibility. The criteria of examination focuses mainly on the use and the analysis of risks concerning the effective end-use of the item. The examination of the potential of misuse and the political analysis of the consignee are the basis for decisions, and demand a very differentiated consideration. Internal procedural instructions may guarantee the standardised application of the laws.[58]

For the risk analysis, the administration examines:

- Whether the application is coherent and conclusive
- Whether the given technical use might be plausible
- The end-use certificate and the consignee or end-user.[59]

However, complex circumstances of cases frequently require a further interagency cooperation. Depending on the level of decision and the field of concern the different departments may meet for coordination in diverse *fora*. For instance, Intelligence information is taken into consideration for the clarification of case facts. While the federal ministries, mainly under lead management of the Federal Ministry of Economy and Technology, may meet – depending on the internal procedural instruction – to decide on politically considerable cases presented by BAFA.

[55] See *Runderlass Außenwirtschaft* of the Federal Ministry of Economy and Technology, No. 10/2003 *concerning collective export licences*, as well as Beutel, H., Richter, A.-K., *op. cit.*, p. 190.

[56] Beutel, H., Richter, A.-K., *op. cit.*, p. 190.

[57] Directive 2009/43/EC of the European Parliament and Council of 6 May 2009 *simplifying terms and conditions of transfers of defence-related products within the Community.*

[58] Weith, Wegner, Ehrlich, *op. cit.*, pp. 222-226.

[59] *Ibid.*, p. 231.

This may involve the Foreign Office, Federal Ministry of Finance, in some areas the Ministry of Defence, or even the Federal Chancellery with a co-ordinating function. Such *fora* might be the German Export Committee concerning cases regarding WMD or the Federal Security Council, a Committee of the Federal Cabinet, deciding on cases concerning exports of military equipment with special importance.[60]

In the context of delivered authorisations, the German export control system knows three types of licences. Besides the classical "individual export licence" and the "collective export licence",[61] possibly the most convenient and important facilitation – the "general licence" – shall be mentioned. Once published in the Federal Gazette, a general licence applies for the specified items to be exported to the specified countries. After registration at BAFA the exporter has to notify the use of the general licence. Currently this facilitation includes thirteen sub-types, which permit within certain conditions the export of specific graphite, computers or items concerning telecommunications and information security.[62]

Finally, the exporter may file an objection at BAFA within one month if the application has been denied.

Moreover, Germany offers a special service in comparison to other EU Member States. If the exporter would like to check in advance whether his project would get a licence, he can make a "preliminary request". Although if the answer is positive it does not replace a licence but could have a prejudge effect at the time of application for a licence. Furthermore the authority may deliver a "blank notice" stating no licence is required for the export.[63]

The Dialogue with Industry

Being aware of the high responsibility given to the exporting companies, Germany's administration offers many facilities to keep them informed. The website of the BAFA gives a broad overview concerning

60 Ministry of Economy and Technology, *Schlaglichter der Wirtschaftspolitik*, Monthly Report February 2011, 1 February 2011; http://www.bmwi.de/BMWi/Navigation/Europa/WirtschaftsraumEuropa/binnenmarkt,did=376968.html?view=renderPrint. See also Weith, Wegner, Ehrlich, *op. cit.*, p. 175.

61 For more examples see BAFA, *Praxis der Exportkontrolle*, Köln, 2006, p. 56, and BAFA, *Brief Outline: Export Controls*, Edition 25 July 2009, p. 14; www.ausfuhrkontrolle.info.

62 BAFA, "*Praxis der Exportkontrolle*", Köln, 2006, p. 55; www.ausfuhrkontrolle.info/ausfuhrkontrolle/de/verfahrenserleichterungen/allgemein genehmigungen/index.html.

63 BAFA, *Brief Outline: Export Controls*, edition 25 July 2009, p. 19.

export control, new developments, the legal provisions, up to leaflets, brochures and reports concerning almost all parts and kinds of problems in the area of export control. A newsletter gives monthly information about international, European and national topicalities. Moreover one can download most of blanks.

BAFA is very keen on providing as much information as possible. Hence BAFA publishes the "Handbook of the German Export Control", which is regularly updated and includes commentaries, broad explications and all the necessary legal provisions. To cope with all technical standards this book is also available online. Moreover BAFA edited a book with a particular view to companies and from companies in its "*Praxis der Exportkontrolle*".

To get in touch with companies BAFA organizes the yearly "Day of Export Control" in cooperation with the University of Münster and the Centre of Foreign Trade Law. This event represents a communication and network platform for companies to meet and exchange views on current topics with representatives of the licensing authority and involved ministries and administrative bodies at the national, European and International level.[64]

The eighty chambers of industry and commerce (IHK) represent another important information channel. Domestic companies have the legal obligation to be member of a chamber of industry and commerce.[65] They incorporate all branches of trade and sizes of enterprise. It is evident that they play an important advisory function in the area of export control by organizing seminars, publishing leaflets or just as point of contact. The same holds for German trade and business associations[66] concentrating on interests of particular branches. They also represent a powerful position in Germany's political landscape.

To some extent IHK and central associations provide information to the exporter on early warning lists of the Federal Ministry of Economy and Technology in order to prevent the involvement of German companies in unintended proliferation activities. These confidential lists include general information concerning end-users of concern.[67]

---

64 Speech of the President of BAFA, Dr. Wallraff, A., on the "Day of Export Control" on 24 February 2011 in Münster; Claudia Topp, "*1. Exportkontrolltag in Münster*", AW-Prax, May 2009, pp. 195 and following.

65 Except crafts enterprise, liberal profession and agriculture holding. See: http://www.dihk.de/wir-ueber-uns/wer-wir-sind/ihk.

66 VDMA, for example, represents the local machinery and industrial equipment manufacturers, www.vdma.org.

67 See Haddex, volume 1, part 1 margin, No. 39 (34 supplemental set, December 2003) and Weith, Wegner, Ehrlich, *op. cit.*, p. 123.

Moreover the IHK disposes of several application forms, *e.g.* about the advice on the list of goods, a special service of BAFA. In case of the exporter's uncertainty he may ask whether the item is covered on the export list. This question arises on the customs side if the Commodity Classification of Foreign Trade Statistics does not permit the conclusion that the good is (not) listed. The advice on the list of goods certifies to the customs that the item is not listed in the export list without establishing a final administrative decision.[68] BAFA published a correlation list which can be downloaded on its website.

In this context the Foreign Trade Academy (*Außenwirtschaftsakademie*, AWA) has to be mentioned, offering basic or individual seminars as well as in-house trainings for companies in the field of export control or customs.[69]

The Sanctionary System: Precondition for Effectiveness

Since the involvement in any export scandal may hurt not only the company's reputation but, even worse, the external relations and the security interests of Germany, violations are severely sanctioned. After all, sanctions ensure an effective export control system.[70]

As in most countries, the customs authority represents the classical enforcement authority in export control matters. On the one hand, they check the compliance with foreign trade provisions, specifically likening requirements, and at latest date when the good will be exported – at the border or while clearing the goods for export.[71] On the other hand, in case of infringements or violations of export control provisions, the Customs Criminal Investigation Office (ZKA) is in charge to initiate, coordinate and analyze investigations. In this framework, as a matter of course, the public prosecutor's office gets also involved.[72]

Moreover, companies have diverse reporting, notification and register obligations whose compliance is monitored regularly in audits. With a view to export control issues BAFA may participate in such audits carried out by the customs administration.[73]

---

68 See BAFA, *Einstieg in die Exportkontrolle*, August 2009, p. 8, and Weith, Wegner, Ehrlich, *op. cit.*, p. 186; See also: www.ausfuhrkontrolle.info.

69 See: http://www.foreign-trade-academy.com.

70 On the other hand each EU Member State has to be consistent with Article 24 of the Dual-Use Regulation in absence of a EU competence in this matter.

71 See Section 9 AWV.

72 Weith, Wegner, Ehrlich, *op. cit.*, pp. 174, 175 and 198.

73 *Id.*

The penal provisions regulate a wide range of cases. On the one hand offences are mainly stipulated in the Foreign Trade and Payments Act in its Section 33, which further refers to the AWV providing an extensive catalogue of elements of offences.[74] The degree of penalty in the form of fines can rise up to Euros 500,000.

On the other hand the penalty of criminal acts[75] can be sanctioned with fines or imprisonment, while the latter could even reach a maximum penalty up to fifteen years.[76] Further incidental legal consequences of the criminal act could be the forfeiture of assets or an occupational ban.[77]

In addition to the penal provisions, legal violations could deploy many painful administrative sanctions, such as the already mentioned denial or suspension of licences in case of unreliability or the refusal of particular procedure facilities.[78]

Conclusion

Exports are Germany's economical basis. Export control is, thus, understood as a vital element to support the foreign trade sector and to protect companies' reputations and Germany's image abroad, particularly given some previous scandals. Therefore, export controls have to meet high standards of responsibility and security, on the one side. On the other side, these controls need to be targeted and have to be carried out effectively in order to avoid interferences with legitimate trade. Against this background, the fact that Germany deals with the highest quantity of export licensing applications in the EU yearly marks a continuous challenge in order to reach this aim. An extensive network system and close information channels through, chambers of industry and commerce, business and trade associations, Foreign Trade Academy and exchange platforms, between the exporting community and the administration are key factors to live up to an effective control system. One important result of this approach is, that the responsibility within foreign trade activities is mainly placed on the companies. The broad functions and duties of the export control officer represent one example of an effective instrument within the German export control system and could serve as a model in the framework of European harmonisation efforts.

---

74 Section 33 AWG in conjunction with Section 70 AWV.

75 Section 34 AWG.

76 Weith, Wegner, Ehrlich, *op. cit.*, p. 235, and BAFA, *Praxis der Exportkontrolle*, Köln, 2006, p. 193.

77 Weith, Wegner, Ehrlich, *op. cit.*, p. 245.

78 *Ibid.*, p. 236.

United Kingdom

Maryna TSUKANOVA

Researcher, Université de Liège

Introduction

Since the beginning of the establishment of an international export control framework, the United Kingdom (UK) has always been among the State Parties founding the main multilateral agreements. This might be partially explained by the responsibility towards the world community, which weighs upon the UK as a nuclear-weapon State.[1] Moreover, taking into account a pace of globalisation, the effective export control can only be conceived via the cooperation on a regional or even on an international level.

Hence, the UK was one of the first states to sign the three seminal *treaties* of international export control structure, which include the Treaty on the Non-Proliferation of Nuclear Weapons (1968), the Biological and Toxin Weapons Convention (1972) and Chemical Weapons Convention (1993). It is rather difficult to access the efficiency of these treaties. On the one hand, they are undoubtedly legally binding for the States Parties; on the other hand, the provisions thereof are often vague and general, which usually gives rise to a divergence in national interpretations. This relative frailty has given birth to quite a few more politically restrictive binding agreements, also known as *international regimes*. Thus far, the UK has actively contributed to the establishment of the following regimes: Australia Group (Chemical weapons), Missile Technology Control Regime (military dual-use items), Nuclear Suppliers Group (nuclear dual-use items) and Wassenaar Arrangement (mili-

---

1 According to Article 1 of the Treaty on the Non-proliferation of Nuclear Weapons, "[e]ach nuclear-weapon State Party to the Treaty undertakes not to transfer to any recipient whatsoever nuclear weapons or other nuclear explosive devices or control over such weapons or explosive devices directly, or indirectly; and not in any way to assist, encourage, or induce any non-nuclear-weapon State to manufacture or otherwise acquire nuclear weapons or other nuclear explosive devices, or control over such weapons or explosive devices".

tary dual-use items). The last legally binding export control initiative by which the British membership benefits is a *regional cooperation* within the EU. Given that the dual-use issue is the main subject of this contribution, it shall be emphasised that the Court of Justice of the European Union recognised this domain as a Community competence.[2] Therefore, the United Kingdom has a legal obligation to respect the European law in this area.[3]

National Export Control Legislation

Furthermore, within this three-level supra-national export control structure, the United Kingdom obviously has its own national provisions. The first export act was outlined in 1939 as an "emergency legislation" adopted on the eve of the Second World War.[4] In particular, Section 1 provided the Secretary of State with an extended power to apply import and export controls on specific items. This temporary measure has nevertheless endured until the early 1990s, notwithstanding the fact that it was largely criticised for the lack of democratic approach.[5] In addition, the last decade of 20th century has brought up some perturbing findings about the loopholes in British export control mechanism.[6]

In order to address gaps in the current legislation, the British Parliament has adopted the Export Control Act 2002.[7] Since then the Act has become "the main UK legislation on export controls for military and

---

2 See Case C-70/94, *Fritz Werner Indusrie-Ausrüstungen GmbH v. Germany* (1995) and Case C-83/94, *Criminal Proceedings against Peter Leifer, Reinhold Otto Krauskopfand Otto Holzer* (1995).

3 See Council Regulation (EC) No. 428/2009 of 5 May 2009 *setting up a Community regime for the control of exports, transfer, brokering and transit of dual-use items* (*Official Journal* L 134, 29.05.2009, p. 1).

4 Import, Export and Customs Powers (Defence) Act 1939, c. 69 (Regnal. 2 and 3 Geo 6), Section 9.

5 The Scott Report has pointed out several shortcomings of the Act, *i.e.* the lack of democratic control over the secondary legislation adopted under the Act as well as a confused explanation regarding the motivation to impose the export controls. For more information, see the Sir Richard Scott's Report of the *Inquiry into the Export of Defence Equipment and Dual-Use Goods to Iraq and Related Prosecutions* in February 1996 (HMSO, 0-10-262796-7).

6 In fact it has been often put forward that the British Government has *de facto* assisted Iraqi armament in preparation for the Persian Gulf War. Indeed, subject to government approval, the Matrix Churchill Group headquartered in Coventry was largely involved in exporting machine tools equipment to Iraq. For more reading, see M. Phythian and W. Little, "Parliament and Arms Sales: Lessons of the Matrix Churchill Affair", *Parliamentary Affairs*, 46 (3), 1993, pp. 293-308.

7 The Export Control Act 2002 was brought into force on 1 May 2004.

Dual-Use goods".[8] Its principal achievements may include a greater transparency of export control legal framework, an extended accountably with regard to the Parliament,[9] as well as empowering the Department for Business, Innovation & Skills (BIS) to consolidate existing secondary export control legislation on and to regulate strategic export controls.[10] Moreover, the Act provides the Secretary of State with "order-making powers to introduce controls on the export of any goods and to make provision about matters connected with the imposition of export controls. It is intended that the existing controls on the export of goods will be reviewed and (where necessary) revised under this power".[11]

The UK Government has put in practice this provision by setting a scope of secondary legislation, including Export of Goods, Transfer of Technology and Provision of Technical Assistance (Control) Order 2003 or "Main Order", Trade in Goods (Control) Order 2003, Trade in Controlled Goods (Embargoed Destinations) Order 2004 and Technical Assistance Control Regulations 2006. These orders have been merged in a single provision, *i.e.* the Export Control Order 2008.[12] Henceforth, the Order is a principal export control legislation owing to the fact that it controls the export of main strategic items along with the transfer of related technology and technical assistance.

Licensing Authority

National export legislation is put in practice by the British licensing authority for strategic goods known as the Export Control Organisation (ECO). This body is an integral part of the Department for Business, Innovation & Skills. During ECO, the establishment of a single licensing body was a key concern, it would encompass personnel involved in strategic exports management from diverse departments, such as the Ministry of Defence, the Foreign & Commonwealth Office, the Depart-

---

8 See Export Control Act 2002 pages on Business Link website: http://www.businesslink.gov.uk/.

9 According to Section 10 of the Act the Secretary of State shall submit an annual report to the Parliament on the operation of any order under section 1 "Export Controls" of the Act. See Export Control Act 2002, c. 28, Section 10. In addition, the Parliament has a right of scrutiny of secondary legislation under the Act. See Export Control Act 2002, c. 28, Section 13.

10 See Export Control Act 2002, c. 28, Section 1. It shall be noted that Section 1 refers to the Department of Trade and Industry (DTI) and not the BIS, which is actually responsible for strategic export controls. This can be explained by the fact that the BIS was created in June 2009 from the merger of the Department for Business, Enterprise and Regulatory Reform (DTI until 2007) and the Department for Innovation, Universities and Skills.

11 See Explanatory note, Subsection 1 of Export Control Act 2002, c. 28, Section 1.

12 The Export Control Order 2008 was brought into force on 6 April 2009.

ment for International Development, etc. The ECO staff has been gradually reduced over recent years, it currently counts around 100 people.

The main mission of ECO is to "promote global security through strategic export controls, and facilitating responsible exports".[13] In aiming towards this achievement, the organisation continuously tries to find an adequate equilibrium between safety requirements and the necessity to stimulate British economy.

With regards to safety aspects, ECO strives to prevent the proliferation of weapons of mass destruction via strict controls of strategic items as well as by taking part in government's counter proliferation initiatives. It also intensively collaborates with the Foreign and Commonwealth Office (FCO), thereby contributing to the management of FCO global issues such as weapons proliferation, conflict prevention and counter terrorism.

However as a part of BIS, ECO also plays an important role in "building a dynamic and competitive UK economy".[14] Hence it benefits from collaboration with a number of stakeholders representing NGOs and industrial groups, such as, the Export Group for Aerospace and Defence, and the Export Control Awareness Committee. In addition, ECO provides a set of instruments (Goods Checker, OGEL Checker, SPIRE online application system, Notices to Exporters) destined, on the one hand, to help UK exporters to understand the British export control framework and, on the other hand, to assist them in proceeding with their business.

Broadly speaking, ECO is in charge of legislating, assessing and issuing export licences for controlled goods. Thus, it is competent for export transactions in dual-use, torture goods, radioactive sources as well as military items. Since trafficking and brokering of arms and dual-

---

13 ECO also has a number of additional missions such as:
"Participate in the shaping of global arms control policies [...] and working with other government departments on counter-proliferation activities;
Develop the UK's export licensing policy and legislation working in consultation with a diversity of stakeholders from industry and non-governmental organisations (NGO);
Take part in FCO-led international outreach work to promote good export licensing practice in other countries;
Update the UK Strategic Export Control Lists;
Audit and ensure company compliance;
Record statistics about licence applications;
Provide help and advice to exporters".
See, BIS, *Introduction to the Export Control Organisation and to Export Controls*, March 2010, p. 4.

14 For further information about BIS targets and priorities, see BIS website: http://www.bis.gov.uk/about.

use items is conditional upon authorisation, ECO is also responsible for delivering trade control licences for these goods.

Is should be noted that ECO is subject to the scrutiny of the British parliament. Since 1999 the Committees on Arms Exports have been examining the UK Government's policy, administration and expenditure on strategic export controls.[15] In addition, the Committees are in charge of evaluation of reports on export controls provided by ECO on a quarterly and annual basis.

Moreover, ECO closely collaborates with other departments such as FCO, Ministry of Defence (MOD), Department for International Development (DFID) and HM Revenue & Customs (HMRC). Indeed the FCO, MOD and DFID directly participate in decision making processes regarding the issue of licences, whereas the HMRC is competent for proceedings against exporters who breach UK strategic export control regulations.

As already emphasised, ECO is constantly balancing between security considerations that generally emanate from multinational joined actions, as well as a necessity to support and encourage the UK business sector. The next section will, therefore, be dedicated to the analysis of UK export legislation which has been largely inspired by the international and regional export control instruments. After this analysis is completed, the relationship between ECO and British industries will become the major subject for consideration.

Scope of the UK Export Control Regime

As it was established in the previous section, the UK legislation for the export of strategic items is strongly influenced by the supra-national national. This is especially true with respect to dual-use items taking into account the legally binding nature of the Regulation 428/2009. Generally speaking the UK export control regime relies on three pillars that will or will not give rise to a licence requirement.

The first pillar concerns items to be controlled. Notwithstanding that the rule is of free trade, commerce of certain goods might be restricted as a result of their potentially dangerous nature. The extent of such restriction differs, *i.e.* it could be either a simple restriction or an outright prohibition. As regards the UK, it maintains a number of specific national control lists along with these stemming from multilateral regimes and especially from the EU law. In order to facilitate the com-

[15] The Committees on Arms Exports is a House of Commons Select Committee, which includes Business and Enterprise, Defence, Foreign Affairs, and International Development Select Committees.

prehension the BIS publishes a single document also known as *the consolidated list of strategic military and dual-use items that require export authorisation.*[16] This list "summarise[s] the text from the appropriate strategic export control legislation (excluding any Sanctions Orders)"[17] that remains in force for UK exports for the time of its issue. The dual-use aspect is put forward by Schedule 3 of Export Control Order 2008 (UK Dual-Use List) that lists prohibited dual-use goods, software and technology.[18] In addition, the list incorporates three relevant Annexes of Regulation 428/2009,[19] which emphasises the importance of the EU law.

The second pillar refers to a country of destination. Indeed in order to somehow maintain the countries that might be considered as worrisome for the international peace and security, States all over the world put in to practice various types of political leverage. The most widely used among them are sanctions and embargoes which cover a wide range of sanctions, *i.e.* trade and export restrictions, travel bans, asset freezes, bans on imports. With regards to EU Member States, they usually apply restrictive measures decided on by the United Nations (Security Council) and the European Union (Common Foreign and Security Policy goals). Moreover, sanctions and embargoes may also stem from the Organisation for Security and Co-operation in Europe. Thus, the UK must comply with its international engagements and implement the sanctions in British law. The secondary legislation adopted under the Export Control Act 2002 points to the BIS as a competent body for the administration of sanctions and embargoes. Characterised by Kofi Annan as "a middle ground between worlds and war", sanctions and embargoes constitute not only an efficient tool of external policy but also an additional burden for British exporters and brokers.[20]

---

16 The current list came into force on 31 of August 2010. The list is available on the BIS website: http://www.bis.gov.uk/assets/biscore/eco/docs/control-lists/uk-consolidated-list.pdf.

17 See BIS, *Strategic Export Control Lists: Contents and Introduction*, August 2010, p. 2.

18 See articles 4 and 5 of Export Control Order 2008.

19 These annexes are respectively Annex I (dual-use items subject to authorisation if exported to the non-EU member States), Annex II (dual-use items covered by the Community General Export Authorisation No. EU001) and Annex IV (dual-use items subject to authorisation if exported to both non-EU and EU Member States).

20 Current Country list of British sanctions and embargoes can be found at Foreign & Commonwealth Office website: http://www.fco.gov.uk/en/about-us/what-we-do/services-we-deliver/export-controls-sanctions/country-listing/.

Finally the third pillar deals with a transaction to be undertaken. The UK legal structure includes a set licence categories which, broadly speaking, cover export, overseas trade, and transhipment.

According to the specific features of an *export* undertaking, an exporter might apply for one of following licence types. He or she might opt for an Open General Export Licence (OGEL) that authorises any economic operator to export a particular listed item to a specific destination. With regards to dual-use the UK has established a set of OGELs such as Export After Exhibition, Dual-Use Goods: Hong Kong Special Administrative Region, Export After Repair/Replacement Under Warranty, Export For Repair/Replacement Under Warranty, Exports of Dual-Use Goods to UK diplomatic Missions of Consular Posts, UK Forces Deployed in Non-Embargoed Destinations, and finally, Oil and Gas Exploration.

If a particular exporter intends to export a determined quantity of specific items to specific destination, he or she can apply for a Standard Individual Export Licence (SIEL). According to Business Link this type of licence is the most commonly used by the UK licensing authority. Generally speaking the SIEL is solicited if conditions of issue of OGEL cannot be met.[21]

In the case where an individual company brings an application for an export authorisation, an Open Individual Export Licence (OIEL) might be issued covering several shipments to several destinations.

With regard to *overseas trade* that involves a transfer of listed items between two third countries, the UK imposes a Trade Control Licence for every broker (natural or legal person) resident or established on its territory who provides brokering services in goods listed in Annex I of Regulation 428/2009. Additional conditions requires the broker to be informed that these items are or may be intended, in their entirety or in part, for a use related to weapons of mass destruction (WMD).[22] An example of brokering services includes arranging supply from overseas factories/warehouses; arranging intra-company transfers; a drop shipping; or acting as a "project manager" for a project in one third country who sources supplies for that project in other third countries.[23] It shall be

---

21 The Business Link website provides an exhaustive overview of the UK strategic export legislation. The dual-use pages are available at: http://www.businesslink.gov.uk/bdotg/action/layer?r.l1=1079717544&r.l2=1084228483&r.s=tl&topicId=1084483507.

22 This authorisation was introduced in order to implement Article 5 of Council Regulation 428/2009. See the Export Control (Amendment) (No. 3) Order 2009, No. 215.

23 See BIS, *Guidance on Brokering (Trade) of Dual-Use Items – Council Regulation (EC) No. 428/2009*, Export Control Organisation, BIS, March 2010, p. 4.

emphasised that with respect to such services only a Standard Individual Trade Control Licence (SITCL) may be granted by the ECO.

Finally it may occur that the specific *transhipment* operation could be subject to licence requirements. Usually a transhipment of listed dual-use items does not entail a licence application. However, if a risk should occur in connection with an item or a final destination, a transhipment licence will be imposed. For that reason goods from the UK Dual-Use List require a transhipment licence when they are destined for Iran or North Korea.[24] A transhipment licence might be either an Open General Transhipment Licence (OGTL)[25] or a Standard Individual Transhipment Licence (SITL) if conditions required by OGTL cannot be met.

Thus far, a general review of licences provided by the UK reveals that this state strictly follows the European prescriptions. Moreover, British law goes sometimes even further by imposing licence requirements for transactions not covered by Regulation 428/2009, *i.e.* transhipment dealings.

Industrial Operator Awareness

Taking into consideration recent geopolitical shifts that have led to the reappraisal of current threats, it seems that only a united approach is likely to strengthen international security. Therefore the significance of national industrial operators countering international terrorism along with the proliferation of WMD cannot be underestimated. It is often true that exporters are those who know best not only the specificities of goods they intend to export but also their clients. Hence, they might represent one of the most adequate information sources for the licensing authority. For that reason the latest tendencies in export control legislation lean toward the extension of industrial responsibility. With regards to the EU law on strategic goods, it contains a number of provisions that gives exporters a greater sense of responsibility as, for example, different catch-all clauses[26] or terms of implementation of internal compliance procedures.[27]

---

24 For more reading see BIS, *Note on Trade "Transit and Transhipment" Controls, Review of Export Control Legislation (2007)*, Supplementary Guidance, Export Control Organisation, March 2010, 27 p.

25 Presently a specific dual-use OGEL is available for Hong Kong Special Administrative Region (HKSAR). The current licence is dated 18 March 2009 and entered into force on 6 April 2009.

26 See articles 4(4) and 5(1) of Regulation 428/2009 as regards respectively exports and brokering services of non-listed dual-use items. If an exporter (broker) is aware that these goods are intended, in their entirety or in part, for WMD related uses, he or she

With respect to the British industrial sector, the companies have three following commitments to observe; regulatory compliance, knowledge of the UK legal framework and information update. The compliance with these commitments is provided by ECO Compliance Inspector visits. In order to pass these inspections the companies are invited to create internal compliance programs (ICP). It shall be noted however that Regulation 428/2009 does not contain an express ICP requirement. Therefore, it seems that there is no legal obligation for UK companies dealing with strategic items to put in to practice the compliance procedures. Nevertheless, this approach appears essential for the facilitation of licensing procedures.

With a view to assist companies in the accomplishment of their internal compliance programs, ECO has established a Compliance Code of Practice. Outlined in close cooperation with industries, this document "aims to promote effective compliance with the law relating to strategic export control".[28] It shall be emphasised that the Code of Practice is not a legally binding instrument; its main purpose is to provide companies with a series of best practices regarding ICP implementation.

The British ICP is formed of a number of elements that broadly cover every stage of ICP implementation, starting from the preparatory measures and concluding with provisions for record keeping. Hence, the company should firstly make a *commitment to compliance* and engage itself to strictly respect British export control laws and regulations. This statement is generally made by higher-ranking personnel and is then communicated to the entire staff.[29] The second step consists in the *appointment of a person responsible for export control issues*. This person has to be part of a board of directors, however he or she is free to entrust others with specific tasks. Since 2004 it is particularly important for each employee to be aware of the existence of such a person, bearing in mind that the export of technology via electronic means is henceforth subject to authorisation. As already mentioned, one of the responsibilities of British exporters urges them to be up-to-date with the export

must notify the national authorities which will decide whether a transaction in question should be subject to authorisation.

27 According to several legal instruments of the EU law on strategic goods, an implementation of an ICP might contribute to a positive reliability assessment of an industrial operator. See, for example, Article 9(2) of Directive 2009/43/EC of the European Parliament and of the Council of 6 May 2009 *simplifying terms and conditions of transfers of defence-related products within the Community* (*Official Journal* L 146, 10.6.2009, p. 146).

28 See BIS, *Compliance Code of Practice*, Export Control Organisation, March 2010, p. 4.

29 Annex 1 of Code of Practice provides an example of compliance statement.

control requirements. Therefore, the companies are supposed to establish all the necessary mechanisms, *i.e. information and training*, aimed to spread relevant export control information.[30]

According to the Code of Practice, *company compliance procedures* as drawn up by British industries must be "effective for the business concerned and reflect as far as possible the best practices illustrated in this code".[31] Even if an establishment of an ICP is not a legal precondition for handling strategic exports, this measure is crucial "to ensure that everything is done to prevent an export of licensable goods being made without valid licence".[32] An average ICP might typically include the following stages: determination, on the one hand, of goods and activities that might require a licence and, on the other hand, of the most suitable type of licence; strengthening of end-user controls; customers assessments; optimization of procedures for licence applications; providing export and freight services; and record keeping. In addition, the Code of Practice provides a checklist of relevant elements that should be considered while setting up an ICP. Among them one can find checking products, destinations and licences; checking on receipt of inquiry or order; checking export procedures and checking records. The guiding lines are presented either as a sequence of steps to follow or as a questionnaire to observe.[33]

Moreover, an ICP can only be effective if a day-to-day vigilance is part of a company's management approach. The Code of Practice invites businesses to consider the development of awareness among staff that will contribute to *identify the suspicious enquiries and orders.*[34] This measure might evade firms from getting involved in risky activities that may potentially be illegal. Another suggestion of the Code of Practice concerns a *record keeping* which has recently become a keystone of the non-proliferation endeavour.[35] In addition, in order to prepare an external compliance audit carried out by ECO, British companies may initiate a programme of systematic *internal audit*. This regular export control appraisal might, inter alia, consist in a verification of a checklist of

---

30 Annex 2 of Code of Practice provides a set of useful references as regards legislation, published guidance documents, training materials, awareness and training, etc.

31 See BIS, *Compliance Code of Practice*, *op. cit.*, p. 10.

32 *Id.*

33 For more reading on this subject, see Annex 3 of Code of Practice.

34 Annex 5 of Code of Practice provides a series of indicators of suspicious enquiries.

35 See, for instance, Article 20 of Regulation 428/2009 or Article 7 of UN Protocol against the Illicit Manufacturing of and Trafficking in Firearms, their Parts and Components and Ammunition. As regards Export Control Act, the Section 29 thereof provides that the records should be kept for up to four years.

questions;[36] or a firm can delegate this procedure to a specialised body. The final recommendation of Code of Practice relates to the integration of export control practices with *quality management systems*. The importance of export issues brings about a conclusion that hereinafter has to be considered equally with others business procedures.

To conclude the section on industrial awareness, it should be noted that British economic operators have access to a large panel of informative sources provided not only by government departments implicated in strategic trade, but also by specific government initiatives for the business sector.

Thus, one of the most exhaustive export control issue overviews is provided by the UK Department for Business Innovation & Skills.[37] The BIS website offers a wide range of information about the international export control regulatory framework as well as about the British policy in this domain. It also contains an extensive description of the role and functioning of ECO. Moreover for transparency reasons, BIS website publishes annual and quarterly ECO rapports on strategic export controls.

It should be kept in mind that ECO has developed several practical tools aimed at helping national businesses in obtaining relevant export control data as well as in accessing potential licence requirements. Indeed, two online applications, *i.e. Control List Classification Search Toll*[38] and *Goods Checker*,[39] are accessible to support British companies in self-rating of goods they wish to export. However if an exporter still has doubts about the possibility of a licence requirement, he can ask for assistance from the ECO's Technical Assessment Unit, which is in charge of *Rating Enquiry Service*.[40] Moreover ECO has initiated a specialised information service for the attention of British exports. Thus, they might subscribe for an email notification service, also known as "Notices to Exporters", which will provide them with the latest updates regarding export control legislation and sanctions.

---

36 Annex 5 of Code of Practice provides a checklist of questions to be examined during an audit of internal compliance.

37 For more reading, see: http://www.bis.gov.uk/policies/export-control-organisation.

38 Control List Classification Search Toll is available at SPIRE website: https://www.spire.bis.gov.uk/eng/fox/espire/LOGIN/login (registration required).

39 Goods Checker is available at: http://www.ecochecker.co.uk/goodsChecker/ (registration required).

40 Rating Enquiry Service is a free service provided by the Technical Assessment Unit, which consists of engineers and scientists who supply a technical advice to exporters and governmental bodies. It shall be noticed that rating applications for more than four items will not be considered.

Finally, for over ten years ECO has created the UK Export Control Training and Skills Academy, which offers various export control trainings carried out by ECO personnel. The Academy addresses its services not only to companies, partners and individuals, but also to international organisations and governments.

National Jurisdiction

It would not be wrong to assert that an issue of national jurisdiction encompasses both compliance and enforcement procedures.

Compliance mechanisms are ensured by ECO, more precisely, the Compliance Unit. This body manages company audits, and controls the respect of conditions of the issued licences. The foremost objective of compliance audits is to confirm that companies export under the appropriate authorisation. The frequency of such visits depends on risk assessments (use of licence, types of licences, compliance records, volume of exports) and varies between three to twelve months, up to maximum thirty-six months. They usually tackle the companies holding Open Individual Licences, Open General Licences along with Standard individual Licences that cannot be decremented by HM Revenue & Customs, *i.e.* Standard Individual Trade Control Licences and Standard Individual Export Licences for the electronic transfer of technology and software. Each compliance visit is usually announced at least four weeks in advance by a confirming letter accompanied by a questionnaire to be filled out by the company. Subjects to be covered usually refer to the internal licensing and export processes, awareness procedures, keeping up-to-date mechanisms, etc.[41] After the audit, which consists of various checks of records of transactions and supporting documents, the Compliance Inspector usually holds a summing up session when he or she will draw up principal conclusions and will present follow-up measures. In the case of non-compliance, the Inspector will propose remedial action to undertake before the next compliance audit. If a re-visit discovers that the non-compliance continues to occur, ECO will consider a suspension of the licence(s) concerned.[42]

Apart from the licence suspension exporters might also be subject to criminal sanctions. The investigation and prosecuting of exporters in breach with UK export control legislation is provided by HM Revenue

---

41 For a comprehensive list of subjects that might be covered by ECO Compliance Unit, see Annex A of BIS, *Compliance Visits Explained*, Export Control Organisation, March 2010.

42 For more reading on the procedure of suspension of company's licences in case of non-compliance with the requirements of the Licence or relevant export control legislation, see Annex C of *Compliance Visits Explained*, Export Control Organisation, *ibid.*

& Customs and the Revenue and Customs Prosecutions Office. Consequently HMRC is informed about every irregularity detected during compliance or about any suspicious customs activity. Taking into account that Article 24 of Regulation 428/2009 requires that each Member Sate shall lay down the effective, proportionate and dissuasive penalties, the UK has established a scope of sanctions for the offences related to prohibitions and restrictions of this Regulation. Hence a person who commits an offence may be liable to a summary conviction of a fine not exceeding Euros 1,000 or an imprisonment from six months to ten years.[43] The actual penalty will usually depend on the category of offence and on the degree of exporter's intentionality. Besides HRMC can apply other enforcement mechanisms as, for instance, a seizure on a compound penalty.

Lastly, another means of dissuasion could be a publishing by BIS of the press releases on export control prosecution and compound penalty cases, also known as Export Control Prosecutions Notices.[44]

Additional Elements

The leading objective of this section is to bring forward a few practical aspects of UK export control regime. As already mentioned, ECO is a responsible authority for the issue of licences for military and dual-use goods. Each export licence is therefore delivered on case-by-case after a rigorous assessment against the Consolidated EU and National Arms and Export Licensing Criteria.[45] This list is a merger between the UK national criteria announced by the Foreign Secretary, Robin Cook, on 27 July 1997[46] and so-called EU Code of Conduct on Arms Exports.[47] It might be interesting to note the UK national criteria contained an explicit reference to the UK national interests, including "the potential effect on the UK's economic, financial, and commercial interests, including our long-term interests in having stable, democratic trading partners; and the protection of the UK's essential strategic industrial base". The

---

43 See Subsection 35 of Export Control Order 2008, 2008, No. 3231.

44 Export Control Prosecution Notices are available at the BIS website: http://www.bis.gov.uk/policies/export-control-organisation/eco-press-prosecutions.

45 See House of Commons Hansard Written Answers Index for 26 October 2000: Column 200W – 203W – regarding the Ministry of Defence, Foreign & Commonwealth Office and Department of Trade and Industry (2000).

46 A full speech of Mr Robin Cook is available at the National Archives website: http://webarchive.nationalarchives.gov.uk/+/http://www.dti.gov.uk/export.control/policy/statement.htm.

47 See Council Common Position 2008/944/CFSP of 8 December 2008 *defining common rules governing control of export of military technology and equipment* (*Official Journal* L 335, 13.12.2008, p. 99).

Code of Conduct also includes mention of national economic interests that are, however, not considered as a definite criterion. The Code simply recognises that "Member States, where appropriate, may also take into account the effect of proposed exports on their economic, social, commercial and industrial interests",[48] but in any case these factors will not affect the application of the criteria of the Code. Moreover since 2002 an additional series of criteria has been applied by ECO for transactions of component goods that "are to be incorporated into products for onward export". Taking into account the globalisation of military and dual-use industries, the British system has introduced so-called Incorporation Factors to be assessed before authorising the export of UK incorporated goods.[49]

However effective and efficient, export controls can only be conceived if an industrial sector consents to participate in it. The significance of industrial responsibility and the increasing role of economic operators in countering terrorism and WMD proliferation have already been highlighted. Hence, a question of compliance has gradually become crucial for the success of national export control regimes. For that reason, in 2009 a compliance study was initiated to "help ECO further improve its contribution towards improving UK competitiveness [and] raising awareness of and compliance with strategic export controls".[50] This study revealed that around 91 percent of respondents considered themselves to be compliant with dual-use regulations and for the most part the degree of compliance was higher amongst the firms that had already been in contact with ECO. Moreover 83 percent of respondents representing industries (commercials and intermediaries) rated an understanding of UK export control legislation within their organisation as quite good or extremely good. Besides companies, which have already been in contact with ECO, believed at more than 80 percent to have a good comprehension. To sum up, this study attested, on the one

---

48 See Article 10 of Council Common Position 2008/944/CFSP of 8 December 2008, *ibid.*

49 The licensing authority should examine following elements: "The export control policies and effectiveness of the export control system of the incorporating country; the importance of the UK's defence and security relationship with the incorporating country; the materiality and significance of the UK-origin goods in relation to the goods into which they are to be incorporated, and in relation to any end-use of the finished products which might give rise to concern; the ease with which the UK-origin goods, or significant parts of them, could be removed from the goods into which they are to be incorporated; and the standing of the entity to which the goods are to be exported". See Foreign Secretary's Statement on Incorporation Issues, 8 July 2002: Column: 651W.

50 See BIS, *Export Control Organisation – Dual-Use Compliance Study*, Summary of Results and Key Findings, November 2009, p. 3.

hand, that deliberate non-compliance with dual-use controls was not "widespread" and, on the other hand, that a significant majority of respondents (88 percent) confirmed that export control compliance is taken seriously by the British industry.

Final Conclusions

This outline of the British export control regulatory framework has confirmed that the UK considers itself as one of the key actors of international combat against terrorism and WMD proliferation. With regards to the dual-use issue, besides its membership throughout international export control regimes, the UK takes an active part in the implementation and enforcement of the relevant legislation drawn out by the European Union. Therefore, the UK legislation is constantly influenced by supra-national regulations, which are rigorously implemented by British legislators.

This is particularly true with regard to the recent tendencies in international export regulations, such as the extension of responsibility in the industrial sector. Considering the transformation of modern threats, the economic operators have become one of the cornerstones of efficient strategic controls. Henceforward businesses have to assume a more active role in detecting suspicious enquiries via so called catch-all clauses. Moreover they are expected to establish a set of requirements such as the ICP and internal compliance audits, and to keep records on transactions involving controlled items. Faced with this new reality, businesses often look for the advice of national likening authorities. The UK case illustrates that such dialogue can be successful. British licensing authority shows itself open and ready to assist the industry either by making the relevant export control information available online, or by providing direct email or phone advice. It also puts at the disposal of the industries a number of online tools that facilitate an assessment relative to licence requirement (Goods Checker, Control List Classification Search Toll) as well as considerably faster licence application procedure (SPIRE).

Such successful cooperation leads to rather optimistic conclusions, taking into account that approximately 91 percent of industrials feel themselves fully compliant with UK export control legislation.[51] In addition, a general impression of the UK licensing authority is "overwhelmingly positive".[52] Despite that there are still several challenges

---

[51] *Ibid.*, p. 13.

[52] Indeed, the ECO study attests that 87 percent of respondents have expressed a favourable opinion about the organisation. *Ibid.*, p. 14.

that remain as, for example, a lack of awareness, a complexity of regulations, an undue bureaucracy, etc.

Nevertheless, this partnership between State authorities and the industrial sector appears to be a pledge of success in the modern export control structure. Although it should be kept in mind that with respect to strategic exports, a promotion of the national business should always be attended with a security risk assessment.

France
From Security to Competitive Security

Sylvain PAILE

Researcher, Université de Liège

Introduction: French Export Control System's Geopolitical Characterisation

France is a Member State which clearly attaches great importance to the objective of securing the international flow of arms and impeding the proliferation of weapons of mass destruction (WMD). On the international scene, it proved to be an active member in the adoption of counter-proliferation measures, all along their evolution. It is a member of all major international *fora*, most often since their creation. In the framework of the North Atlantic Treaty Organisation (NATO), it was a member of the CoCom, which was dissolved in 1994 and substantially replaced by the Wassenaar Arrangement. France is also a member of the Australia Group (biological and chemical products), of the Nuclear Supplier Group (NSG),[1] the Chemical Weapon Convention (CWC), and the Missile Technology Control Regime (MTCR, dealing with delivery means of WMD) which are also – together with the NSG – international export control *fora* encompassing dual-use items and technologies' trade. As a full member of these instances, it seats legitimately in the technical group, which prepares the plenary meetings and initiates the development of counter-proliferation measures at the international level. Finally, France as a Member State of the European Union (EU) has complied with all the European regulations issued on the control of dual-use items' trade since 1994.[2]

---

1 The creation of the NSG, besides, was intrinsically linked to the French refusal to join the Non-proliferation Treaty before 1992.

2 Council Regulation (EC) No. 3381/94 of 19 December 1994 *setting up a Community regime for the control of exports of dual-use goods*, OJ L367, 31 December 1994. This Regulation was invalidated by the European Court of Justice on the basis of the arguments formulated by the Commission establishing that the control of dual-use trade was primarily a trade – Community, therefore – matter and not security. France

France also has considerable experience in the trade of sensitive items. It is, indeed, the fourth world exporter of weapons and ammunitions, the second in the EU, behind United Kingdom, with an estimated value of Euros 8 billion in 2009.[3] Consequently, France attaches great importance to the regulation of the European market in this area. The Common Position 2008/944 CFSP, adopted in December 2009 under the French EU Presidency,[4] which replaces the Code of Conduct in arms trade (1998), is particularly relevant in this context since it establishes a certain number of principles aimed at organising progressively fair competition between industrial operators.

The interest in these regulations, notably when it comes to a sound competition, is also met in the sub-section of the export of sensitive items, which are the dual-use items and technologies' trade. According to the French Service of Dual-Use Goods,[5] the value of the international export of these items amounted to Euros 20 billion for the year 2009. Each year, the French authority for dual-use goods and technologies delivers between 2,000 and 3,000 licences, and these numbers are constantly increasing. The economical weight of this sector is thus considerable. The French export all rest with an industrial structure composed notably by "heavy weight" actors, such as Areva,[6] Thalès[7] and Safran.[8] The numbered data on these three operators adequately illustrates the statistical importance of trade of sensitive items, in particular dual-use goods and technologies, both economically and socially for France, which overall exports amounted to Euros 406.1 billion in 2008. However, one must not forget that the French dual-use picture is completed by numerous small and medium-size companies which, while they do not have the same sensitive export control culture as these big competitors, may be unfamiliar, or even unaware, of the rules of the game. Their vision is most probably oriented toward one or two specialised products, which form the core of their business. The question of their (non) knowledge of the regulations is therefore particularly important for their survival on the market.

---

had already implemented the Regulation into its national legislation at the time the Court so decided.

3 Estimate of the *Direction Générale de l'Armement* (DGA, Ministry of Defence).

4 Common Position 2008/944 CFSP of 8 December 2009 *defining common rules governing controls of exports of military equipments and technologies.*

5 Interview conducted at the Service of Dual-Use Goods (SBDU) in August 2010.

6 Source: Areva (http://www.areva.com/).

7 Source: Thalès (http://www.thalesgroup.com/).

8 Source: Safran (http://safran-group.com/).

The licences delivered by the French authority[9] concerns almost exclusively "exports", in the meaning of the European Regulation 428/2009.[10] Very few demands or licences – for reasons that will be developed later in this contribution – concern transit, brokering, or even "catch-all". Furthermore, there is only little use of the possibility offered of global licences. Substantially, the licences delivered in France encompass almost all[11] categories of the European list of dual-use items and technologies in annex I of Regulation 428/2009: categories 1, 2, 3, 5 (which may be characterised as a *spécialité française*), 6, 7, 9, and 0 of course. The breakdown of French licences with regard to the international regimes dealing with these items and technologies may be estimated as follows:[12]

Regime	Percentage of the licences delivered by the French dual-use authority
Wassenaar Arrangement	55%
Australia Group	23%
NSG	17%
MTCR	3%
EU sanctions against Iran	1%
Catch-all	1% (less)

The Regulatory Corpus and Licensing Authorities

Although the data emphasizes the long-standing position of France in the trade of sensitive items, the French legislation may be seen as the evidence of a real culture in the management of the risks represented by these sensitive businesses. Indeed, France requires an authorisation prior to an export of armaments (since 1939) and prior to an export of dual-use items (since 1944).[13] The evolution of the corpus of norms accurately demonstrates the importance of this cultural dimension when it comes to the analysis of the export control system. Until 2001, a certain parallel between the export control of armaments and dual-use items could be formally observed. The respective regulatory instruments, even though they were substantially distinct, were adopted the same day, as a sort of

9 Interview conducted at the Service of Dual-Use Goods (SBDU) in August 2010.

10 Council Regulation (EC) 428/2009 of 5 May 2009 *setting up a Community regime for the control of exports, transfer, brokering and transit of dual-use items.*

11 However, this list is not exhaustive. It is aimed at illustrating the most important areas in which France is statistically active.

12 Interview conducted at the Service of Dual-Use Goods (SBDU) in August 2010.

13 Décret-Loi of 18 April 1939 and Décret of 1944, respectively. It must be noted that, in the French law at that time, a decree-law had a legislative value although a decree had a regulatory value.

"sensitive trade" package.[14] It was not the case anymore in 2010 when France came to the "implementation" of Regulation 428/2009. This step marks a philosophical de-connection of the dual-use sector from the intrinsically security-related sector of armaments. An effective and recent emancipation of a dual-use export control culture from the more global sensitive trade culture can therefore be observed. Nevertheless, this evolution does not challenge the strategic characteristics of the dual-use items in the vision of the French authorities.[15]

The security of French dual-use export items is monitored and controlled by a number of authorities. This mosaic is worth presenting while it accurately reveals the evolution of the French *pensée* on the export control of this category of items. Before the 1st of April 2010, the Authority for the delivery of dual-use export licences was the External Trade Titles Service (SETICE), which is an organ of the Directorate General for Customs and Indirect Taxation (DGDDI) placed under the tutorship of the Customs Minister. The SETICE remains today and is still the delivery authority for the export licences of military items, of items listed in the "Torture Regulation"[16] and, together with the customs, the import documents. Since the 1st of April 2010 and the most recent "dual-use regulatory package" adopted in March 2010 for implementing Regulation 428/2009, the main competence for the dual-use items has been transferred to a newly created organ named Dual-Use Goods Service (SBDU).[17] The SBDU, created within the structure of the Directorate General for Competitiveness, Industry and Services (DGCIS), has been placed under the authority of the Minister of Industry, thus evolving from a "hard security" to a more "competitive" perspective, symbolically. Its mission is to study the applications and to deliver the authorisations under the authority of the Minister, who acts through the SBDU. It must be noted that the SBDU is also competent for the export of explosive powders designed for civilian purposes. For the authorisation of the export of items of category 5 of the European Regulation ("telecommunication and information security"), an expert agency, the Information Systems Security National Agency (ANSSI), provides opinions to the SBDU. It is also similar to the Swedish model of "interactive network" between the administration and the industries,

---

14 On the 13 December 2001, for example, five regulatory acts were adopted. Two related to the trade of armaments, three to the trade of dual-use items.

15 Circulaire des douanes No. 6590 of 26 January 2004.

16 Council regulation (EC) 1236/2005 of 27 June 2005 *concerning trade in certain goods which could be used for capital punishment, torture or other cruel, inhuman or degrading treatment or punishment.*

17 Arrêté du 18 mars 2010 *portant création d'un service à compétence nationale dénommé "service des biens à double usage".*

in that it is a centre for the information of the economic operators.[18] Under this hat, it may notably assist the producers – *e.g.* small and medium-size companies – in the definition of their exports of complex items according to the European dual-use lists. However, the SBDU does not have dedicated teams of experts who would be exclusively available for this task, as in the United Kingdom, even though its staff is mainly composed of engineers. The SBDU took over the – relatively small –[19] personnel and procedures which were until then used by the SETICE, meaning that although the Service is young it has already a considerable experience of its mission. For example, it is already engaged in EU outreach activities in Morocco, Tunisia and China.

If the SBDU, under the authority of the Minister, is the Authority in the sense of the European Regulation, there exist also other organs that play an active role in the French export control system. For example, the Ministry of Economy and Finances formally publishes a list of countries subjected to restriction on exports. But the most important role, to this regard, is played by the technical ministries, such as that of Defence or Environment, and the Ministry of Foreign Affairs, which must be consulted by the SBDU when a decision is to be taken on the export of particularly sensitive items or to sensitive destinations. In order to favour and formalise the communication in this area, the regulatory package adopted in March 2010 allowed the creation of a Dual-Use Items Inter-Ministerial Commission (CIBDU)[20] within the Ministry of Foreign and European Affairs. Its mission is to provide opinions with regard to the export, brokering, transit, classification of dual-use items when an application regarding competences of several ministries is received or, more generally, on aspects of the applicable legislation. It may also provide opinions related to imports, meaning the international import certificate (IIC) or the delivery control certificate. It is informed of all applications and their outcomes by its secretariat, which is assured by the SBDU. It is chaired by the Ministry of Foreign Affairs and includes representatives from the technical ministries, which may seize it, even urgently when necessary. Finally, it is worth mentioning the recent creation of a Nuclear Policy Council (CPN)[21] in the nuclear sector, which is tasked with the definition of the general orientations of the French nuclear policy, notably with regard to the exports. The CPN is chaired by the President of the Republic, who gathers the directors of the nuclear agencies as well as the ministers of defence and economy,

---

18 As prescribed notably in Regulation 428/2009 in the Article 19 paragraph 5.

19 Less than twenty people as of January 2011.

20 Décret No. 2010-294 du 18 mars 2010 *portant création d'une "commission interministérielle des biens à double usage".*

21 Décret No. 2008-378 du 21 avril 2008 *instituant un conseil de politique nucléaire.*

and may hear representatives from the industry on aspects of nuclear policy.

Items and Flows: Comprehensive Controls and Merged Approach

The French "legislation" – composed of regulatory acts – claims a strict attachment to the European Regulation. In the "Notice to the Exporters",[22] which is a regulatory and binding document drafted by the authorities to the attention of the exporters, the applicable legislation is summarized. It clearly states that the French system is "essentially based" on the European Regulation. The definitions, such as that of a dual-use good, are indeed the same in the Notice and the Article 2 of the Regulation and a look at the customs regulatory acts does not contradict this observation. The term "essentially" suggests, however, that France uses its margin for manoeuvre in the process of implementing the European text, which will be developed in this section.

From a philosophical perspective, the most remarkable specificity of the French export control system with regard to the European legislation is its merged approach of the movements that must be controlled. In the French legislation, indeed, a paradox may be observed. The regulations, which legitimizes the controls, clearly contain in their titles direct references to the "export, transfer, brokering and transit" of dual-use goods[23] although only "exports" are referred to in the text. It is, here, a key for understanding the French dual-use export control system: any transboundary movement of a dual-use item – exception made of the European "transfers" – is considered to be an "export" and falls therefore in the framework of application of the French regulations. Concretely, this merged approach means that the controls apply to all the movements of items leaving France for a destination located outside the EU – exports, transit, brokering, transhipment – even if these movements are intangible, such as technical assistance. It must be noted that other texts may exist, besides those which regulate the authorisation procedures, notably in the customs area for the effective controls, *e.g.* for transit or intangible exports. There is, at the time being, no particular project for differentiating these movements from the – more generic – term of "export", even though the SBDU engages in sensitizing

22 *Avis aux exportateurs de biens et technologies à double usage*, 31 mars 2010.

23 Décret No. 2010-292 du 18 mars 2010 *relatif aux procédures d'autorisation d'exportation, de transfert, de courtage et de transit de biens et technologies à double usage et portant transfert de compétences de la direction générale des douanes et droits indirects à la direction générale de la compétitivité, de l'industrie et des services.*

measures for the industry on some specific aspects such as the risks represented by the intangible transfers.[24] It is a specificity of the dual-use sector, in the context of the French export control system, since there are distinct national regulatory texts dealing with the transit and brokering in the armaments' trade rules. Beyond the legal simplification of the dual-use legal corpus that this merged approach allows, another advantage of this abstraction is that European catch-all clauses apply to all the movements. For example, Article 5 of the European Regulation allows the application of catch-all to the brokering of dual-use goods, which this merged approach implements at the French national level.

Concerning items covered by the dual-use legislation, France again goes further than the European legislation. It requires, an authorisation prior to the export of "tear gas and riot control agents" as well as some "civil helicopters and their spare parts".[25] This authorisation may be granted through a general licence. Furthermore, on items of category 5 of the Annex I of the European Regulation, France requires also an authorisation – given by the ANSSI – for their European transfers, which is more restrictive than the words of Article 22 paragraph 9, which leaves the possibility for the Member States to require "additional information".

Regarding the licences that may be granted for the export of dual-use items, mainly by the SBDU as presented above, France uses the four types of licences which are described in the European Regulation: individual, community general export authorisation (CGEA), global, and general licences. The practice of the individual licences or the CGEA, which is delivered by the SBDU "on behalf" of an abstract "European authority", does not reveal real French specificity. Global licences, furthermore, are not extensively applied for in France – except for some cryptographic or electronic items – at the time being. However, the shape of the French general licences reveal the singular particularity of the export control system, not only because of the principle of use of such alternatives proposed in the European legislation but also because of the concrete use that is made of these licences. Four general licences are proposed, corresponding to categories of items:

---

24 Interview conducted at the Service of Dual-Use Goods (SBDU) in August 2010.

25 Avis aux exportateurs du 28 juin 1995 *relatif à l'exportation de gaz lacrymogènes et agents anti-émeute vers les pays tiers* and Avis aux exportateurs du 18 mars 1995 *relatif à* l'exportation de certains hélicoptères et de leurs pièces détachées à destination de pays tiers, respectively.

- Industrial goods;[26]
- Graphite;[27]
- Chemical products;[28]
- Some biological products "genetic elements and genetically-modified organisms".[29]

These general licences can be used for items and end-user States[30] listed and defined by regulations, and are valid throughout the EU territory. In order to benefit from this possibility, five criteria must be fulfilled by the export for the award of a general licence:

- The exporter must assure the non-diversion of the export;
- The exporter must warn the end-user that the item must not be re-exported toward a country not-listed for this licence;
- The exporter must inform the SBDU of changes of the end-user;
- All the export documents must contain a notice stating that the export was duly authorised;
- The exporter must keep all information on all exports made under the licence.

Furthermore, the exporter must sign a formal document – sort of "exporters' charter" – stating its intention to comply with these five criteria. In addition to these four general licences, a fifth one may be added: the general licences, also called "licences 02" on tear gas and riot control agents and some civilian helicopters and their elements. However, these licences are very specific with regard to the picture of the French dual-use general licences, and while they have been created through two notices to the exporters, the four others have been created through regulations[31] (*arrêtés*), and that, even though they are given by the SBDU, an inter-ministerial procedure is very likely owing to the

26 Arrêté du 18 juillet 2002 (modified 21 June 2004 and 18 March 2010) *relatif à la licence générale "biens industriels" pour l'exportation des biens industriels relevant du contrôle stratégique communautaire.*

27 Arrêté du 18 juillet 2002 (modified 21 June 2004 and 18 March 2010) *relatif à la licence générale "graphite" pour l'exportation de graphite de qualité nucléaire.*

28 Arrêté du 18 juillet 2002 (modified 18 March 2010) *relatif à l'exportation des biens à double usage chimiques et à la licence générale "produits chimiques".*

29 Arrêté du 14 mai 2007 (modified 18 March 2010) *relatif à la licence générale "produits biologiques" pour l'exportation de certains éléments génétiques et organismes génétiquement modifiés.* It has been signed not only by the Minister for Economy but also by the Minister of Agriculture and the Minister of Health.

30 Including some of the French overseas departments and territories.

31 However, like the *arrêtés*, the notices to the exporters are published in the *Official Journal.*

particular nature of these items. Finally, France is actively engaged in the discussion taking place at the European level on the creation of European general licences for export, brokering and transit of dual-use goods.[32]

Regarding the criteria that are used by the SBDU for its decision on whether or not to grant a licence for an export, it must be stated that the French legislation does not provide specific guidelines. Even the reasons for objecting to an export authorised by an other Member State or the "national security interests", in the meaning of the European Regulation, are defined on a case-by-case basis, which explains that such objections have rarely been opposed in fact. Such criteria, however, are available in the legislation when it comes to armaments: respect of international law, of human rights, behaviour of the end-user State in general, adequacy of the export with the real technical needs, risks a diversion of the exports. However, for France, the principle in weapons' exports is the prohibition and the exception is the export although the principle in dual-use goods' exports is the authorisation and the exception is the denial. Therefore, the application of pre-defined criteria does not correspond to the French vision even though a dual-use culture progressively emancipates itself from the "all-security" culture in arms' export. In the particular case of catch-all, for example, no particular legislation is foreseen. The criteria that are followed by the SBDU are formulated by the Ministry of Foreign Affairs, thus highlighting the challenge of an effective and efficient inter-ministerial communication. As regards the international embargoes, as stated earlier, these conditions are made available to the industries via information through the Treasure. As regards the criteria, the information is somehow centralised in the French system at the level of the SBDU, which must act on a case-by-case basis and faces, in fact, a constant increase in the demands for information from the industries[33] that are looking forward to assure more predictability for their exchanges. If no assurance on the criteria is given to the French industries at the moment, clues of these criteria may be found, nonetheless in the provisions concerning the internal procedures that are required from exporters applying for a global licence.

Authorities and Industries: Toward a Permanent Dialogue

The awareness of the rules and active role to be played by the exporters is a particularly important challenge in the French dual-use

---

32 Six propositions of European general licences have been formulated and would deal with: safe countries, low-value exports, fixing/replacement, exhibitions, calculators, telecommunications, and chemical materials.

33 Interview conducted at the Service of Dual-Use Goods (SBDU) in August 2010.

export control system since the statistical reality, as developed earlier, demonstrates the diversity and global weight of the industry. The trend, in the French legislation is, as introduced above, to enhance communication channels between the authorities and the primary actors. Unlike the French armaments' export legislation, the dual-use regulatory acts do not formally set the possibility for an exporter to ask the Authority for an advisory opinion, prior to the application for a licence. Nevertheless, in the texts and in the practice, the SBDU commits to communicating as much as necessary with the exporters, notably in answering questions when they occur. Information is thus at the heart of the relationship between authorities and industries. More formally, the compliance "charter" that must be signed by the exporters when they apply for a general licence can be seen as a first personal link between the industry and the Authority. Eventually, an internal compliance programme (ICP) is the most advanced connection possible between the Authority and the exporter since it is close to an actual registration of the exporter, prior to the delivery of a global licence. It is aimed at easing the interaction between these two and enhancing responsibility for the industry, notably for the application of suspicion clauses. Under the national regulations,[34] the implementation of compliance "procedures"[35] is controlled by the SBDU. They must deal with six kinds of obligations:

- The internal verification of the nature of the goods to be exported with regard to the end-use;
- An internal list of people responsible for the compliance of the export with the dual-use export regulations;
- An internal audit programme verifying the compliance with the procedures;
- A procedure that would help identifying customers, which may infringe the export control rules;
- A training programme for the staff dealing with the exports under global licences;
- A specific system of accounting for and archives containing information on all the operations realised.

[34] Arrêté du 13 décembre 2001 *relatif au contrôle à l'exportation vers les pays tiers et au transfert vers les Etats membres de la Communauté européenne de biens et technologies à double usage*, Article 10 modified by the Arrêté du 18 mars 2010. It must be noted that this modification substituted the terms "(the exporter) shall indicate that the measures will be communicated and effectively applied" to the terms "shall endeavour to communicate (...)", which goes deeper in the direction of exporters' liability.

[35] The French legislation does not use the term "internal compliance programme".

As introduced earlier, however, France does not have a solid culture of the ICP since the global licences are relatively less used.

The relationship between the authorities and the industries, beside the informative or consultative role of the SBDU, is also administrative since the procedures have an important role to play, notably with regard to the communication between the EU Member States. The documents in the French procedures, called CERFA, are drafted at the national level and they essentially correspond to the models presented in Annex III of the European Regulation. The application document for individual, global and general licences (CERFA No. 10994*03) reproduces the exact words of the European model with a slight difference: it includes a mention for the knowledge of the exporter of a risk of diversion of its export for a WMD proliferation purpose, which may be legitimately seen as a French implementation of the European suspicion clause. The CERFA (No. 11892*01) for the CGEA is simplified, in comparison with the other licences and, at the time being, a CERFA for the licences "02" is still in preparation. There is also a specific CERFA for the "torture Regulation" items. Finally, other CERFA were established for the end-user certificate (No. 12659*01), the international import certificate (No. 11030*1) and the delivery verification certificate (No. 11030*01). The former and the latter must be accompanied by additional commercial documents. The SBDU centralises these applications for licences and import-related certificates before dispatching them to the relevant authorities.

In parallel, the exporter must cope with the customs procedures for its exports and, in the French system, there is no systematic correspondence between the list of dual-use items – as established at the European level – and the customs' tariffs classification, which adds complexity and extends the timelines of the overall procedure. In order to diminish this constraint, France is currently engaged in a process of dematerialization of the procedures in making the administrative documents available to the industries on the customs and dual-use export control websites, which would allow the exporters to become more familiar with the documents before they have to complete them in real situations. Before that, the CERFA could only be obtained from the national publication office on the request of the exporter.

The gain of time, indeed, is a real challenge for the French industries – not exclusively the "big" companies – for which time is a precious ally not only in the commercial negotiations but also in the production. Multinational companies are an example of the globalised manufacturing processes that imply that the item must be exported several times, and comply with the export control rules of each of the production countries. Furthermore, one must not forget that the re-export of dual-use items must be authorised by all the countries, according to the international regulations. In the French texts,[36] the regulatory timeline for a decision by the Authority is nine months, after which it is denied. If this delay may be considered as quite long for and by the industry, practice[37] showed that average timelines depend on the nature of the licence applied for: fast for a CGEA – while it is close to a "registration" process –, two months maximum for global and general licences – while inter-ministerial discussions may be required. Prospectively, the purpose of the SBDU is to decrease this average to a one-month timeline, notwithstanding delays caused by issues of classification of the good or registration. The small team of the SBDU presents, indeed, the advantage of reducing bureaucratic delays to the possible extent and, in fact, it is already able to punctually provide decisions within twenty-four hours when the adequate conditions are met.

Jurisdiction, Sanctions and Denials

Under the French legislation, the control of transboundary movements is the left to the competence of the customs agents with regard to the investigations, definition of the offence and sanctions. For both the armaments and the dual-use goods, be they civilian or military, the law[38] states that the cooperation between police, gendarmerie and customs forces is necessary. Exporting without a licence is considered as an offence in the Customs Code[39] and may be sanctioned by a maximum three-year imprisonment, the seizure of the good, the means of transportation and all items used for hiding the fraud as well as a fine amounting once to twice the value of the fraud. If the criminal intent is established, meaning that there is an actual intention for trafficking, the Criminal Code foresees in its chapter on "the fundamental interests of the Nation" that the "exporter" be punished with a ten to thirty months imprisonment and a Euros 150 to 450,000 fine. A case law has been established along the long-standing French experience of the dual-use export control rules. Other infringements may be characterised besides the illicit export, such as that the exporters must legally set a system of accounting for, and archives of all their dual-use exports that must be kept available to customs services for at least for a three-year period.

---

36 Décret No. 2001-1192 du 13 décembre 2001 (modifié par le Décret No. 2010-292 du 18 mars 2010) *relatif au contrôle à l'exportation, à l'importation et au transfert de biens et technologies à double usage*, Article 9.

37 Interview conducted at the Service of Dual-Use Goods (SBDU) in August 2010.

38 Loi No. 92-1477 du 31 décembre *1992 relative aux produits soumis à certaines restrictions de circulation et à la complémentarité entre les services de police, de gendarmerie et de douane.*

39 Code des Douanes (Customs Code), articles 38 and 414.

With regards to the denial by the authorities of licences for an export or any other movement of dual-use items, the applicants may formally appeal within two months under the French regulations. Nevertheless, if the circumstances of the export have changed, for example for a denial based on a catch-all, the industries are encouraged to resort to the permanent dialogue with the Authority and, eventually, to make a new application. Dialogue is also a key word with regard to the procedures set by the European Regulation in the case of divergences between Member States themselves. Until now, the SBDU has never faced obstacles – such as those foreseen by articles 11 paragraphs 2, 13 and 16 – that could not be quickly solved by diplomatic means. Despite the absence of a European structure for communication on these aspects, France relies on the connections and dialogue between diplomatic and intelligence services and on the informal communication between the export control authorities of the other Member States in order to avoid potential undercut conflicts.

Conclusion: Challenges and Way Ahead

The French dual-use export control system is now engaged into a transition aimed at evolving from an exclusively "security" assurance to a more competitive position on the international market. This trend, however, does not, and will not sacrifice security concerns, as is demonstrated by the enhancement of greater inter-ministerial cohesion through the structure of the CIBDU. The challenge is thus, for both the authorities and the industries, to reach a satisfying balance of both security and competitiveness in the French culture of dual-use export control. The new SBDU is also in a developing process itself. It is, at the time being, integrating additional staff – from four in the previous structure to almost twenty – and shall first establish itself as a team and a structure. Nevertheless, as early successes, it rapidly began defining priorities and acting in accordance to them. It seeks to appear as a centre for information of the industries, notably through the development of its website and the publication of the CERFA, but also as the guardian of the French dual-use culture and know-how, for example in organising training and conferences for the industries and the students, or in publishing a newsletter of the export control rules and best practices.[40] Naturally, industry hopes for an increased importance of the competitive aspect in the balance, with view to assure more concrete predictability for their commercial exchanges, the needs of technological cooperation, and the globalisation of their production. Major progresses have been

[40] The newsletters are titled "Janus Express" and are available at the following address: http://www.industrie.gouv.fr/pratique/bdousage/sbdu-janus.php.

attained by the French system to this regard under the influence of the industries, such as the ongoing dematerialisation of the administrative – both authorisation and customs procedures – or more simply the availability of the SBDU for the information to the industries. Additionally if the question of legal timelines for the decision of the Authority remains a concern for the applicants, practice of the SBDU is driven by the care for a smoother trade. Nevertheless, industry in general does not look forward to sacrifice security, either. In the spirit of the ICP for global licences, voices have been raised for a system of authorisation based on a reinforced partnership with the authorities[41] as it already exists, for some customs procedures with the status of "certified economic operators". This status, aimed at increasing the self-responsibility of the exporters with regard to their exchanges and their consequences for international security, allows them to gain time in the procedures once they are certified. In the dual-use picture, translating such a system would imply that the licence would be awarded not for items listed but for a specific exporter. This may be a possible development to be discussed at the European level – perhaps in connection with the European general licences that are projected – but, on a shorter term perspective, the implementation of the ICP by the exporters may likely lead to compensations in terms of timelines for the authorities' decisions.

Finally, one of the most important challenges, shared by all the EU Member States, will be the enhancement of formal exchange of information and best practices between the dual-use authorities themselves in order to assure the overall cohesion of the system at the European level, since many of the rivals of the French industries are European.

[41] Cédric Paulin, "Les exportations et transferts européens de biens et technologies à double usage", in Fondation pour la Recherche Stratégique, *Annuaire stratégique et militaire 2005*, Paris, Odile Jacob, 2005, pp. 233-263.

Poland

Irena Kołakowska

Warsaw School of Economics

Introduction

In the early 1990s – an era of major political and economic changes in Poland – arms export control like many other state activities underwent a complete reform. One of the symbols of a new approach was that Poland had become a founding member of the Wassenaar Arrangement. By the mid-1990s export control had steadily gained a new, more visible, place in the realm of foreign security policy. This new order was confirmed by an act of law on export control adopted in 1997, and soon replaced by a new legislation (in the year 2000), which better reflected Western solutions.

Since then Poland has come a long way. Today the country is a member of all non-proliferation and export control regimes as well as other dedicated forums. The Polish system has nevertheless, been improving continuously and has adapted to the new requirements.

This article elaborates on the main features of arms and dual-use goods export control in Poland. It outlines the organisation and functional schemes. The first part provides an overview of the international dimension of export control. It presents the Polish system against this background by mentioning steps to accommodate new EU regulations. The second part describes the national economic and political environment of the export control system. It also contains a general picture of Polish defence and the dual-use goods industry, and the scope of their export activities.

Next, the article develops on the relationship between industry and export control authorities from the perspective of one advisory body (Ministry of Foreign Affairs). The following part is devoted to security and non-proliferation considerations. Finally, the author gives opinions on how the economic interests of defence industry is viewed in framework of export policy.

International Context of the Polish Export Control System

The history of modern export control in Poland starts after the year 1989. Before this date decisions regarding the transfer of arms were part of a wider geo-strategic policy, constructed and executed along the paradigms of the Warsaw Pact. In the 1990s Poland made a great leap forward, also by the fact that it became a member of all export control and non-proliferation regimes. Today, many factors that influence Polish policy and law stem directly from international arrangements. Law of the European Union plays central role here.

The legal basis for executing control constitutes:

1) Council Regulation (EC) No. 428/2009 of 5 May 2009 *setting up a Community regime for the control of exports, transfer, brokering and transit of dual-use items* for dual-use goods (directly applicable in the domestic law);
2) Common Position 2008/944/CFSP *defining common rules governing the control of exports of military technology and equipment.* The Common Position describes EU Common Criteria in Arms Export;
3) Directive 2009/43/EC *simplifying terms and conditions of transfers of defence-related products within the Community* (Intra Community Transfers Directive) for arms export.

Although the Common Position and the Directive are legally binding, they require additional implementation to the national legislation.

Undisputable, the United Nations Security Council sanctions and European Union sanctions are part of national legal system and are applied directly. Poland also fulfils sanctions adopted by OSCE. Other political decisions or documents adopted by non-proliferation regimes like Wassenaar Arrangement are given due consideration in daily decision-making.

Overview of the Polish Export Control System

In Poland, control on trade in arms and dual-use (DU) goods is integrated into one system. Its organisation and functioning is defined by the Law of 29 November 2000 on *foreign trade in goods, technologies and services of strategic importance to the security of the state and to maintaining international peace and security* (further referred to as the Law on the export control).

Organisation of the System

The Minister of Economics is the export control authority in Poland. His office is responsible for managing the decision making process and issuing licences on trade in arms or DU goods. Every decision is made after an obligatory consultation with:

- The Minister of Foreign Affairs,
- The Minister of Defence,
- The Minister of Internal Affairs,[1]
- The Minister of Finance,[2]
- The Chief of Internal Security Agency (counterintelligence agency),
- The Chief of Intelligence Agency,
- The President of National Atomic Agency.

An export control system would not be effective without enforcement. In Poland these tasks are assigned to the Custom Office and the Internal Security Agency.[3]

Scope of Control

Concerning the scope of commodities controlled, it can be said that Polish dual-use goods and military item control lists are fully compatible with the respective EU and therefore Wassenaar Arrangement's lists. Regarding the spectrum of trade activities, the system covers the following:

- Export of arms,
- Import of chemical weapons and toxins,[4]
- Export of dual-use goods,[5]

---

1 MoI is also responsible for supervision over gun ownership, internal arms trade and manufacturing.

2 A supervisor of the Custom Office.

3 It should be also noticed that Poland is very active in the Proliferation Security Initiative and regularly organises regional exercises. The aim of PSI is to enhance international and national cooperation of enforcement authorities in order to prevent proliferation of WMD, namely trafficking of weapons and components for their production. For more details visit: http://www.psi.msz.gov.pl/index.php?document=18 or http://www.state.gov/t/isn/c10390.htm.

4 Items listed in category 7b, 7j and 7k of the military list. For import of other military items a licence is not required. However an indirect control is exerted through authorisation by the control authority of end-user assurances or issuance of international import certificates.

5 It should be noticed that import of selected category of dual-use items, namely cryptographic ones, is supervised by the Internal Security Agency. Their import should be notified to the Agency. In this case the scope of control covers: cryptographic items (category 5 of DU items list: part 1 "Telecommunication": 5A001a and 5A001b4; part 2 "Information security").

- Intangible technology transfers from Poland,
- Brokering on arms and dual-use goods,
- Provision of technical service (repairs, modernisation, etc.).

Polish national regulation envisages the catch-all clause for arms and dual-use goods transfers (Article 6.7 of the Law on the export control). That means that even if an item to be transferred is not listed on control lists, but an exporter is aware that it might be used for WMD or military related purposes, an export licence must be applied for.

In daily practice, special emphasis is put on the verification of end-user declarations including the reliability of end-user and the purpose which the goods are supposed to serve. End-user assurances and other contractual agreements are central for assessing related risks, and thus admissibility of the transaction.

Penal Sanctions

Penal sanctions concerning trade in arms and dual-use goods are described in chapter 6 of the Law on the export control. According to provision of Article 33, a person undertaking trade without a licence, even not deliberately, is subject to an imprisonment of a duration of one to ten years. A fine of up to Euros 50,000 is also envisaged. A person violating conditions of a licence may be imprisoned for no longer than two years or a restriction of his freedom might be imposed. A fine of Euros 25,000 is then a discretional measure. Moreover, according to Polish Penal Code (Article 121) a production, trade, or other actions concerning WMD taken against international or national law are subject to one to ten years of imprisonment. Thus a violation of an international embargo on WMD activities, even before it is implemented into national law, is penalised.

Additional Requirements for Enterprises

A legal or natural person wishing to engage in the foreign trade in arms or dual-use goods needs to fulfil certain conditions before applying for a licence. In the case of a company, it must be registered in Poland. A natural person should possess Polish citizenship. For both it is necessary to follow an internal compliance programme (detailed presentation of the Programme will be given in the next section). Last but not least, every person wishing to trade in arms must obtain an authorisation for handling in arms on the territory of Poland, (trade, manufacture, storage, etc.) which is issued by the Minister of Internal Affairs.

Internal Compliance Programme

As has been indicated, any entity wishing to trade in arms or DU goods in international markets needs to implement an internal compliance programme (ICP).[6] ICP was designed to introduce elements of self-control over compliance with Polish and international laws and norms, especially international sanctions or EU Common Criteria in arms export. This mechanism was intended to share responsibility but also has a clear educational function. It implies some efforts on the side of an exporter to do a preliminary assessment of planned activity against criteria before engaging itself in pursuing business objectives.

Implementation of ICP in an enterprise results in introducing internal regulations and procedures regarding:

- Main tasks of company's bodies,
- Responsibilities of an employee who is in charge of self-control (a licence application presented to the control authority needs to be signed by the employee responsible for the ICP),
- Procedures of cooperation with the state administration,
- Regulations concerning recruitment of personnel,
- Regulations concerning training, internal audit and order execution.

An appropriate introduction of the ICP in an enterprise is examined by an external body and is certified according to the ISO 9000 standard. A verification of proper functioning of the ICP is made every six months by the body. However, this requirement is going to be changed – with a frequency of control extended to every twelve months.

Channels of Communication between Authorities and Industry

Polish law on export control offers to the representatives of industry a possibility to formally consult the intended transaction with export control authorities. Such inquiry can be done before licence application is formally submitted. This allows companies to obtain necessary guidance before employing time and resources for completing the transaction.

Firstly, a company may ask whether it has classified an item properly according to the dual-use goods or munitions lists. Not surprisingly, nearly all questions concern the dual-use goods. In one of the recent

---

[6] According to the law in force by February 2011. However changes in Polish law were on the way at time of writing the article with a prospect to cancel the requirement of ICP for trade in dual-use goods.

cases we delivered an opinion regarding chemicals which may also be used for nuclear purposes.

Secondly, an exporter may request for a clarification as to whether a catch-all clause should be applied. There are three to four such cases recorded annually. Most of them concern chemicals or machine tools.

Moreover, the Ministry of Foreign Affairs offers to the industry informal pre-licensing consultations. A company should present in writing a detailed description of a planned transaction, including at minimum information on importer and end-user, item description, quantity, and planned end-use. The Ministry assesses the intended transactions and presents its advise in writing. This response however is not legally binding. Official decisions can only be issued when a complete application is properly submitted and full information on the deal in question is enclosed, including an end-user certificate.

According to the Common Position 2008/944/CFSP, if an exporter is informed about a negative decision on the above-described request, export control authorities might then submit a notification about denial. The Polish Ministry of Foreign Affairs takes advantage of this opportunity, as it considers information exchange and transparency as a key aspect of export control. Such a notification is important information that prevents circumventing negative decisions by re-applying for an export licence in another EU country.

Additional communication platforms are seminars for industry organised by the Ministry of Foreign Affairs. Recently discussed topics include: the international commitments of Poland in the area of export control, EU Common Criteria in Arms Export, and transparency among the EU and Wassenaar Arrangement countries. Experience shows that the EU criteria and transparency measures, including information sharing on denials, are not yet recognised by the industry as a positive function.

Planned Improvements of the System

At the moment Poland is in the process of finalizing the implementation of the recent EU regulations (CP 2008/944, CR 428/2009, Directive 2009/43) and introducing some other adjustments into the national legislation. Current law on export control was passed ten years ago, and the perspective of the time passed offers a good opportunity for its overall assessment.

The revision process aims at making the system more efficient in terms of risk assessment. It also intends to make the law more user-friendly by lessening the administrative burden on companies and speeding up the decision-making process. There is also a need to define more clearly responsibilities of bodies involved in the process. Last but not least, additional channels of communication between authorities and exporters will be established to allow better access to information.

In order to obtain these goals the following changes will be introduced:

1. Certification of the internal compliance programme will no longer be required to obtain an individual licence on export, service and brokering of dual-use goods. This change will bring about a considerable decrease in financial and administrative difficulties for businesses. It should be noted that Poland is the only EU country where an introduction of the ICP is a formal condition to engage in trade in arms or DU items. However, experience shows that the programme has not contributed to major changes in terms of increasing the self-reliability of exporters. Moreover, the obligation could have discouraging effects on small companies wanting to engage in the trade of DU goods. Nevertheless, the ICP is still required for companies that trade in arms.
2. A separate licensing for the freight of exported goods will be cancelled (until now the licensing authority gave a licence for export of goods to an exporter and a licence for the freight or shipping of the same items to a shipping company). In practice it proved to be a redundant activity that did not contribute to security or non-proliferation objectives.
3. A clearer sharing of responsibilities between the licensing authority and advisory bodies will be established. For example the Ministry of Foreign Affairs will no longer have to accept the end-user certificates or international import certificates concerning imports to Poland – as it does not posses instruments to supervise companies and goods imported to the country.
4. New regulations concerning data collection on licensed issued goods exported will increase transparency and enable better reporting. At the time being it is impossible to indicate the real volume of export from Poland – national and EU reports contain only a number and value of licences issued, but not of an actual export.
5. Finally, new formal channels of communication will be established in order to enhance the flow of information between authorities and enterprises applying for licence. For example every authority will have the right to demand additional information regarding application (currently this remains the prerogative of an advisory body only).

Volume of export

Table 1: Number of individual export licences for arms and dual-use goods issued every year[7]

	Military Items	MI denials	Dual-use goods	DU denials
2003	191	1	62	1
2004	230	0	51	2
2005	266	3	56	0
2006	284	3	37	0
2007	345	1	41	0
2008	322	2	33	0
2009	460	0	27	0
2010	700	1	18	0

Source: database of Ministry of Foreign Affairs of Poland.

What can be observed is that the trade of arms is unquestionably more significant in terms of number of licences issued and accordingly, value of items exported. As the table indicates, the amount of applications is constantly increasing. The reason for this is a growing activity in the international markets of the Polish defence industry, and increasing involvement in global cooperation. Not less important, particularly for figures from the last two years, is the rise of international defence corporation projects in Poland.

On the other hand, the export of dual-use goods from Poland is clearly diminishing every year. This decrease is caused mainly by a steady introduction of the EU regulations. Firstly, there was a cancelation of the individual licences for the export of dual-use goods to the EU countries which are major importers of Polish DU goods. Secondly, there have not been many, or actually none, very sensitive items exported that would need a licence (items listed in annex IV to Council Regulation No. 428/2009). Finally, the Polish industry may take advantage of general and global licences for export to countries listed in annex II to the above-mentioned Regulations. The list includes Australia, Canada, Japan, New Zealand, Norway, Switzerland and United States – some of them are important final destinations of the Polish DU industry.

Polish Defence and Dual-use Goods Industry

One of the partners in the dialogue for the direction and conditions of Polish export policy are the national defence manufacturers. The Polish

---

7 Please note that these figures do not include global licences nor individual ones for brokering and service.

defence industry can be divided into two subgroups: state owned and private owned companies. The first group consists mainly of about 30 defence companies consolidated within the Bumar capital group. The Private sector counts a couple of dozen small companies and few large ones (WB Electronics) but is becoming stronger. A distinctive feature of the state-owned sub-branch is that it specialises mainly in production, modernisation and trade of post-Soviet equipment. This is a defining feature of potential export markets. The private enterprises specialize in communication, electronics systems as well as others. An increase of direct investments of European and American defence companies is also visible, mainly in the aviation sector. The segment of DU goods is significantly smaller in terms of revenues. The trade in dual-use goods in Poland is in the domain of private companies.

Non-Proliferation and Security Considerations

Export criteria taken into account in the Polish export control system are a consequence of the international obligations of the country and its security interests. The most crucial are those stemming from legally binding international law: provisions of United Nations Security Council resolutions and European Union's law. However, not less important are various politically binding decisions of international organisations or export control regimes, for example OSCE or the Wassenaar Arrangement.[8] Every licence application[9] is checked against all criteria listed beneath by a licensing officer in the Ministry of Foreign Affairs:

1. UN Security Council, EU and OSCE[10] sanctions on arms or DU transfers. Embargoes are valid since their entrance is by force. Nevertheless, international sanctions are implemented in the Polish legal system by a Regulation of the Council of Ministers which establishes a list of countries and persons to which a transfer is forbidden or restricted.[11] The list covers all UN and EU sanctioned end-users (including Al Qaida accomplices). Additionally, some

---

8 Article 2 of the Law on the export control stipulates that trade in arms or DU goods is prohibited if conditions set out in, *inter alias*, international agreements and other international obligations has not been fulfilled. According to article 15.1.2, the licensing authority denies a licence if this is required by international treaties, agreements or alliance agreements, including those referring to the control and non-proliferation of arms and dual-use goods.

9 It concerns also applications on brokering, technical assistance and intangible technology transfers.

10 Although the latter ones are only politically binding, Poland follows them.

11 Regulation of Council of Ministers of 20 October 2009 *on introduction of prohibitions and restrictions on trade in goods of strategic importance to the security of the State*.

national restrictions are listed due to the security and defence needs of Poland. Also a global prohibition of the export of anti-personal mines is included.

2. Risk of Weapons of Mass Destruction (WMD) proliferation.[12]
3. Defence and security interests of Poland.[13]
4. European Union's Common Criteria in Arms Export. In practice, criteria which are most often a matter of concern in the case of export licence applications are: 7 (risk of unauthorised re-export or transfer to another end-user), 2 (human rights violations), 3 and 4 (internal and regional instability). Related to the fourth criterion of the EU Common Criteria are the Wassenaar Arrangement's *Elements for Objective Analysis and Advice concerning Potentially Destabilising Accumulations of Conventional Weapons*. Some of EU Common Criteria are indicated in Polish law as a ground for denial (sanctions, risk of diversion, human rights violations, regional stability and terrorist activity). However, there is still a need to explicitly list all eight criteria as a possible basis for a negative decision.
5. End-user assurances (end-user certificates or international import certificates) and other contractual arrangements. These play a central role in assessing related risk, and thus the admissibility of the transaction.
6. Last but not least, a planned transaction is assessed against best-practices guidelines of: OSCE (Small Arms and Light Weapons Handbook) and the Wassenaar Arrangements (on export of Small Arms and Light Weapons, MANPADS, arms brokering, intangible transfers of technology and Best Practices to Prevent Destabilising Transfers of SALW through Air Transport).

Additional Measures

Control authorities analyse a proposed transaction in all its aspects with the purpose to decide whether an introduction of some additional requirements and security measures is necessary in order to diminish the risk involved.

The supplementary measures might refer to fulfilment of provisions of UN Security Council resolutions describing the conditions of export of arms to sanctioned countries (detailed information on shipment,

---

[12] Article 15.2 of the Law on the export control explicitly prohibits granting a licence if goods in questions could be used to WMD production purpose.

[13] According to Article 15.1.1 of the Law on the export control. Please note that also security needs of our allies are taken into account as a transaction must be in compliance with alliance agreements of Poland.

submission of additional documents verifying the end-user, etc.). There are also various requirements regarding handling of small arms and light weapons (SALW) including: proper stock management by an end-user, obligatory marking of every weapon, post shipment inspections, implementation of certain procedures concerning theft or loss. These are all described by OSCE and Wassenaar Arrangement best practices and are in accordance with the UN Programme of Action on SALW, other related agreements and the EU Strategy on SALW. If this is the case, Ministry of Foreign Affairs would demand from an exporter to present documents (shipping documents, amendments to contracts, agreements on a post shipment inspection) proving compliance with the above mentioned obligations.

Crucial for a proper risk analysis is intra-agency cooperation and information sharing among all partners involved, including an exporter. If a state company is involved in a planned transaction, then the authority responsible for supervising state companies (Minister of Treasure) is also included in the process. Close cooperation between industry and authorities is crucial because of the necessity of increasing mutual trust and the proper implementation of safety measures.

Economic Interests

The export control authorities should not neglect economic considerations. The system serves primarily to safeguard security interests of the state and its allies, but also it maintains a facilitating role in conducting legitimate trade. This implies certain duties on the side of controlling bodies. First of all, industry ought to be well informed on rules governing this business. The best way of doing so is to have a transparent law and consequent policy. All relevant criteria for licence examination should be explicitly pronounced and state policy should remain steady regardless of internal political considerations. A regular outreach to industry where the policy is explained as to the merits and interests taken into account proves to serve this objective well. Clear rules thus prevent criticism but also diminish effectively the risk of wrong business decisions by companies.

EU Export Policy Convergence

An instrument of securing interests of arms exporters would be an universal adherence by all EU Member States to provisions of the Common Position 2008/944/CFSP which concern policy coordination in the field. In practice this means aiming at no undercutting of other state's denials. Provisions of the Common Position include: policy information exchange (Article 9), denial notification (Article 4) and obligatory consultations (Article 4). They should prevent a situation when an exporter in one EU country is denied a licence for export to a third country, but an exporter in another EU country receives a positive decision in an identical case. However, it should be acknowledged that as long as a final verdict is the sovereign decision of each state, the risk of undercutting cannot be totally excluded.

State Support to Industry

Last but not least, national authorities can use their resources to support arms and dual-use exporters in markets that are considered admissible. This may take the form of establishing contacts with local authorities or political lobbying. However, one should remember that according to the above-mentioned Common Position economic calculations must not outweigh security considerations. On the other hand, foreign policy activities involve protection of interests of the defence industry at the international *fora*.

Conclusions

One of the most challenging aspects of export control is risk assessment. Although most of the cases are black-or-white, the number of those with more complex backgrounds are constantly growing. An in-depth analysis leaves, then, more doubts than answers. In this aspect, transparency, cooperation among agencies, and dissemination of information to industry take on a special meaning.

In this process much depends on the professionalism of the controlling staff. From the perspective of ten years of experience in applying control in Poland, it could be said that know-how, expertise, and specific wisdom comes steadily with time, and results from numerous discussions, enquiries, comparisons or even internal disputes that often serve as very good verifying mechanisms.

Additionally, export control is not set in a constant environment. Therefore, regular improvements of the export control system are necessary to keep up with changing political and economic circumstances. National export control law should be always up-to-date in terms of requirements and obligations. From a perspective of private companies it is of paramount importance to have a clear picture of them. In this context outreach seminars are the main platform for pursuing dialogue between government and businesses, and are a necessary part of export control policy. Finally, a well functioning internal compliance system can serve as a warning system for a company discouraging it from investing money and resources in an inadmissible export activity.

In order to support industry interests, authorities should also take advantage of measures offered by EU mechanisms. This is mostly to prevent unfair behaviour of other EU companies or states that favour a more liberal approach, and create opportunities for undercutting issued denials. Of course at the same time, this internal EU cooperation stimulates convergence and creates a level playing field, thus should be cherished and strengthened.

Hungary
ICP from the Perspective of the Export Licensing Authority

Laszlo STEFAN

Senior Counsellor, Authority of Defence Industry and Export Controls

Hungary has been a member of the European Union since 2004. As an effect of this, the European Union's export control regime must be implemented. Where applicable or otherwise empowered by European binding legal acts, national legislation regulates trade control. Each European nation has peculiar national provisions in export controls. A mandatory internal compliance programme (ICP) in Hungary may be one worth analysing further.

Internal compliance programmes form an integral part of companies' lives in dealing with exports of dual-use items in Hungary. A mandatory prerequisite for any foreign trade activity with strategic goods and technology was introduced by the legislator in 1999, with the amendment of the Government Decree which regulated this area at that time. Since then, thanks to the flexible wording used by the legislator, no changes were made in these provisions, though the world around us has undergone major changes. The basic principles and objectives for introducing these stipulations have remained unchanged and valid the whole time: handling the operators as partners, assuming responsibility of their actions through self-governance in exchange of administrative advantages. Perhaps in times of cutbacks in the administrations, and rapid growth in world trade, a wide acceptance and standardisation of ICP might be a point which should be further scrutinised.

This paper has the intention of tracing out the incentives of the legislator for introducing an obligatory ICP for exporters in the field of export controls; as well as the advantages and challenges associated from the perspective of the Authority; finally the author will try to draw some conclusions on possible future developments. The reader must bear in mind that these facts and themes were developed based on Hungary's experience and stay thus limited to this premise.

To our knowledge, legally binding provisions on ICP exist primarily in national legislations, and even they are quite limited in number, there is no consensus on this topic in the export control regimes (informal and primarily politically binding *fora*) either. There have been attempts to lay down the foundations of the forms of "Best Practice Guidelines" in some export control regimes (*e.g.* Wassenaar Arrangement) but even this attempt has remained limited due to a number of reasons.

Paragraph 2 of Article 12 of Regulation 428/2009/EC states however, that in cases of global export authorisations, in addition to the general criteria to be applied when assessing licence applications (in paragraph 1) "Member States should take into consideration the application by the exporter of proportionate and adequate means and procedures to ensure compliance with the provisions and objectives of the Regulation and with the terms and conditions of the [global] authorisation". Most EU States thus require an ICP to be in place at the operator before issuing global licences (or other general licences, because these types of licences imply a great amount of trust). The EU legislator does not venture further.

The focal point for regulating ICP requirements is the national level; even there, states preferring and promoting the use of ICP oblige operators to introduce ICP in exchange for global or general licences, and evade making it a general condition for all licensable transactions.

Hungary inherited a different outset. A system of registry was and still is a precondition for the inception of any foreign trade activity with dual-use items. A mandatory system of registry stems from the transition period to a market economy. Hungary was not denied transfers of strategic goods and technology anymore; however a robust control over imported items was a prerequisite for any export of strategic items. Import certificates and delivery notifications had to be endorsed by the licensing authority as a proof of this surveillance and control activity. To help the control powers of the licensing authority a system of registry was created to strengthen controls in both directions of trade flow: imports and exports. With Hungary's political integration into the NATO and the European Union and into the world's export control community (being a participant of all regimes) as well as economical integration into the European and world markets, import controls ceased to play a role.

ICP has become the core element of the registration. The act of registration may be regarded as automatic and has three main elements: identification of the operator (tax No, authentic signature of the person with the right of representing the entity), the point of contact (full details of the person who may be reached from the Authority for export control matters at the operator) and finally an ICP duly endorsed (by the director (-general) of the legal person or partnership).

The legislator had an immediate aim to eliminate *ad hoc* "post-box" companies by requiring all of these documents to be at the disposal of the Authority in charge of issuing the licences in order to establish the basic facts and evidence on the exporting company. Information in the registry is then used before deciding on licence applications or when the Authority conducts (retrospective) compliance checks or for other reasons.

The licensing authority analyses the presented ICP before entering the operator into the registry. ICP content requirements are covered by national legislation. The legislator defined four elements in Article 3/A of Government Decree 50/2004 on licensing of foreign trade with dual-use items which a company should cover in its ICP.

The first: (internal) *regulation of tasks, competencies and responsibilities of persons* in charge of export control matters. This basic criteria aims to identify who are the responsible persons in a company, the key people in charge of export controls, and where are they placed in the organisation of the entity. Furthermore their responsibilities and powers regarding issues in export controls should be clear. The responsibilities for the person in charge for exports (preferably in the management), his coordination powers, the overall organisational structure of the operation and the chains of responsibilities, including the powers to interfere in the sake of export controls should be revealed and visible.

At larger companies a unit is established explicitly for export control matters or together with other areas such as trade compliance. An independent unit for the sake of compliance helps to integrate possible tasks in different organisational sections and parts of the company. They can dedicate and devote their time to establish user-friendly tools to comply with foreign trade obligations. Intranet or quality management systems may serve as a good example here. A person responsible for export control or the head of the unit responsible for export control should help the decision makers of the operator by submitting proposals for an appropriate organisation and a system for work flow so the overall activity of the operator becomes "water tight" in terms of export controls. Ideally a central responsible unit or responsible person should be appointed holding all relevant information and serving as a point of reference in all export control issues with a focused responsibility. This unit or person should work out and maintain the self-regulating and auditing framework of the company that is foreseen in an ICP. As licence applications must be signed by the person whose signature has been sent for the sake of registration, there is an indirect pressure on this person (usually director general) to follow the company's export control relevant cases or be in contact with the unit/person in charge of export controls. The right to represent a company implies a top management position. With the reform of our national legislation, endorsement of an export application may be delegated.

Second element: (internal) *regulation pertaining to the obligations of relevant legal acts*. This point has the aim of establishing the internal rules and procedures for the implementation of relevant export control legislation within a company. Under this topic the Authority checks if there is a sort of commitment of the company for compliance. The existence of a published corporate commitment is not a legally prescribed obligation, but becoming a wide spread tool to deliver a message on a culture of compliance to its business partners; this commitment and dedication of the management trickles down to the employees and helps in their orientation of actions. This dedicated message on devotion might help raise awareness among the employees who in certain cases can step up where they find a gap in the internal regulatory tools of the firm.

Under this point manuals and internal regulators are checked by the Authority which describe what ought to be done and what is to be evaded. This includes the procedure of how to achieve these goals. We try to establish whether all the internal stages of the company are regulated relevant to export controls. There is naturally a major difference in a high tech R&D or a multinational production firm and a small trading company. Particulars such as who rates the items, at what stage, how it is verified, etc. at the operator are crucial in our understanding. Main issue is to verify if the company has a reasonable system of risk analysis on the end-user and end-use. Clearly the company will know the end-user and most probably the end-use far better than the Authority. The obligation of the exporting firm to get to know the partner – substantiate some knowledge on his activities – is always stressed by the Authority (difficult thing to do if orders are received in fairs or exhibitions, etc.) On the other hand if risk indicators, red-flags are fed into a risk analysing system (especially if it is open to catch-all controls) as part of a transaction screening function, (which is spread out into the core areas of the company's activity from development till shipment) illicit orders may be realised at a relatively early stage and dropped as soon as possible; as a result economic loss is kept as low as possible. This implies – depending on the size of the company – that an appropriate IT system supports the company and risk analysis system is operating. Quality management or enterprise resource planning systems (company software models, ISO standards) are commonly used by the operators and are very useful tools. American firms are aided by different risk indicator services in exchange for larger sums of money.

Updated information should include relevant export control legislation aligned with the appropriate changes, including the list of items, furthermore embargoes and the control lists thereof.

The nomination of a responsible person in charge of export (control) matters was mentioned above. This person should be from the management and should be equipped with necessary powers reflected in the internal rules and procedures or manuals. This person or unit should be responsible for working out or at least for reviewing the relevant workflows and manuals. The point is that responsibility should not be dispersed and hidden away in complicated rules and manuals. An employee, who is personally responsible for export controls with potential criminal sanctions, will likely be better motivated to take actions to comply with the law.

The company should be aware of its obligations regarding intangible transfer of technology. This does not only cover the electronic transfer of data or its availability, but includes the entire area of technical assistance for controlled technology, both inside and outside our borders. These rules cause some headaches to companies that have many subsidiaries scattered around the world who use the principle of division of labour (and technology). Flexible solutions such as global licences may decrease the administrative hurdles and illicit technology transfers. ITT remains still one of the most challenging areas to control exports from the perspective of the Authority.

A new tendency at large multinational operators is to outsource some activities and central functions of the company to countries outside of the EU. We shall discuss the problems associated with sharing controlled information with outsourced activities, and seek to know how this is regulated internally.

The subsidiaries pose a challenge: most Hungarian international companies are subsidiaries of large international companies. This means, that quality management systems are transferred including ICP. On one hand, this fact improved tremendously the quality of those ICP imposed domestically. Irrespective of their sophisticated organisational aspects, the heaps of information and data, including foreign regulations, however, revealed a weakness on the other hand: as these ICP come "fix-und-fertig", moreover the compliance or export control sections and personnel are usually integrated into the parents' organisational structure, Hungarian subsidiaries run the danger of not transposing the national/European peculiarities of export controls, because they might be intimidated by the give and take system and structures. Any amendment attempts run the risk of condescending criticism from the central office or head quarter. The Authority also faced similar remarks (at a multinational company): "we took the strictest regulations in the world (read: US) in order to comply with the rest of the world's expectations" (read: which should be more relaxed).

Record keeping rules and procedures principally pose no obstacles to the companies. The general rule of five years counting from the date of the establishment of obligations is in line with other relevant record keeping rules (*e.g.* tax and excise rules). Attention should be paid to the obligations that all documents relevant to export controls are kept for retrospective checks and audits. Yearly reporting requirements on the use of global and general licences should be borne in mind when designing this module of the ICP. A good system of record-keeping helps convince the Authority that the operator is orderly and disciplined.

The last prescribed part of an ICP is the *operational plan for the reparation of consequences in case of violation* of relevant (export control) regulations. Here the Authority asks what action plan the company has (according to its internal rules) in cases where relevant regulations are violated: does it foresee the shipments to be blocked or interdicted; is there an obligation to report the case to the Authority; what internal sanctions does a responsible person face in case of breaching internal/legal obligations; does it lead to a revision of the activities of the company including the ICP, perhaps an extraordinary internal audit and revision of the ICP. Naturally the Authority aims to achieve realistic goals here and in all areas of work. According to the Hungarian Criminal Code nobody is obliged to reveal a criminal act he committed. Besides the above, this point addresses the need to prevent failures by suggesting to impose a revision clause, which based on self assessment methods or external audits, which are in turn based on random or systematic checks, or even periodic revisions, depending on the system in place.

Though not stipulated by legislation we welcome any internal training or forms of education on this topic, especially for new comers at the company or regular updates for staff who may be potentially involved with matters relevant to export control. Conducting internal trainings is one of the most important tasks of the person responsible for export control matters.

The Authority does not offer a ready sample or model of ICP. This has to do mainly with the fact, that the companies should not have to take over automatically ready and established models, "just for the sake of the legislator". The intention of the absence of such a model is to serve as an incentive to establish a (self-) tailored model that fits the company to its best. Self-chosen and flexible solutions in the field of self-governance is a basic right of the companies. One size will not fit all. It must be mentioned here, that natural persons who have the right to export obviously do not have the requirement to establish an ICP. Micro companies are treated very differently compared with firms who employ 1,000 persons or above. ICP should therefore be proportionate.

The ICP is the core element of the registry; the legislator stipulates in paragraph 4 of Article 3/A that *the Authority controls without delay if the above conditions are fulfilled.* This is the moment, where the Authority in most cases visits the company. This visit has many aims: firstly to enable the operator to explain and elaborate on the presented ICP, but also to give the licensing authority a chance to pose questions and comment on the received information. An appropriate slogan may be used here: we analyse its efficiency and comment on deficiency. Another point is to establish personal contacts with the operator, and to explain in detail the licensing procedures; we shed light on the decision making process for licence applications and the stakeholders involved. We gather information on the possible export markets of the operator; and in exchange we explain the sensitive destinations and make them aware of suspicious inquiries, critical routes etc. Legislation is explained and awareness is raised at the premises of the company right at the inception of the exporting activity (for dual-use items). The aim is to establish mutual trust and co-operation. We visit the production site and have the company explain to us the export control relevant dual-use items, characteristics of their products, the main trading partners, maybe the operator's known rivals, how orders are taken, how partners are found and contacts established. This is a mean to establish a profile of the exporter and serve as a basis for decisions on applications. These visits essentially help both parties in their duties: the Authority gets to know its exporters, who constitute the first line of defence; the operator becomes aware of its obligations regarding export controls and at the same time finds ideally a supporting partner in its exporting endeavours: the licensing authority. Newcomers to export controls pose a risk. The mandatory registry including the ICP helps minimise the risk of illegal exports. Furthermore it helps the authorities to establish a sound case with clear responsibilities in the cases of violation of exports.

There is no official sample for an ICP offered by the Authority. There is however an obligation to give guidance to the companies on their ICP. Legally speaking the Authority has no right anymore to oblige a company to amend or rewrite its ICP. HTLO has the obligation to check and control the legally set criteria in the ICP. If there are however reasonable doubts concerning the functional capability, effectiveness and adequacy of the presented ICP, or if important comments would not be taken on board, this would be a sufficient reason not to register a company or to put pressure on the operator otherwise, if it is already registered. Paragraph 5 stipulates namely, that operators are registered (automatically), *except if the Authority establishes according to paragraph 4 that the ICP does not meet the criteria laid down in paragraph 3.*

In our experience companies have always cooperated, especially if privileges linked to licensing decisions were at stake (and they are essentially always at stake).

The merits of a mandatory registry and underlying ICP is that the operator is at the earliest possible point confronted with the rules and regulations on export controls. Responsibility is shared with the most important stakeholder of export controls: the exporter. To assume the main role in responsibility the exporter is provided by the legislator a mandatory tool to use as efficiently as possible according to its own needs. The Authority on the other hand supports the operators by providing them with as much information and help as possible, this involves bilateral meetings as often as needed and other well established methods. The licensing authority can take decisions easier and quicker in the licensing phase, because the reliability of the exporter is assured to a certain extent in the pre-licensing phase. It can dedicate its efforts to concentrate on the difficult export cases and work on areas where the operators cannot.

Future aspects

A very important sector of potential exporters of controlled items (which includes technology) remains a serious challenge to the licensing authority, namely research institutions and academia. Without going into details it goes without saying that the nature of their activities and their habits of exchanging information and data (including controlled ones) causes great difficulties for the licensing authority and the enforcement community. We need to gain experience from other states with regards to how they have succeeded with these institutions to comply with the authorities and as a second step to set up ICP for self-regulation. Promotion of an efficiently functioning ICP to assist both the Authority and the operators, including academia and R&D institutions to fulfil their obligations has been sufficiently underlined above.

It seems that the world is becoming more complex as world trade and the interaction of people (and the enabling tools) keeps steadily increasing and improving; so does the risk of illicit procurements and clandestine activities. The same applies for the fact that high technology is being ever widely used for civil end-use; the risk of misuse increases proportionately. ICP is a self-assessing and self-regulating tool to apply for the industry and other stakeholders involved in strategic transfers, to reduce or eliminate the risk of illicit exports. A well functioning ICP helps to reduce the unnecessary administrative burden and should be thus beneficial to both exporters and the authorities. Besides, a company can gain international reputation (which is an asset) by being compliant to export controls based on its own incentive and decision. The Authority on the other hand needs only to monitor its companies and can concentrate more on problematic cases.

Certification of ICP implies a body with the right to attest them. The most authentic body is the export licensing authority, but the latter has usually no capacity to screen the operator in depth and know the overall structural and functional needs of the company; consulting firms specialised in certifying quality management systems run the danger of not being up to date with all relevant information and law in force (as we had the chance to experience). Market needs and economic interests may possibly further distort the certification process.

As a next step a standardised ICP would help setting up common premises. In Hungary at least the basic pillars of an effective ICP is laid down in legislation. If some type of common standards were accepted at least on the level of the export control regimes the implementation practices would be better harmonised. As practising licensing officers we strongly recommend and support these efforts!

Italy
Export Licensing of Dual-Use Goods

Elisa GIANGRASSO

Ensign, Italian Coast Guards

Introduction: The Export Control Policy

In a modern global economy, where the forces of the international trade operate at the fast "speed of business", commercial exchanges flow as freely as possible and controls by countries on their own exports tend to be rather soft. One relevant exception concerns military and dual-use goods, whose exports are generally under strict control in order to prevent the risk of weapons of mass destruction (WMD) proliferation and the stockpiling of conventional arms in critical area of the globe.

The export control system for sensitive items, in particular dual-use ones, is a complex political phenomenon standing in a grey area between security and trade and the great challenge of this policy is to find the correct balance between the need to guarantee Security and the interest of facilitating a country's economic development.

The objective of assuring security in the international environment is common to all Countries, but export control policies require an approach stressing the dynamics of the economic and political specificities of each State. For this reason, the export controls on dual-use items can be described as a multilevel policy in which different elements interact on two main levels:

- The policy making structure, where the political actors set the essential political decisions, *e.g.* principles, objectives, lists of goods and destinations; and
- The policy implementation structure, which establishes administrative licensing procedures that are able to ensure the effectiveness of the controls, the compliance and the enforcement of the rules.

In the field of WMD non-proliferation and dual-use items, the first level is based on international legally binding treaties banning nuclear, chemical and biological weapons, on the cooperation agreements between like-minded States, such as the Nuclear Supplier Group and Wassenaar Arrangement, and of the Europeanization process which has established between the EU Member States a common system for export controls of dual-use items.

However, national prerogatives still persist and the implementation and enforcement of EU rules are in the hands of the Member States: they have discretion to interpret the provisions and there is always a possibility that those rules are not applied uniformly.

Aware of the need and of the importance to have adequate regulation in this sector, since the beginning Italy has participated in all the European and International forums that oversee the regulation and the control of the transfers of armaments materials and dual-use items in order to prevent WMD proliferation, has assimilated their basic principles through revisions of its national legislative framework, and contributes to the exchange of information, such as the denials to authorize export operations, with other major members of the abovementioned regimes.

The object of the present work is to illustrate the Italian system of export controls on dual-use items, focusing on Italian industrial capacity, the administrative procedures, and sanctions set out by the national laws.[1]

Industry of Sensitive Items in Italy

States are sensitive about maintaining a final say on the decisions on export control regulations mainly because most companies producing sensitive items – defence and dual-use – are usually the ones with high technological capabilities and are strategically important industries for the Countries which are, therefore, concerned with their competitiveness and employment.

For the Italian economy, the Industry of sensitive items is a driving sector, employing about 64,000 people and producing, in 2009, about 1 percent of the national GDP. According to SIPRI, Italy takes the 7th place among the world arms producers and one third of the entire national defence production is exported abroad.[2] The value of the total export operations authorized by the Ministry of Foreign Affairs in 2009

---

1 This report presents the results of a review of Italy's export licensing system for dual-use goods, which has involved the examination of legal materials, *i.e.* legislative Decree No. 96/2003 and Law No. 185/1990, and interviews to the Director of Dual-Use Unit of the Ministry of Economic Development; the diplomat of the Ministry of Foreign Affairs responsible for multilateral economic and financial cooperation; and an Official of the Customs Agency of Catania.

2 See: http://www.iai.it/pdf/Oss_Polinternazionale/pi_n_0003.pdf.

has been a record, counting almost five billions Euros and being the only sector which has not suffered the international economic crises of 2009.[3]

Dual-use industry is a less impressive industrial section, but important as well for the Italian economy, due to the great variety of items included in this sector. In particular, Italy boasts very good high tech competences in the production of machine tools and in 2009, despite the dramatic economic situation, Italy remained the 4th producer of machine tools (Euros 4,093 billions) – after China, Germany and Japan – and third exporter worldwide (Euros 2,527 billions) – placed after Germany, but before Japan, Taiwan, China, and USA.[4] Most of the Italian production of machine tools has been destined to other European Countries and during the first half of 2010, the main market for the Italian supply was China, then United States, France, India, Russia, Iran, Brazil, Spain and Poland.[5]

The System of Export Controls on Dual-Use Items in Italy

Although the industry of sensitive items and their exports is a fundamental source for the Italian economy, Italy has formally submitted its economic interests to a "Security priority", undertaking commitments at international and European level regarding the creation of a licensing system where exporters are required to have an authorisation to sell sensitive goods abroad.

The Italian system of export controls for defence items is founded on the national Law of 9 July 1990 No. 185, and described as "amongst the strictest and most advanced legal instruments in the world to ensure transparency and control in arms export", and establishes the appropriated licensing procedures relying on the action of the Ministry of Foreign

---

3 The main destinations have been Saudi Arabia, Germany, United States, United Kingdom, Qatar, India, Romania, Spain, United Arab Emirates and Morocco. The major Italian exporter companies are: Finmeccanica (aeronautics and defence systems), Avio (aerospace propulsion), Fincantieri (merchant, passenger and war ships) and Iveco (tactic and logistic trucks). *Report of the President of the Council to the Italian Parliament on export, import and transit of armaments materials (2009)* http://www.governo.it/Presidenza/UCPMA/Rapporto2009/rapporto_2009.pdf. Before 2005, excellent products made in Italy such as the patrol boats "Levriero", IVECO trucks and engine Isotta Fraschini have often bought by the Iranian regime for its defence system.

4 See: http://www.modena.legacoop.it/rassegna/2009/12/pressline20091218_141746.pdf and http://www.ucimu.it/ucimu/ita/index.cfm?id=644.

5 Data provided by *Centro Studi Ucimu*'s survey based on Istat data: 36 percent in Italy; 21 percent EURO Countries; 43 percent other countries.
See: http://www.ucimu.it/ucimu/ita/index.cfm?id=657.

Affairs and the Ministry of Defence.[6] Instead, export control systems for dual-use items is established by the more recent legislative Decree, 9 April 2003 No. 96, adopted in order to implement the provisions of EC Regulation 1334/2000 and Joint Action 2000/401/CFSP.[7] After the entry into force of EC Regulation 428/2009, which extends the controls to brokering and transhipment, replacing the EC Regulation 1334/2000, Italy has started an evaluation of the existing national legal framework in order to comply with the new EC provisions. Although a legislative act, replacing or integrating the existing legislative Decree No. 96, has not been adopted yet because of the complex national amendment procedure, the Regulation 428/2009 is immediately applicable and the existing licensing procedures are applied to the new activities.

The Italian export control system for dual-use items is articulated around a single national licensing authority: the IV Division of Directorate General for International Trade Policy within the Ministry of Economic Development (MED). Nevertheless, other public administrations, representing relevant national interests, plays a role in the field, especially when controls are to be extended to unlisted items according to the catch-all clause set in Article 4 of the EC Regulation 428/2009. In particular, the Ministry of Foreign Affairs embodies specific national foreign policy interests and is the main political actor representing Italy within multilateral export control regimes and EU, where it contributes to the international negotiation. The Ministry of Defence is important insofar as military and security aspects are concerned, while Intelligence and Police bodies support the MED in gathering information and carrying on preventive risk assessments inherent to some export operations. Although the single Authority rests in the MED's hands, an inter-ministerial cooperation is somehow guaranteed through a consultation process within the Consultative Committee, which is a subsidiary body within the MED structure, composed of eleven members belonging to the most concerned Ministries. Its function is to express an obligatory, but not binding comprehensive opinion before the MED grants any authorisation (Article 11 legislative Decree No. 96).

---

6 HOLM K., "Europeanising Export Controls: The Impact of the European Union Code of Conduct on Arms Exports in Belgium, Germany and Italy", *European Security*, Vol. 15, No. 2, 213-234, June 2006. http://www.prio.no/sptrans/365467078/2006kh001.pdf.

7 Legislative Decree No. 96 is accompanied by the Decree of the Ministry of Productive Activities 4 august 2003 on the General National Authorisation http://www.mincomes.it/dualuse/dualuse_norme/d040803.pdf.

Scope of Application

According to EC rules, Italy applies export controls to materials listed in Annex I of EC Regulation 428/2009 (Annex I, II and IV of Regulation 1334/2000), and any modification of the mentioned lists is immediately and directly applicable in the Italian legal system (Article 1 of the legislative Decree No. 96).[8]

For Italian law, any economic operator trading with third countries can apply for a licence, without the need to fulfil any preliminary obligations, except for the case when the name of the exporter demanding a "general" authorisation is enrolled in specific national records. Moreover, the economic operators are free to carry on the pre-contractual negotiations according to their economic interests, without any obligation to inform the national Authority. Therefore the procedure usually starts with a presentation to the MED of a specific licence request for an export operation which is subjected to a formal and substantial analysis in order to verify its consistency with the requirements set by law.[9]

There are four types of licences: Individual Specific; Individual Global; National General; Community General. The first two kinds of licences require stricter conditions to be fulfilled, while the general ones represent facilitating procedures for particular Countries of destination.

The Individual Specific Authorisation (Article 4 of the legislative Decree No. 96) is to be accompanied by an "End-user Declaration" reporting all the details about the object of the export operation and the involved subjects. In certain cases the MED can require an authentication of the end-user declaration by the competent Authority of the end-user's country and/or by the Italian Diplomatic Authority in that country.

The Individual Global Authorisation is not granted to occasional exporters and may have a validity of three years maximum, with a possibility for extension. The request must include a document subscribed by the legal representative of the exporter, where the exporter commits himself not to breach the licence conditions and to demand the consignee and/or end-user a statement declaring not to re-export or divert during the shipment the dual-use items to be used only for civil purposes. Thirty days before the end of each calendar semester, the exporter has to transmit to the MED a list summarizing the operations carried out under its individual global authorisation.

---

8 See: http://www.mincomes.it/dualuse/dualuse_norme/dl090803_it.pdf.

9 The Ministry takes into account different factors such as the obligations deriving from Italian membership to the international non-proliferation system, the reputation of the exporter; the sensitivity of the items; the end-user; the country of final destination with particular reference to its membership of non-proliferation systems, last but not least the national foreign and security policy.

Italy has introduced a National General Authorisation, which extends the facilitating conditions of the Community General Authorisation to Antarctica – Italian base – Argentina, South Korea, Turkey (Article 6 of legislative Decree No. 96). Each time a General Authorisation (national or community) is granted, the Customs Agency is promptly informed.

Table 1: Licences granted by the Ministry of Economic Development from 2006 to 2009

Licences	2009	2008	2007	2006
Individual Specific	365	437	346	313
Individual Global	23	28	7	14
National General	68 since 2003			
Community General	139 since 2003			

Source: Reports of the Ministry of Economic Development on the export activity of dual-use items to the Presidency of the Council.

Any licence could be cancelled, suspended, modified or revoked when not consistent with international non-proliferation provisions, national foreign security policies, and obligations set by the licence itself.

Table 2: Licence requests denied by the Ministry of Economic Development from 2006 to 2009

Denials	2009	2008	2007	2006
NSG	10	9	5	7
MTCR	0	0	2	4
WA	0	2	1	1
AG	1	2	2	7
Tot	11	13	10	11

Source: Reports of the Ministry of Economic Development on the export activity of dual-use items to the Presidency of the Council.

The law does not provide any time limits for when the licensing process should be concluded, nor provisions about the possible inertia from the Authority, in any case the MED usually grants the authorisation within 60 days.

The Catch-all Clause

The catch-all clause represents the only case in which the entire procedure starts with a preliminary phase of interdepartmental coordination for the acquisition of the necessary information and risk assessment inherent to a particular export operation; in particular, when the exporter or a public Authority (MED, Ministry of Foreign Affairs, Ministry of Defence or Ministry of the Interior) is aware or has ground to suspect diversion risk (*Suspicion Clause*), the "warning" is assessed in the framework of an inter-ministerial meeting among the concerned departments and notified to the exporter and Customs Agency. After this preliminary phase, if the company is still interested in carrying on with the export operation, it starts the procedure with the presentation of a licence request.

The catch-all clause has a duration of three years and any identical export operation has to be subjected to the dual-use provisions.

In practice, this clause has required the strong efforts of the MED in order to comply with the numerous appeals from the international regimes and a constant coordination activity among the MED, Customs Agency (both at central and peripheral levels) and the Presidency of the Council, aimed at sharing information on the items and destinations and assessing the sensitivity of export operations. This collaboration has been focused especially on exports towards Iran, according to the restrictive measures of the UN Security Council and the EU.

Table 3: Catch-all clauses from 2005 to 2009

2009	2008	2007	2006	2005
31	24	22	33	2

Source; Reports of the Ministry of Economic Development on the export activity of dual-use items to the Presidency of the Council.

Control and Enforcement

Control and enforcement mechanisms are crucial components of an adequate and effective administrative framework for the correct application of abstract normative provisions, since without proper end-user checking and enforcement, the entire system could become meaningless.

Article 12 of the legislative Decree No. 96 acknowledges the primary responsibility of the MED for control activities, distinguishing between pre-shipment preventive actions, combined with penalties in case of breaches, and post-shipment checking. For accomplishing its tasks, the MED avails itself of the collaboration of bodies responsible for the protection of the public order and security, such as the Customs Agency, the Revenue Guard Corps (*Guardia di Finanza*) and Police, in order to collect information and making the necessary inspection activities.

During the last years, the main instrument of control used by the Italian Authority has been record checks and commercial documentation on the exported goods the companies have the duty to keep for at least three years. The MED has not been able to carry out inspections and physical post-shipment controls, as required by Article 12 of the Decree and by the UN Resolution 1540, because of a lack of necessary financial resources.

Concretely, a prominent role is played by the Customs Agency, at central and local levels, which acts on the basis of its general mandate as customs formalities controller (Article 52 paragraph 4-10 Decree of the President of the Republic No. 633/72) and judicial police, (articles 55, 57, 347 and followers of the Code of Criminal Procedure). Its activity is carried out with the support of the Revenue Guard Corps, which has the power to make visits, inspections and checks.[10]

Specific controls on dual-use items exports and the methodologies used by the Customs Agency and Revenue Guard Corps are confidential information, which are not accessible to the public. Data regarding the attitude of the companies are restricted in order to avoid an unfair competition from foreign suppliers, which could have negative consequences on export flows and Italian economy.

Enforcement is one of the more problematic issues of the export licensing of dual-use goods, in Italy and elsewhere, because *ex post* controls are very resource intensive and extremely difficult to be implemented, and it is not easy to detect trails of illegal traffic in case of triangulation, false end-user, front companies, fraud documents, especially when financial and human resources are insufficient. The Customs Agency and the Revenue Guard Corps usually carry out controls at random. More specific and targeted controls are done when imposed by the computer information system of the Customs Agency (AIDA) which analyses real-time any export declaration, or in case of an international warning.[11]

Sanctions System

Any functional national control system has to impose effective proportionate and dissuasive sanctions to repress illicit acts. For this purpose, Article 16 of the legislative Decree No. 96 sets specific adminis-

---

10 The crucial role of the two Corps was demonstrated in September 2009, when the Customs Agency of Orio al Serio, near Milan, detected and seized two cargos of dual-use items, respectively thermoregulation instruments directed to Pakistan and technological software destined to Iran, without the necessary authorisation. See: http://www.agenziadogane.gov.it/wps/wcm/connect/408bb900442290e68e34bf4e7aaa0be0/cres20090929130328.pdf?MOD=AJPERES&amp%3BCACHEID=408bb900442290e68e34bf4e7aaa0be0.

11 This is the case of Sniper Operation, occurred in March 2010, when the Revenue Guard Corps of Milan seized a cargo of military and dual-use items directed to Iran. Nine people (5 Italians and 4 Iranians) were arrested with the accusation of criminal conspiracy aimed at illegal export of arms and dual-use towards Iran. The successful operation occurred after 8 months of inquiries, started after warning deriving from English and Romanian customs agencies and thanks to the instrument of phone tapping. See: http://www.loccidentale.it/articolo/l%27arresto+delle+spie+iraniane+%C3%A8+una+prova+del+%27nuovo+corso%27+fra+roma+e+teheran.0087238.

trative and criminal sanctions. In particular administrative fines – from Euros 15,000 to 90,000 accompanied by possible suspension or revoke of the licence – are inflicted in case of "documental incompliance" (*e.g.* when the exporter does not inform promptly the MED about any relevant change to the information provided or he does not keep the documents for at least three years), but in concrete the export operation is in line with non-proliferation rules.

Criminal sanctions, instead, are inflicted for facts connected with the actual realization of an illegal export operation (*e.g.* export operations without licence or with a licence obtained thanks to false information; inconsistency with the obligations set in the licence document; violation of Article 4 of the EC regulation on the duty to inform the MED about its awareness or suspicion on the risk inherent to an export operation) and Italian system sets the existence of pecuniary penalties and prison sentences – from two to six years of prison and fines from Euros 10,000 to 250,000 – as equal option for each crime, it is up the judge to decide the kind of penalty to apply.

Moreover Italy fully complies to the EC rules on the restrictive measures against Iran, and approved the legislative decree of 14 May 2009 No. 64 setting criminal sanctions (from three to eight years of prison according to the seriousness of the breach) for those who violate EC Regulation 532/2010 provisions.

Unfortunately, information about concrete prosecutions initiated for failure to comply with export controls and sanctions application are not available because of their confidentiality, therefore any evaluation on the efficacy and effectiveness of the abovementioned sanctions cannot be made.

Government-Industry Dialogue

Since it is extremely complex for the government to check every single item exported in such a heavy trade volume, an effective export control system cannot but be the result of the combined efforts and collaboration among the main involved actors: licensing authorities, customs bodies and last but not least the industry. In particular, the instrument of internal compliance programme (ICP) as well as the dialogue between the government and industry are fundamental elements for a successful comprehensive export control which combines security guarantee and economic/industrial development.

Although industry could be considered as a key player in export control efforts, its awareness about its legal responsibility in complying with the rules and its political responsibility in preventing any kind of contribution to the WMD proliferation are in many cases lacking. The problem is especially acute among small companies within the larger countries such as Italy. It is acknowledged that industry's concerns are different than the government ones: companies aim at getting an authorisation, exporting items as fast as possible and not to lose clients, and not rarely they try to minimize the risk of exporting to a sensible end-user, even in case of suspicion.

Italy recognizes the importance of dialogue with industries and commits to persuading them about the pre-eminence of international security interests regarding trade, and to assist them in the correct implementation of dual-use export control rules through "outreach activities" focusing on three main points:

- Raising social awareness in exporting towards sensible countries;
- Enhancing legislation compliance;
- Avoiding risky export operation.

Assistance to the industry has a determinant role and it is externalized by different channels and through different tools such as: the "organization of seminars and workshops" for national exporters to spread knowledge about dual-use issue; "transparency" thanks to an updated MED website section on dual-use items, reporting all the legislative acts, forms and information about dual-use exports; "daily availability" of the Export Control Unit Staff for exporters by email, phone, meeting in the Ministry's premises.[12]

The companies have, anyway, at their disposition other instruments consenting them to verify the dual-use nature of the goods they intend to export, *e.g.* the website of the Customs Agency – section TARIC database – and the *Consiglio Nazionale delle Ricerche* (CNR) technical expertise.[13]

Unfortunately, this "outreach system" presents some weak points, in particular during the meetings there is not sufficient time to clarify all doubts on practical questions; the person from the company attending the meeting, is not generally the one responsible for practical rules application; there is very little awareness and understanding of obligations coming from legislation and a lack of ICP, so that the company does not have any employees officially responsible for rules application and does not provide any basic/updated training. At the roots of these inconveniences there is the lack of sufficient resources for the implementation of the legislation on export controls on dual-use items, its enforcement and control activities.

---

12 See: http://www.mincomes.it/dualuse/dualuse.htm.

13 See: http://aidaonline.agenziadogane.it/nsitaricinternet/TaricServlet.

The Italian Authority, aware of these gaps, is trying to push for the adoption of a new legislative act in line with EC Regulation 428/2009, this could include provisions about compulsory ICP and the appointment of people responsible for the company to implement the rules, as well as the organization of more frequent inspections into the companies with the costs of the visits in charge of the exporters.

Final Remarks

Although there is not a single blueprint for the effective national control system of dual-use items, best practices suggest that any functioning export controls regime relies on five key elements:

- Political commitment to fully undertake the state's responsibilities as part of the international non-proliferation regimes;
- The imposition of a comprehensive legislative framework;
- The creation of an efficient licensing process;
- Effective enforcement mechanisms based on domestic and international inter-agency co-ordination and criminal sanctions;
- Dialogue between government and industry.

From the illustration of the rules and procedures applied by the Italian Government, Italy can be defined as a good complier, tying itself to international regimes and European rules, adopting national laws for a full implementation of those rules, while assuring to its national industries controls as equal as the ones carried out by other countries.

In particular, the strengths of the Italian system are due to its relatively simple administrative structure, with a single licensing body composed of well informed personnel open to dialogue with interested parties; the detailed and updated level of information available on the MED website and the reasonable rapidity of the responses.

Unfortunately, the system presents some gaps regarding the need to provide the Authority with more financial and human resources, as well as advanced information and support from specialists and experts. However, the weakest link, being also the least harmonized elements among EU Member States, is "enforcement", with the difficulty to carry out post-shipment controls and the rare infliction of sanctions, since most times it is sufficient for the companies to invoke their good faith during the export operation for being acquitted of the accusation to export dual-use items without a licence.[14]

---

[14] In October 2005 a cargo of dual-use aluminium T6 7075 produced by the Italian company "Commercial Fond" (based in Modena), usually used for the Ferrari's body, but fundamental for realizing the components of the centrifuges to enrich uranium, was seized in Gurbuluk (Turkey) by the Turkish customs authority which

Thus, the government has the duty to invest in order to assist the companies to know and understand univocally their obligations and to instil the awareness about their legal and political responsibility in the struggle against WMD proliferation. The government's efforts should be accompanied by an active and cooperative participation of other national actors (*e.g.* customs agency, police, intelligence and judicial services) with an actual application of sanctions in case of breaches, in order to affirm the credibility of the entire system.

However a basic problem continues to exist: the incomplete harmonization of the implementation structures between the States creates acute disparities and distorts the competition, which ultimately has negative consequences for the European and international trade flows, and undermines the pursuit of the ultimate aim to protect the peoples from a WMD proliferation threat.

---

had been alarmed by a CIA warning about illicit traffic of dual-use metals involving Alcoa – American industrial giant for aluminium – and directed to Iran. Although the gravity of the event, in that occasion there was not any international letter rogatory, no searches on the items, nor Carabinieri or Revenue Guard Corps' involvement and no imprisonments or sanctions. The managers of the Commercial Fond showed to the Prosecutor the contracts of three years of trading with the STEP Standard (owned by the Iranian family Jafari, expert in import/export from EU to Iran, which meant to sell the items to the Shadi Oil Industries in Teheran – oil company which did not appear in any database and whose official address corresponded to a grocery shop), for a total value of 30,000 euros, declaring to be in good faith and not to know the obligation to demand for an authorisation. In 2006 the criminal accusations were dismissed for lack of voluntary action, modest monetary amounts and lack of circumstantial evidence. Di Feo G., Maurizi S., "Iran la pista atomica – Da Modena a Teheran", *L'Espresso*, 22nd December 2006.
See: http://www.informazionecorretta.it/main.php?mediaId=12&sez=120&id=18825.

Belgium
Local Governance of Global Risks

Sara DEPAUW

Researcher, Flemish Peace Institute

Introduction: Strategic Export Control Regime in Belgium

Profile of Exports in Military Equipment and Dual-Use Items

Strategic export controls include controls in military equipment and trade in dual-use items. This section gives a concise overview of the Belgian military and dual-use market, while the following sections will focus in more detail on the dual-use export control regime.

Belgium is a medium player within the European Union when it comes to trade in military equipment. Based on the latest figures of the EU Working Group on Conventional Arms (COARM), Belgium ranked ninth in the list of exporting Member States (total value of exported licences worldwide issued in 2009).[1] This rating matches more or less its economic size in relation to the EU-27 in 2009 in which Belgium ranks seventh.[2]

In recent years, Belgian export of military equipment has experienced a strong growth. Traditionally, the Walloon Region accounts for the largest share of licensed Belgian arms exports. In 2009, the Walloon Region represented 62.6 percent of the value of Belgian arms exports. The share of the Flemish Region was 25.2 percent. The Brussels Capital Region is clearly the little brother in this picture. In 2009, only

1 *Official Journal of the European Union*, C9/1, Twelfth annual report according to Article 8(2) of Council common position 2008/944/CFSP *defining common rules governing control of exports of military technology and equipment* (2011/C9/01).

2 Eurostat, *European economic statistics*, 2010 edition Table 2.2.1 Comparison of countries' economic size in relation to the EU-27, p. 30. See: http://epp.eurostat.ec.europa.eu/cache/ITY_OFFPUB/KS-GK-10-001/EN/KS-GK-10-001-EN.PDF. In GDP per capita, Belgium ranked eighth in 2009, see: http://epp.eurostat.ec.europa.eu/statistics_explained/index.php/GDP_per_capita,_consumption_per_capita_and_comparative_price_levels#Main_tables.

0.4 percent of the Belgian arms exports were licensed by Brussels. The Federal Government (competent for arms exports by the Belgian military and police forces only) took 11.8 percent of the share. Walloon arms exports mainly consist of "traditional" military equipment such as firearms, ammunition, explosive devices, aircraft components and vehicles. Arms exports from Wallonia are primarily destined for the United States, the European Union and the Middle East. The Flemish defence-related industry, with its high-technology components such as military electronics, visualisation screens, military vehicles and components and aircraft components, exports mainly to the industrial sector in Europe, North America and industrialized countries in East Asia. Arms exports from the Brussels Capital Region consists mainly of aircraft components destined for industry and foreign armed forces in the Middle East and the other Asian regions.[3]

Table 1: Value of approved arms export licences (in million Euros) in the regions of Belgium and the Federal State 2007-2009[4]

	2007		2008		2009	
	Value	%	Value	%	Value	%
Wallonia	621.0	62.1%	688.6	67.7%	805.2	62.6%
Flanders	270.3	27.0%	240.0	20.1%	282.2	25.2%
Brussels	8.9	0.9%	1.4	0.1%	5.3	0.4%
Federal State	99.8	10.0%	264.5	22.1%	150.3	11.8%
Total	1,000.0	100%	1,194.5	100%	1,243.1	100%

Much less clear is the size of the "dual-use industry" within the Belgian territory. Cross-border trade of dual-use items with EU Member States is largely exempted from licence obligation (licences are required only for trade in the most sensitive dual-use items such as nuclear materials). For export of most dual-use items (except for these most sensitive ones) to a limited number of countries outside the EU[5] a Community general export authorisation (CGEA) is granted at EU level. This means that exporters are not required to apply for additional licences for the export of most dual-use items to these "friendly countries". For the export of dual-use items to which no CGEA applies, exporters have to apply for individual or global licences from the regional authorities in Belgium. According to the annual report of the

---

[3] Duquet, N., *Flemish foreign arms trade and trade in dual-use items 2009*, Brussels: Flemish Peace Institute, 2010.

Duquet, N., *Belgian arms exports five year after the regionalization of competences: facts and figures*, Brussels: Flemish Peace Institute, 2008.

[4] Duquet, N. (2010), *op. cit.*

[5] Australia, Canada, Japan, New Zealand, Norway, Switzerland and United States.

Walloon Region for 2009, the Walloon Region issued 26 licences for dual-use items.[6] For Brussels, the number of dual-use licences is not known.[7] Only the Flemish Region publishes detailed figures on the number and the value of the issued licences.[8] Therefore the following table offers only a partial view of the licensed trade in dual-use items from the Belgian territory in 2009. The differences in numbers of licences between the regions make clear that most dual-use exports in Belgium depart from Flanders. This is largely to be attributed to its chemical industry, which is one of the most important sites in Europe (situated in Antwerp), and accounts for 41 percent of the number of individual export licences and 65 percent of the number of global licences in Flanders.

Table 2: Numbers and values of issued dual-use licences by the Flemish Government in 2009 and 2010[9]

	2009				2010			
	Individual licences		Global licences		Individual licences		Global licences	
	Amount	Value	Amount	Value	Amount	Value	Amount	Value
EU Member States	12	51.6 million	-	-	16	32.9 million	-	-
Befriended countries	9	407,877	-	-	20	350,702	1	52,500
Other	67	59.9 million	31	1.3 billion	87	42.7 million	51	492.3 million

6 *Rapport au Parlement Wallon sur l'application de la Loi du 5 août 1991, modifiée par les Lois du 25 et du 26 mars 2003 relative à l'importation, à l'exportation, au transit et à la lutte contre le trafic d'armes, de munition et de matériel devant servir spécialement à un usage militaire ou de maintien de l'ordre et de la technologie afférente, rapport annuel 2009*, see: http://data.grip.org/documents/ 201010271526.pdf?bcsi_scan_7F8B5FB73E9E063D=0&bcsi_scan_filename=201010271526.pdf.

7 *Gouvernement de la Région de Bruxelles-Capitale, Rapport du Gouvernment de la Région de Bruxelles-Capitale au Parlement de la Région de Bruxelles-Capitale concernant l'application de la loi du 5 août 1991 relative à l'importation, à l'exportation, au transit et à la lutte contre le trafic d'armes, de munition et de matériel devant servir spécialement à un usage militaire ou de maintien de l'ordre et de la technologie afférente, periode du 1er janvier 2009 au 31 décembre 2009 inclus*, http://data.grip.org/documents/201012161602.pdf?bcsi_scan_7F8B5FB73E9E063D=0&bcsi_scan_filename=201012161602.pdf.

8 All reports on issued licences of the Flemish Region can be found on the website of the Strategic Goods Control Unit at: http://iv.vlaanderen.be/nlapps/docs/ default.asp?fid=55.

9 Duquet, N. (2010), *op. cit.*

The most important type of items exported from the Flemish region originate from the chemical industry (category 1), the nuclear industry (category 0), materials for processing (category 2), and electronics (category 3). Given the nature of the regulation on trade in dual-use items, the licensing procedures and the limited access to data for the other two regions, it is difficult to provide a full picture of the size of the dual-use industry in Belgium.[10]

Legislative Framework of the Belgian Export Control Policy

Control on trade in strategic goods (both military equipment and dual-use items) is a competence of the regions in Belgium. Following a political debate over a controversial export of arms to Nepal, the Federal Government of Belgium decided in the Summer of 2003 to empower the regions with the jurisdiction over import, export and transit of military equipment, dual-use items and law enforcement equipment. Each region – the Flemish, Walloon and Brussels-Capital regions – is competent for trade in military equipment and dual-use items that takes place from its territory.[11] The Federal Government remains competent for imports and exports of this material directly related to the Belgian army and police forces.[12] Also customs remains a federal competence.

The regions in Belgium are not only competent for the execution of the export control policy, they also possess legislative power to draft legislation in the field of export controls. According to their competences, both the regions and the federal level can adopt proper legislation. All legislative measures remain however subject to a number of limitations resulting from international obligations to which Belgium adheres. Since the regionalisation, neither the regional, nor the federal parliaments have taken legislative initiatives with regard to export controls. Meanwhile, the existing federal legislation remains in force. The most important legislations in force for controlling trade in military items are:

- Federal Law of 5 August 1991 *relating to the import, the exportation and the transit of arms, ammunitions and equipment specifi-*

10 Duquet, N. (2010), *op. cit.*, pp. 117-120.

11 Companies should apply for licences in the region in which their social seat site is based.

12 The Special Institutional Reform Act of 12 August 2003 *modifying the Special Institutional Reform Act of 8 August 1980* empowered the regions in Belgium with jurisdiction over "the import, export, and transit of arms, munitions and equipment specifically intended for military use or law enforcement and related technology as well as dual-use items and technology, without prejudice to the federal competence for import and export with regard to army and police, and in compliance with the criteria determined in the European Union Code of Conduct as far as arms exports are concerned".

cally designed for military use or law enforcement and related technology;

- Royal Decree of 8 March 1993 *implementing the law of 5 August 1991 concerning the import, export and transit of weapons and ammunitions.*

With the adoption of the European Directive on intra-community trade in defence equipment (directive 2009/43/EC) the Belgian export control regime has reached a turning point. The legislation on arms export controls needs to be amended to comply with the provisions of this directive by June 2011. The regional parliaments are competent to adopt these new amendments to the law.[13] New legislation for arms export controls is therefore expected in the course of 2011. For now, the legislative framework is still common to all three regions in Belgium.

Trade in dual-use items is legislated at the EU-level. The legal basis for controlling import, export and transit of dual-use items and related technology is Regulation (EC) 428/2009. The legal basis for the execution of the dual-use regulation is the general Law of August 1962, which monitors exports, imports and the transit of goods and technology as well as implementing decisions.[14] Trade in nuclear materials is also subjected to a preliminary authorisation, regulated in the federal Law of 9 February 1981 bearing on the conditions for export of nuclear materials and technology and its implementing Decree of 12 May 1989 (see *infra*).[15]

---

13 This means that each of the regions can adopt their own legislation according to their political preferences. However, since 1922 Belgium (including its regions) and Luxembourg form a customs union, the Belgium-Luxembourg Economic Union (BLEU). Foreign trade only exists between BLEU and third countries. According to Article 34 of the BLEU Treaty, all regulations concerning import, export and transit licences are common to all BLEU-members. Also trade in defence equipment and dual-use items is subject to the common BLEU control regime. It is unclear though, whether the content of this Treaty will prevent the regions in Belgium from adopting diverging legislation. More information: Flemish Peace Institute, "The Flemish arms export policy: an analysis of the legal framework", pp. 57-60.

14 Law of 11 September 1962 *on the import, export and transit of goods and associated technology*, *Belgian Official Journal*, 27 October 1962.

15 Law of 9 February 1981 *establishing the conditions for export of nuclear materials and equipment as well as technological data*, *Belgian Official Journal*, 10 March 1981.

Royal Decree of 12 May 1989 *on the transfer of nuclear materials, equipment and nuclear technological data and their derivatives*, *Belgian Official Journal*, 15 June 1989.

Export Control Regime for Dual-Use Items

Trade in dual-use items is subjected to Regulation (EC) 428/2009 which is directly applicable in all EU member states.[16] This section describes the export control regime in Belgium, thereby focussing on how the regions in Belgium implement this regulation and where national and/or regional legislation/practices differ from the EU Regulation.

Lists of Dual-Use Items Placed under Control and Catch-All Clauses

The scope of export controls on dual-use items is mainly defined by Regulation (EC) 428/2009. All items listed in Annex I of the Regulation are subject to a licence requirement (Article 3). Moreover, trade in non-listed items can also be subject to licence obligations according to articles 4 and 8 of the Regulation. Article 4 defines the EU catch-all clause for dual-use items, which has been regularly invoked in Flanders (sixteen times between 2007 and 2010, mainly for exports to Iran). A licence is required for non-listed items in the case that an exporter is being informed by the authorities that the items may be related to weapons of mass destruction (WMD), in the case the items will be exported to weapon embargoed countries if they are destined for military use, or when the items will be integrated in military equipment that was exported without a valid licence. Member States may decide to extend the licence requirement to transactions where the exporter has grounds for suspicion that the products to be traded are destined for use in WMD. Thus far, the regions of Belgium have not implemented this law provision in their legislation.

According to Article 8, Member States may prohibit or impose a licence obligation on the export of products that are not listed in the annexes for reasons of public security or human rights considerations. None of the regions in Belgium place extra products under control on the basis of Article 8.

However, in the Royal Decree of 8 March 1993, Belgian authorities adopted a broadly defined military catch-all clause that also affects the control of dual-use items. Belgian authorities may impose a licence requirement for "other equipment and other materials (other than the

16 Council Regulation (EC) No. 428/2009 of 5 May 2009 *setting up a Community regime for the control of exports, transfer, brokering, and transit of dual-use items*, OJ L 134 of 29 May 2009, pp. 1-269.

listed military items) intended to support military actions".[17] As a result of this catch-all clause in the Belgian legislation, all dual-use items not listed in Regulation (EC) 428/2009 to be used in military applications may require a licence on the basis of this military catch-all clause and are treated as military items (licences of military equipment are granted in this case). In Flanders, this happens frequently. Products such as certain visualisation screens and electronics that are not listed on dual-use, nor on military control lists systematically require a licence on the basis of this catch-all clause.

Industry criticized the Belgian catch-all clause because of its broad scope and lack of legal certainty. In the review process of the legislation controlling trade in military equipment, it is likely that this catch-all clause will be redefined.

In current licensing practices, the Flemish licensing authorities agreed with the customs controls that for certain categories of exports of (non-listed) items to specific sensitive countries, customs checks with the licensing authorities whether a catch-all should be invoked or not.[18]

Transactions Placed under Control

Regulation (EC) 428/2009 sets up a Community regime for the control of *export, transfer, brokering and transit* of dual-use items.

For *exports and transfers* of dual-use items, the Belgian export control regime is not significantly different from what is prescribed by the Regulation. For most items, transfers of dual-use items between Member States do not require a licence. For export of dual-use items to other countries outside the EU, a general, global or individual licence is required, depending on the country of destination and the nature of the goods. Only the most sensitive lists of items (such as nuclear materials) are excluded from the free trade principle of the internal market, and require an individual licence according to Regulation (EC) 428/2009.

Extra controls for trade in nuclear items apply not only at EU-level, but also in the Belgian legislation. On 9 February 1981 a law was passed that deals with the implementation of the international agreements on the non-proliferation of nuclear weapons. This law installs a prior federal authorisation requirement for the transfer of nuclear materials, in addition to the existing legislation on import-export and transit licences granted by the regions. The Belgian prior authorisation is thus main-

---

17 Royal Decree of 8 March 1993 *implementing the law of 5 August 1991 concerning the import, export and transit of weapons and ammunitions*, Annex N, 2nd category, A.19.

18 "Outreach Seminar Strategic Goods Control Unit" – Flemish department of foreign affairs, VOKA, Vilvoorde, 2 June 2010.

tained, parallel and complementary to the licensing procedure imposed by the EU legislation.[19] The federal competence on this matter has recently been challenged by the Flemish Government. Following an amendment to the Law of 1981, the Flemish Government appealed in November 2010 against these amendments before the Constitutional Court. The Court will now clarify the division of competences on this matter.[20]

Until recently, no form of control was exercised in Belgium on *brokering* activities for dual-use items, since none of the laws applying to trade in dual-use items contained provisions on brokering. As of 27 August 2009 however, this situation has changed with the adoption of control on specific brokering activities in Regulation (EC) 428/2009. This regulation does not impose a systematic licensing obligation for brokering activities. A licence is only required if the broker has been informed by the competent authorities that the products may be used in relation to WMD (Article 4.1 of Regulation (EC) 428/2009). The Member States themselves decide whether or not to extend this licence requirement to brokering activities with non-listed products in case they may be intended for WMD, for military items on national lists destined for countries under embargo or exported in defiance of the national licensing procedure. Member States may also extend the licensing requirement to transactions where there is a suspicion that the products to be traded are destined for use in WMD. So far, the regions in Belgium have not made use of these possibilities to extend controls on brokering.

There is also a remaining difficulty in the division of competences in Belgium regarding control on brokering. Contrary to the control of import, export and transit of military equipment and dual-use items, the control of brokering activities was not explicitly transferred to the regions in 2003. Since then, it remains unclear whether the control of brokering activities is a regional, a federal or a mixed competence.[21] However, for control of brokering activities in *dual-use items* (contrary to brokering activities related to military equipment), it was agreed to

[19] Van Heuversweyn, K., *Advice concerning the arms trade cooperation agreement, appendix: legal advice on the export of dual-use nuclear items*, Brussels: Flemish Peace Institute, 2008, pp. 10-23.

[20] *Belgian Official Journal*, 23 December 2010, p. 81742.

[21] Van Heuversweyn, K., *The Belgian regime for the control of brokering in military and dual-use items*, Brussels: Flemish Peace Institute, 2010.

appoint the regions as the competent authority to issue the required licences.[22] However thus far, no brokering licences have been issued.

Transit in dual-use items was not placed under control by EU legislation until 2009. Regulation (EC) 428/2009 introduced control on the transit of these items in very specific situations. Member States can prohibit transit of dual-use items, or may impose licence requirements in individual cases if those items are or may be intended for use related to weapons of mass destruction. Member States can also extend the application of licence requirements for transit of non-listed dual-use items in case they might be used for WMD or illegitimate military use as referred to in articles 4.1 and 4.2 of the Regulation. Belgium however, adopted already a ministerial decree in 2000, which extended the scope of Regulation (EC) 1334/2000 to transit of dual-use items.[23] Under the same conditions as for exports of dual-use items, a transit licence is required, except when the country of origin or destination is a Benelux Member (Belgium, Luxemburg or the Netherlands), when no transhipment takes place, or when the transaction is already covered by a Community export licence. Since the adoption of control on transit in the EU Regulation 428/2009, it is debatable whether this Belgian decree still conforms to the EU legislation. Thus far, the Decree has not been withdrawn or amended.

Types of Licences

Exporters in Belgium can make use of the Community general export authorisation, global licences and individual licences for exports of dual-use items. National general licences are issued in none of the regions. Companies who make use of the Community general export authorisation (adopted in Annex II of Regulation (EC) 428/2009), need to register in advance with the regional licensing authorities and are obliged to keep records of their transactions (see also Article 20 of Regulation (EC) 428/2009).[24] It is however unclear whether Belgian authorities collect and verify this data.

---

22 Hendrickx, M., Parliamentary question to Minister Peeters K., Flemish Parliament, 2009-2010, 27 April, No. 198. See: http://docs.vlaamsparlement.be/docs/handelingen_commissies/2009-2010/c0m198bui11-27042010.pdf.

Depauw, S., & Van Heuversweyn, K., *Toetsingskader voor een Vlaams decreet inzake de buitenlandse handel in militaire goederen*, Brussels: Flemish Peace Institute, 2010, pp. 26-27.

23 Ministerial Decree of 28 September 2000 *concerning the procedure governing the transit of dual-use items and technology. Belgian Official Journal*, 20 October 2000.

24 "*L'Article 20 prévoit les modalités d'archivage. Pour toute licence, individuelle ou globale, ou pour toute Autorisation générale communautaire d'exportation, l'opérateur économique doit archiver pour une période d'au moins trois ans les documents commerciaux pertinents (factures, documents de transport, documents*

Other than Community general export authorisation, individual export licences are the rule in Belgium. Individual licences are valid for one year and can be prolonged for one year. They cover specific goods (as identified on the licence application), for a specific amount and to a particular end-user. Companies that can prove their reliability, *e.g.* by proving internal procedures on end-use control and knowledge of relevant legislation,[25] can be granted global licences. Global licences are also valid for one year. They may cover a range of (specified) products to all civil end-users in one or more countries of destination for a maximum value. In specific cases, the Flemish authorities attach end-user restrictions to global licences. In recent years, global licences are used more often. This eases the administrative burden for companies and the administration but decreases the level of transparency in terms of control on end-use, more specifically on countries of (final) destination.

Licensing Procedure

It is unclear whether companies or individuals that intend to export dual-use items to destinations that do not fall under Community general licences need to apply for an export/transfer licence in the region in which their largest production site or rather in the region in which their seat is based.[26] In Flanders, the competent authority (Strategic Goods Control Unit) belongs to the Flemish Department of Foreign Affairs. Currently, the Minister-President of Flanders is competent for foreign affairs and foreign trade and thus bears the political responsibility for trade in strategic goods. In Brussels, the external relations administration processes applications for foreign trade in military and dual-use items. It is the entire Council of Ministers who is politically responsible. In Wallonia, two administrative directions are involved: the *Direction des Licences d'Armes* which forms part of DG06 Economy, Employment and Research and is competent for issuing licences and controlling their use, and the *Service Contrôle Licence* (analyse politique étrangère et droits de l'homme) which belongs to Wallonie-Bruxelles Internation-

douaniers) permettant tout contrôle a posteriori". See: http://economie.wallonie.be/Licences_armes/2U/Divers.html#1.

25 In accordance with Article 12.2 of Regulation (EC) 428/2009.

26 Discussions on the criteria to decide which region is competent are still taking place. Caron B., oral question to Mr Kris Peeters, Minister-President of the Flemish Government on ammunitions of FN, report of the Commission of foreign policy, European policy and international cooperation C 173, 2010-2011, Flemish Parliament, 15 March 2011.

Gouvernement de la Région de Bruxelles-Capitale, *Rapport annuel 2009 du Gouvernment de la Région de Bruxelles-Capitale au Parlement*, p. 28.

Rapport annuel 2009 au Parlement Wallon, p. 30.

al (WBI) and assists DG06 with political assessments. The political responsibility rests with the Minister-President of the Walloon Region.

Exporters need to apply for a licence using standard application forms. The administration will first check whether all necessary documents are present in the file. Then a technical analysis on the nature of the products, control on end-use and the end-user and a geopolitical analysis will take place. Exporters need to provide all the information they have on end-use and will need to provide an end-user certificate or an international import certificate (IIC) according to the destination of the products (see *infra*). The regional authorities can make use of the country files, compiled by the Federal Ministry of foreign affairs in Belgium for an assessment against the criteria of the EU Common Position. The administration will then formulate an advice to the minister who is politically responsible. After the export has taken place, exporters are in principle required to deliver proof of delivery. Not all authorities however, follow up on this and actually require such a document. When the licences expire, they should be sent back to the regional authorities. There are no time limits adopted in Belgian legislation for the duration of the licensing process.[27]

All three regions distinguish sensitive from non-sensitive licence applications. In Brussels and Flanders, a decision of the Secretary-General of the administration (instead of the competent minister) is sufficient in specific situations that are not considered to be sensitive. For sensitive files, consultation among regions may take place. In 2007, a cooperation agreement between the regions and the federal level was concluded.[28] The Walloon region also installed an advisory committee for assessing the most contentious licences. Flanders and Brussels do not make use of such a committee.

As mentioned earlier, for transfers of nuclear items subject to the federal Law of 9 February 1981, a preliminary authorisation is required.[29]

End User Controls

Particular attention needs to be paid to issues of re-export and end-use. Article 9 of Regulation (EC) 428/2009 stipulates that exporters shall supply the competent authorities with all relevant information

---

27 For Flanders, informal guidelines are inclined to suggest between six to ten weeks. "Outreach Seminar Strategic Goods Control Unit" – Flemish department of foreign affairs, VOKA, Vilvoorde, 2 June 2010.

28 The Belgian Federal-Regional Arms Trade Cooperation Agreement, *Belgian Official Journal*, 20 December 2007.

29 For more information see Van Heuversweyn, K. (2008), *op. cit.*, pp. 10-23.

required for their applications for individual and global export authorisation so as to provide complete information to the national competent authorities in particular on the end-user, the country of destination and the end-use of the item exported.

Companies wishing to export dual-use items with individual licences are required to submit either an end-user certificate or an (international) import certificate. Whether the first or the latter is required depends on the country of destination. An end-user certificate is a document, signed by the end-user, which declares the final end-use of the products. The end-use certificate is not a standard document and is drafted by the recipient. Certain guidelines are, however, provided by the regional authorities. In Flanders and Brussels, the authorities adopted the guidelines formulated by the Council of the EU (see *Official Journal of the EU* 2009/C11/01). The document contains a clause which states that the products will not be used for military use or for weapons of mass destruction. Also a re-export clause is included. The Walloon authorities also prescribe minimum requirements for end-user certificates.[30] End-use certificates need to be certified by local Belgian chambers of commerce or by the Belgian embassy in the country of final destination. A procedure of certification may last up to eight weeks.

In Belgium, for exports with individual licences to listed befriended countries,[31] an (international) import certificate can be used. This is a document granted by the competent authorities in the country of destination that proves their knowledge of the import of the products. There is no certification/legalisation needed by the chambers of commerce or Belgian embassies in the country of destination.

For global dual-use licences, no end-user certificate or IIC is required, but exporters are required to sign a document by which they commit themselves to the export or transit of the products to the countries of destination as adopted in the licence and in accordance with the provisions of the licence. Companies commit themselves to keeping records of their transactions and declare to be aware of the legislation in force.

The records of actual exports, the end-use document and the certification of the documents by the local chambers of commerce/Belgian embassies allow governments to maintain control on actual exports and to carry out post-export controls.

---

30 See: http://economie.wallonie.be/Licences_armes/2U/end_user.html.

31 Andorra, Hong-Kong, Malaysia, Singapore, Turkey, South Korea, Bosnia, Iceland, Croatia, Liechtenstein, Macedonia, Serbia and South-Africa.

Outreach Activities and Internal Compliance Procedures

So far, Belgium has not adopted any provisions related to internal compliance procedures for companies in its legislation. Nevertheless, it is clear that outreach to industry has received more attention lately. Outreach seminars to industry organised by regional authorities in cooperation with, for instance, the chambers of commerce in Belgium. The importance of internal compliance procedures (ICP) is stressed during these sessions. Although ICP is not a formal requirement, it is clear that the better a company makes itself known, and the better a company is acquainted with export control legislation and procedures, the more likely a company can make use of global licences instead of individual ones. In addition, a lot of information is made available on the websites of the competent regional authorities. Nevertheless, it remains a challenge to reach those companies active in the dual-use sector who are unaware of the risks involved and the legislation in force.

Transparency

Transparency is a crucial – but often underestimated – aspect of every legitimate export control regime. Democratic accountability is the ultimate means to assess the effectiveness and legitimacy of a governmental export control policy. Without transparency on issued/denied licences, public and parliamentary control is impossible. The Regulation did not adopt any provisions related to public transparency (other than general reports to the European Parliament on the implementation of the Regulation produced every three years), but does lay down some record requirements.

Article 20 of the EU Regulation 428/2009 prescribes that exporters (and also brokers) should keep detailed records of their exports, in accordance with the national law or practice in force in the respective Member States. Such registers should contain:

- The description of dual-use items;
- The quantity of the dual-use items;
- The name and address of the exporter and the consignee;
- Where known, the end-use and end-user of the dual-use items.

These records should be kept for at least three years from the end of the calendar year in which the export (or brokering transaction) took place. They shall be delivered on request to the competent authorities of the Member State in which the exporter or broker is established (Article 20 Regulation (EC) 428/2009).

In the Belgian legislation, there is no provision foreseen on how exporters should keep records, neither are there legal obligations for the government to report on trade in dual-use items to their respective parliaments. However, companies commit one selves to keep registers when they apply for global licences. Also (without a legal obligation to do so) the Strategic Goods Control Unit in Flanders has published monthly reports on their website since 2007. For each individual and global licence application, the recipient country, the country of end-use (in case the end-user does not reside in the recipient country), a description of the items (according to the code in Annex I of the Regulation) and the value of the licence are presented.[32] The other two regions (Brussels and Wallonia) have (so far) not provided detailed data on trade in dual-use. Given the nature of the general and global licences for dual-use, numbers on actual exports would greatly benefit the level of transparency in this field. Since companies are required to keep detailed registers (Article 20 Regulation (EC) 428/2009), it should be possible for competent authorities to collect this data.

Penal Provisions

Article 24 of Regulation (EC) 428/2009 obliges Member States to adopt appropriate measures to ensure proper enforcement of all the provisions of this regulation. In particular, they shall lay down the penalties applicable to infringements of the provision of this regulation or of those adopted for its implementation. Those penalties must be effective, proportionate and dissuasive.

In Belgium, breaches of import, export, or transit regulations in dual-use items are penalised pursuant to provisions in articles 10 and 10bis of the federal Law of August 1962 on *monitoring exports, imports and transit of goods and technology* and the general Law of 18 July 1977 *on customs and taxes* (articles 231, 249-253, 263-284).

Attempts of evasion of a declaration, declarations acquired on the basis of wrong information and falsely acquired licences may be punished with a term of imprisonment ranging from four months to one year. This penalty may be doubled in the event of a second conviction and increased to two and up to five years for every repeated offence. In addition, the goods in question are confiscated and a fine is imposed of ten times the duties evaded. In case it pertains to prohibited products, to which, by definition, no duties are applicable, the fine amounts to twice the value of the goods. In case it pertains to a repeated offence, the fine is doubled. Parties that have an interest in, or insurers of a smuggling offence, will be sentenced in the same manner as the actual smuggler.

---

[32] Duquet, N., *Flemish foreign arms trade and trade in dual-use items 2008*, Brussels: Flemish Peace Institute, 2009, p. 27.

In the event that the declaration is submitted with a licence, but not in line with the conditions of the licence, the goods will be confiscated and, in addition, a fine will be imposed that corresponds with the value of the said goods.[33]

Extenuating circumstances or the acceptance that the violation is due to oblivion or committed by mistake may lead to a settlement. When the violation can be proved beyond doubt, and when deliberate fraud is in clear evidence, a more lenient settlement is not possible. The mentioned penal provisions apply to military material, dual-use goods, as well as to associated technologies.[34]

An additional penalty is the possible denial of every import, export, or transit licence for a period ranging from one month to six months to any person who imports, exports, or trans-ships – or attempts to do this – without a valid licence, who trades in prohibited arms, who collaborates in the circumvention of the commercial traffic, who submits incorrect or incomplete information in order to obtain a licence, or who refuses to cooperate in a control or investigation (Article 10bis Law of August 1962).[35]

Without prejudice to the authority of the judicial police to enforce compliance with the applicable legislation, supervision and control of compliance with all the mentioned obligations are, in practice, chiefly the task of the Customs and Excise Administration officers. They verify whether the declaration corresponds to the transported goods and requests the presentation of the required import, export, or transit licence. This means that the licences issued by the regions are verified by federal officers. For this verification, the customs officers can in turn call upon the expertise of the licensing authorities. In particular with regard to import, export, and transit subject to licensing, including trade in military or dual-use goods, the officials of the Economic General Inspection and the officials or officers appointed to that task by the competent Minister are also authorised to track down and establish violations.[36]

Conclusion

Control on dual-use items in Belgium is largely based on EU Regulation (EC) 428/2009. Belgium has not made use of any of the provisions foreseen in the Regulation to extend its scope. This is not only due to the traditional EU-centric attitude of Belgium, but also to the outdated

33 Based on Article 231 of the general Law of 18 July 1977.

34 Articles 263-284 of the general Law of 18 July 1977.

35 Castryck, G. *et al.*, *The Flemish arms export policy: an analysis of the legal framework*, Brussels: Flemish Peace Institute, 2006.

36 *Id.*

legislation (of 1962) that grounds the implementation of the regulation. Most procedures to be followed by applicants for dual-use licences are not anchored in legislation, but are part of administrative procedures. In these procedures, all regions in Belgium make use of standard documents provided by the EU council (such as examples of end-use certificates among others). The most important points of divergence between Belgium and EU Regulation (EC) 428/2009 concern the control on transit of dual-use items (which are more widely controlled in Belgium), control on nuclear items (for which an extra federal authorisation is required), and the use of a broadly defined military catch-all (which widens the scope of the dual-use catch-all clause). The legal provisions concerned precede the EU Regulation (EC) 428/2009. Moreover some difficulties with its internal division of competences should be clarified (*e.g.* competences on brokering activities and control on transfers of nuclear items). An assessment of the compliance between Belgian legislation and the EU Regulation (EC) 428/2009, followed by an update of its legal framework by regional decrees to ensure the implementation of the Regulation, would benefit legal certainty and clarity for companies active on the dual-use market. This framework should include clear procedures needed for the implementation of the Regulation, *e.g.* for the organisation of control of brokering activities or requirements for reporting and transparency and an update of enforcement procedures.

Local regulation of trade in strategic goods by Belgian regional authorities may benefit from small-size administrations and their proximity to "the field". Yet, it is also challenged by the need for coordination between all actors involved and a complex legislative framework. At a time where the legislative framework for trade in strategic goods is being evaluated and reformed, the regions of Belgium should seize this opportunity to update and align their legislation with EU law and other international obligations in order to implement a clear and efficient control regime that limits global risks.

Sweden

Anna WETTER

Doctoral Candidate, Law Faculty, Uppsala University

Introduction

The topic of export control of dual-use items often revitalizes the question on how to balance trade interests against security interests. How should licensing authorities behave in order to create good business environments while at the same time ensuring that national and international policies for combating the proliferation of weapons of mass destruction are not being challenged? How many resources should the customs authorities allocate to the physical detection of smuggled items? And how much time should the national prosecution agencies spend on learning the complex regulations in order to detect those (assumingly) relatively few cases where the illegal export is conducted for the purpose of proliferating weapons of mass destruction? Is it not reasonable that most resources go to combating more common crimes to civil society?

The main rule is that the questions raised above are to be answered at the national level of the EU Member States. At the same time the Member States are obliged by EU law to take appropriate measures to ensure fulfilment of the obligations that arise from the treaties or secondary EU legislation.[1] This means that the Member States must ensure an effective enforcement of EU law that includes establishing effective systems for law enforcement and prosecuting breaches of EU law.[2] With this in mind it is more difficult to argue that the Member States have exclusive possession over the question of how many resources should be allocated to those law enforcement agencies that bear the responsibility for ensuring the effective enforcement of EU laws.

---

1 Article 4(3) of the Consolidated Version of the Treaty on European Union, published in the *Official Journal of the European Union*, C-83/13 on 30 March 2010.

2 See *e.g.* Judgment of the Court in Case C-304/02 of 12 July 2005 and Judgment by the Court in Case C-64/88 of 11 June 1991.

The discretionary power held by EU Member States gives room for the Member States to decide also on the attitudes the authorities should take in their relations with the exporting industry. In other words, the Member States are free to decide in what way and somewhat also to what extent export control should be carried out. At the same time they must balance this freedom against the obligation to carry out a *de facto* control. Should the control mechanism turn out to be completely ineffective it is most likely that the national system would meet international critique. Nevertheless, control mechanisms may be regulated by laws such as are those of accountancy (in Sweden at least) or they may be based on softer laws where the authorities act on a feeling rather than on an obligation to carry out systemic controls on specified intervals. The Swedish Agency for Non-Proliferation and Export Controls (ISP) and the Nuclear-Power Inspectorate (for nuclear materials, facilities and equipment) share the responsibility for issuing licences for exports of dual-use items in Sweden.[3]

The Swedish licensing authorities have a European reputation of maintaining a rather unique relationship with the export applicants based on a business-like relationship. In belief that compliance records will benefit from the industry's notion that the authorities show confidence in the Swedish export industry, the authorities avoid giving its export applicants the feeling that each and everyone is a proliferation suspect. In the Authority's perspective this kind of relationship can be maintained as long as the law enforcement authorities and the intelligence services do their work. Hence, the system depends on a well-established cooperation between the authorities. The contrast to the Swedish example can be found in other EU Member States such as Germany, the Netherlands or the United Kingdom where the licensing authorities are generally more focused on tracking down the export culprits than what can be seen in Sweden. The differences in approach between the European states may be explained by differences in criminal records where Sweden historically has fewer cases of intentional illegal exports of dual-use items in comparison to Germany, the Netherlands and the United Kingdom. Whether this depends on a malfunctioning detection system in Sweden, low criminal activity or anything else is impossible to say.

---

[3] Paragraph 4 of the Act on the Control of Dual-use Products and Technical Assistance (*Lag om kontroll av produkter med dubbla användningsområden och av tekniskt bistånd*) Svensk Författningssamling (SFS) 2000:1064 and paragraph 7 of the Regulation on the Control of Dual-use Products and Technical Assistance (*Förordning om kontroll av produkter med dubbla användningsområden och av tekniskt bistånd*) *Svensk Författningssamling* (SFS) 2000:1217.

This chapter will describe the Swedish system for enforcing export controls of dual-use items and technology. To some extent the described system is also a reflection on the Swedish interpretation of what type of system is necessary in order to effectively enforce the framework EC regulation that is applicable in all EU Member States.[4] However it cannot be concluded that the Swedish system provides no more than the minimum level of law enforcement since EU Member States can decide on higher protection as long as the national systems do not conflict with European trade policies. With this in mind it is difficult to judge the choices made in the Member States in balancing between trade and security interests.

Setting the Scene – Sweden's Geopolitical Context

The geopolitical context of Sweden is simple and yet very complex. Sweden chose the line of neutrality during the Second World War. At the same time little doubt remains concerning the Swedish Government's creation of safety lines during the war that were to be secured by the North Atlantic Alliance in the case Swedish neutrality policy would fail.[5] The Swedish Government has a tradition of taking the issue of non-proliferation of weapons of mass destruction seriously. However, up until the late 1960's Sweden had not yet abandoned the idea of creating a nuclear weapon and to make it part of the country's defence posture.[6] This was presumably an idea sprung from the conviction to remain neutral throughout the cold war. However, since the decision to abandon the idea of a national nuclear weapons programme and the signing of the Non-Proliferation Treaty in 1969 the country has consistently supported international non-proliferation initiatives. Furthermore Sweden signed the Chemical Weapons Convention (CWC) in 1995 and the Biological and Toxin Weapons Convention (BTWC) in 1975.[7]

---

4 Council Regulation (EC) No. 428/2009 of 5 May 2009 *setting up a Community Regime for the Control of Exports, Transfer, Brokering and Transit of Dual-use Items*, published in the *Official Journal* L 134/1, onwards referred to as the EU regulation.

5 For more reading on Swedish neutrality during the Cold War, see the Swedish Commission on Neutrality Policy, "Had There Been a War: Preparations for the Reception of Military Assistance 1949-1969", Report of the Commission on Neutrality Policy, Translation of *Statens Offentliga Utredningar* 1994:11 (Statsrådsberedningen: Stockholm, 1994).

6 For more reading on the Swedish nuclear weapons program, see Jonter, T., "Sweden and the Bomb – Swedish Plans to acquire Nuclear Weapons, 1945-1972", Nuclear Weapon Research in Sweden, 2001, ISSN 1104-1374; p. 33.

7 1995 Convention on the Prohibition of the Development, Production, Stockpiling and Use of Chemical Weapons and on their Destruction opened for signature on 13 January 1993 and entered into force on 29 April 1997. The Convention on the

Throughout the years the support has also taken the format of direct initiatives to combat the proliferation of weapons of mass destruction. For example in 1982 a Commission headed by then Prime Minister Olof Palme of Sweden submitted a report which argues that the nuclear arms race and mutual assured destruction (MAD) could destroy human civilization and that security could only be attained through cooperation and disarmament.[8]

On the proposal of the then Under-Secretary-General of the United Nation, Jayantha Dhanapala, the Swedish Government set up the Weapons of Mass Destruction Commission in 2003 that was to be mainly funded by the Swedish Government. The Commission published a final report, which includes recommendations on general principles of action in support of non-proliferation of weapons of mass destruction.[9] Earlier, in 1966, the Swedish Parliament established an independent international institute, the Stockholm International Peace Research Institute (SIPRI) which was commissioned to conduct research in areas of conflict, armaments, arms control and disarmament. The area of export control of dual-use items has been part of the institute's research for several decades. Although an independent institute the institute keeps a frequent dialogue with the Swedish Government.

On the international arena, Sweden participates in all of the four multilateral export control regimes and in the Zangger Committee.[10] A Swedish ambassador, Sune Danielsson, has been the Head of Secretariat for the Wassenaar Arrangement since 2002. As already mentioned Sweden has signed all three of the international non-proliferation agreements (the NPT, the CWC and the BTWC) and supports the Proliferation Security Initiative.[11] As a member of the United Nations,

---

Prohibition of the Development, Production and Stockpiling of Bacteriological (Biological) and Toxin Weapons and on their Destruction was simultaneously opened for signature in Moscow, Washington DC and London on 10 April 1972 and entered into force on 26 March 1975. The biological, chemical and nuclear weapons are covered by the Swedish acts; Military Equipment Act, Svensk Författningssamling (SFS) 1992:1300 and the Military Equipment Ordinance, Svensk Författningssamling (SFS) 1992:1303.

8 Common Security, by the Independent Commission on Disarmament and Security Issues, Simons and Schuster, 1982.

9 United Nations, "Weapons of Mass Destruction Commission, Weapons of Terror: Freeing the World of Nuclear, Biological and Chemical Arms", July 2006, published by the United Nations.

10 The multilateral export control regimes are; the Wassenaar Arrangement, the Nuclear Suppliers Group (NSG), the Australia Group and the Missile Technology Control Regime (MTCR).

11 The Proliferation Security Initiative (PSI) is a voluntary grouping of states which cooperate to work against the illegal transfer of WMD. It was established in 2003.

Sweden is additionally obliged under Resolution 1540 of the Security Council to ensure that export controls of dual-use items are effective and properly enforced.[12] It should be added in this context that Sweden has an international reputation of being loyal to its international legal commitments.

Regulations and Law Enforcement Mechanisms

The first two sections of this paper describe the Swedish perception of the threat of weapons of mass destruction and the government's response to that threat in very general terms. This description, however, does not explain the shape which the general policies concerning non-proliferation take when translated into national regulations and practices by the law enforcement authorities. The following sections of this chapter will focus on the legal context related to the export control of dual-use items and technology – an area which has been identified by the international community as a crucial component of global efforts to combat the proliferation of weapons of mass destruction. The description of the regulatory framework will be supplemented by a description of the system for licensing procedures, and will conclude with some remarks concerning law enforcement.

The Regulatory Framework

Sweden became a member of the European Union in 1995. Since then Swedish exports of dual-use items and technology have been regulated by EC Regulation 428/2009 in *setting up a Community regime for the control of exports, transfer, brokering and transit of dual-use items* and previously by its predecessors.[13] A Swedish law from 2000 supplements the EU regulation with provisions concerning sanctions for violations of the EU regulation and law enforcement.[14] According to the act, anyone who intentionally exports items that are regulated in the EU Regulation without a licence should be sentenced to a fine or a maximum of two years imprisonment.[15] The same punishment should also be applied to anyone who intentionally and without a licence submits technology through electronic media transfers (which are also laid down

[12] Security Council Resolution 1540 of 28 April 2004, operational paragraph 3(c).

[13] Council Regulation (EC) No. 428/2009 of 5 May 2009 *setting up a Community Regime for the Control of Exports, Transfer, Brokering and Transit of Dual-use Items*, published in the *Official Journal* L 134/1.

[14] 2000 Act on the Control of Dual-use Items and Technical Assistance, (SFS) 2000:1064.

[15] Paragraph 18, section 1 2000 Act on the Control of Dual-use Items and Technical Assistance, (SFS) 2000:1064.

by the EU regulation).[16] Finally, the same punishment should be applied to anyone who intentionally violates the provisions concerning transit.[17] If the offences are considered particularly grave the act provides for a prison term of between six months and six years.[18] In the judgment of the gravity of the crime the court should consider whether the offence was part of criminal activity carried out systemically or on a large scale or whether it has challenged a significant public interest.[19] Furthermore the act criminalizes gross negligence for all of the aforementioned offences provided that the offence is not of a minor character. Gross negligence can lead to a fine or a maximum two years prison sentence.[20]

The transfer of technical assistance to non-EU Member States without a licence can lead to a fine or imprisonment of a maximum of two years provided that the technical assistance is intended for use in connection with the development, production, handling, use, maintenance, storage, detection, identification or proliferation of chemical, biological or nuclear weapons. Grave offences may lead to a prison sentence between six months and six years.[21]

In addition to the sanctions listed above anyone who intentionally or by negligence submits false information in an application for an export licence may be sentenced to a fine or a maximum of six months imprisonment.[22] This statute refers to articles 4, 5, 20 and 22 in the EU regulation which provides for the requirement to notify the competent authorities on several occasions, including in the event that a broker has knowledge about an illicit end-use of the items. Minor offences of the notification requirement are exempted from criminal sanctions. Furthermore the act refers to the Swedish Penal Code for penalties for

---

16 Paragraph 18, section 2 of 2000 Act on the Control of Dual-use Items and Technical Assistance, (SFS) 2000:1064.

17 Paragraph 18 a, section 1 of 2000 Act on the Control of Dual-use Items and Technical Assistance, (SFS) 2000:1064.

18 Paragraph 18 section 3 and paragraph 18a section 2 of 2000 Act on the Control of Dual-use Items and Technical Assistance, (SFS) 2000:1064.

19 Paragraph 18 section 4 and paragraph 18a section 3 of 2000 Act on the Control of Dual-use Items and Technical Assistance, (SFS) 2000:1064.

20 Paragraph 19 of 2000 Act on the Control of Dual-use Items and Technical Assistance, (SFS) 2000:1064.

21 Paragraph 20 sections 1 and 2 of 2000 Act on the Control of Dual-use Items and Technical Assistance, (SFS) 2000:1064.

22 Paragraph 22 of 2000 Act on the Control of Dual-use Items and Technical Assistance, (SFS) 2000:1064.

attempts to carry out unlicensed exports of those items that are listed in the EU regulation.[23]

Export offenders may in addition to the aforementioned statutes be prosecuted under the 2003 Act on Criminal Responsibility for Terrorist Offences but only if the offence would seriously risk damaging a state or an intergovernmental organization and the offender's intent would be to (amongst a list of alternative criteria) seriously intimidate a population or a group of a population.[24] The criminalization also covers the financing of crimes through the Act on Criminal Responsibility for the Financing of Particularly Serious Crime in some cases.[25] The Act on the Transport of Dangerous Goods regulates amongst other things the transhipment through Swedish territory and domestic transfers of certain human pathogens, animal/zoonotic pathogens, plant pathogens, and dual-use equipment.[26] Finally, the act on penalties for smuggling should be mentioned in this context as it includes some provisions that could be relevant for export offences.[27]

In addition to the criminal sanctions mentioned above, the Swedish act provides for the confiscation of property. For example items that have been subject to crime according to the Act on the Control of Dual-use Items and Technical Assistance, alternatively the corresponding value of such product may be confiscated unless it is not blatantly unreasonable.[28]

Licensing, Detection and Prosecution Procedures

The Swedish Agency for Non-Proliferation and Export Controls (ISP) was established in 1995 replacing the former licensing authority

---

[23] Chapter 23 of the Swedish Penal Code (*Brottsbalken*) Svensk Författningssamling (SFS) 1962:700.

[24] Act on Criminal Responsibility for Terrorist Offences (*Lag om straff för terroristbrott*), Svensk Författningssamling (SFS) 2003:148.

[25] Act on Criminal Responsibility for the Financing of Particularly Serious Crime in some cases (*Lag om straff för finansiering av särskilt allvarlig brottslighet i vissa fall*), Svensk Författningssamling (SFS) 2002:444.

[26] The Act on Transport of Dangerous Goods (*Lag om transport av farligt gods*) Svensk Författningssamling (SFS) 2006:263.

[27] Act on Penalties for Smuggling (*Lag om straff för smuggling*), Svensk Författningssamling (SFS) 2000:1225. In the 1990's, an Iranian born Swedish citizen was prosecuted under the Act on Penalties for Smuggling for having illegally, without a licence, exported dual-use goods to his cousin in Iran. For an analysis of this case see Anna Wetter, *Enforcing European Union Law on Exports of Dual-Use Items*, published by Oxford University Press in 2009, ISBN 978-0-19-954896-5.

[28] Paragraph 23 of Act on the Control of Dual-use Items and Technical Assistance, (SFS) 2000:1064.

which was found within the Swedish Ministry for Foreign Affairs.[29] The reasons for the reform are several. One reason was to facilitate for industry by introducing one coherent licensing authority that would deal exclusively with export licences. All export applications were to be addressed to ISP which would refer applications only of principle relevance to the government. Mainly, such applications would concern war weapon material and only to a very marginal extent applications concerning dual-use items and technology. Another reason (although along the similar lines) was to create better conditions for the Ministry for Foreign Affairs to concentrate on the applications of principle relevance. By concentrating on these the Ministry was to develop coherent guiding policies in the area of export control. It was believed that this objective could only be achieved if the Ministry could be released from the huge amount of export control applications.[30]

The Swedish approach to combating illegal exports of dual-use items and technology builds on the principle that early prevention is more effective than detection at the border. Thus, the focus is on licensing procedures and on effective intelligence to facilitate the detection, disruption and prosecution of illegal export activities. Recently, ISP has taken measures to improve inter-agency cooperation with authority allies such as the Customs Agency, the Intelligence Services (both the civil and the military, SÄPO and MUST) the National Defence Radio Establishment (FRA) and the Swedish Defence Research Agency (FOI). This arrangement is complementary to the establishments that already exist. Another recent initiative by the ISP is the introduction of cooperation between the Agency and the National Prosecution services. The initiative was taken in belief that there was work to be done in the area of bringing effect to the Swedish law in this field at the prosecution level. Experience shows that national prosecutors in Sweden find the export control regulations complex and difficult to apply.[31]

There are two distinctive features in ISP's licensing procedure for dual-use items. According to one system, let us call it the surveillance system; the point of departure is taken in the end-use of the items. This type of licensing procedure emanates from ISP's suspicion that the end-user will use the items in a weapons program that Sweden does not approve with. As already mentioned the surveillance system kicks in whenever there is a suspicion of illicit end-use. The suspicion usually

---

29 ISP became operational in 1996.

30 *Ny myndighet för kontroll över krigsmateriel och andra strategiskt känsliga produkter*, Regeringens proposition 1995/96:31, p. 24.

31 This experience was collected by the author in 2008 during and in preparation for the Stockholm seminar on Investigating and Prosecuting Offences related to the Illegal Export of Dual-use Items in EU Member States on 10-12 September 2008.

emanates in information collected by ISP and other authorities. The surveillance system is largely dependent upon a close cooperation with the Customs Agency, the Swedish civil and military intelligences service, the National Radio Defence Establishment and the Swedish Defence Research Institute. The organs work together to detect suspicious activities related to the export of weapons and weapons materials.

Other systems, such as the product control system, take their point of departure from the control lists. Licensing applications by companies with good compliance records and with long established relations with ISP are the most likely to follow the product control system. This system is supplemented with audits done by ISP and other auditing actors such as the Customs Agency.

The surveillance system requires extensive resources. It requires that ISP carry out systematic investigations of business, organizations and persons in the search for those who may be assisting end-users with proliferation objectives. If suspicious end-use is identified the Authority may add the product to a provisionary list, using the catch-all instrument provided for in accordance with the EU Regulation. According to ISP officials the catch-all instrument is fundamental for stopping suspicious items to sensitive destinations.

In recent years ISP has developed new procedures for making more resources available to sensitive licensing applications. One such initiative is the work done on the refinement of procedures for issuing global licences. ISP notes in its 2009 yearly report to the Ministry for Foreign Affairs that a more frequent use of global licences creates better opportunities for the Authority to focus on sensitive applications.[32] It further notes that the use of global licences is also good for industry as the licences may speed up the licensing procedure.[33] ISP finally notes that, importantly, the conditions for applying global licences must be subject to ISP's control of the company's internal control programs.[34]

Sweden applies three different groups of licences which each may include further types of licences. The three groups include i) general licences, ii) global licences, and iii) individual licences. The general licences apply without a prior application procedure to the licensing authority. The general licences, which are at the disposal of the exporter, include the Community General Export Authorisation (CGEA) and the

---

32 *Strategic Export Control – War Material and Dual-use Items and Technology*, 2009 Annual Report to the Swedish Ministry for Foreign Affairs, Government Communication, 2009/10:114, p. 67.

33 ISP 2009 Annual Report, *op. cit.*, p. 67.

34 *Id.*

national general licence.[35] The CGEA is applied to all items that are listed in Annex I of the EU regulation and are provided for exports to Australia, the US, Japan, Canada, New Zealand, Norway, and Switzerland. When a company applies it for the first time it must notify ISP at the latest thirty days after the first use. The Swedish national general licence is applied on items that are only temporarily exported outside the EU, for example, for demonstration or reparation purposes. The national licence may be used for exports to 42 states around the globe.[36] The use of general licences may be prohibited if a certain product has become subject to a catch-all warning issued by the Swedish authorities.

As mentioned above ISP has recently been developing the procedures for issuing global licences. The use of the licence requires that enterprises have well developed internal systems for export control. ISP controls these companies by ensuring that they have good internal compliance systems (ICP). Global licences are given to individual companies but may apply on a non-established number of the defined product. The shape of the licence varies depending on factors such as the company's needs and the sensitivity of the items. Global licences are only provided for civil end-use. The licences may be valid for a number of years before they need to be renewed.

Finally, the individual licences are provided for exports of particularly sensitive items. They are in most cases used for defined contracts between a Swedish exporter and a particular customer in a state outside the EU. Licences are not authorized unless, after a cautious examination, it cannot be ruled out that the end-user will use the items for manufacturing weapons or weapons of mass destruction.

In 2007, the Swedish licensing authority introduced a new internal code of conduct for the licensing process. In the year of 2008, this new system showed its effects. Despite the increase of applications, the time period for the licensing process was reduced considerably. In 2009, 73 percent of the licensing applications for dual-use items could be managed within a period of two weeks.[37]

---

35 Currently, Sweden is one out of seven EU Member States that make use of the national general licence. The others are: France, Germany, Greece, Italy, the Netherlands and the United Kingdom.

36 The provisions concerning the application of the national licence are laid down in the Instructions of the Swedish Agency for Non-proliferation and Export Control, Tullverkets Författningssamling (TFS) 2000:24 with amendments laid down in Tullverkets Författningssamling (TFS) 2004:35. The 42 countries are listed on ISP's website, www.isp.se.

37 *Strategic Export Control – War Material and Dual-use Items and Technology*, 2009 Annual Report to the Swedish Ministry for Foreign Affairs, Government Communication 2009/10:114, p. 18.

Sweden applies a system of preliminary decisions. This is type of service provided by the licensing authority aims at giving companies a first hint of what the final decision on a licence application will be. This way companies may dare to proceed with export contracts although they will not know for sure whether their applications will be authorized until ISP makes the final decision. The number of requests for preliminary decisions has increased considerably over the past few years. ISP sees this development in the light of the suspected WMD-programs in North Korea and Iran.

Little has been said about the work carried out by the Swedish Customs Agency in this field. This is not because the Customs Agency is not doing any work in the field. However, the main responsibility for ensuring that items of dual-use items and technology are not exported illegally outside the EU remains with ISP for which this paper has focused on its functions and procedures. Nevertheless it shall be stressed that the Customs Agency is an important co-partner for ISP, as are the intelligence services.[38]

As mentioned earlier, ISP has recently established new networks for cooperation with the Swedish Prosecution Service. Seen in a historical perspective few violations of export controls of dual-use items and technology has led to prosecution. It is difficult to know why this is, but seen in the light of the prosecutors own witnessing it could be because they have little experience.

Table 1: Export applications concerning dual-use items in the years 2007-2009[39]

Export applications	2006	2007	2008	2009
Total amount, incl. general, global and individual	305	508	491	786
Wassenaar arrangement	173	277	291	406
MTCR	16	5	4	1
NSG	13	11	9	49
Australia group	103	190	187	227
Sanctions		25	39	83
Non-controlled items				20

38 For more reading on the operational functions of the Swedish Customs Agency in the area of combating illegal exports of dual-use items, see Wetter, A., *Enforcing European Union Law on Exports of Dual-use Items*, SIPRI Research Report 24, Oxford University Press, 2009, pp. 110-112.

39 *Strategic Export Control – War Material and Dual-use Items and Technology*, 2009 Annual Report to the Swedish Ministry for Foreign Affairs, Government Communication 2008/09:114, p. 64 and *Strategic Export Control – War Material and Dual-use Items and Technology*, 2009 Annual Report to the Swedish Ministry for Foreign Affairs, Government Communication 2009/10:114, p. 81.

Audits and other Control Mechanisms

Both ISP and SKI conduct regular audits. ISP holds responsibility for inspections of the majority of the items that are listed in the EU regulation for which this section will focus on its supervision. The yearly number of inspections carried out by ISP has gone up since 2005. In 2005 the number of inspections was nine. This has gradually increased over the years with seventeen inspections in 2006 and twenty in the year 2007.[40] This should be seen in the context that ISP has approximately fifty registered customers that trade in dual-use items.

ISP's inspection procedures begin with a telephone call to the company in due time to prepare it for ISP's visit. During the visit the Authority focuses on ensuring that the company has good knowledge about the export control laws and that export control procedures are well integrated into the working habits of the concerned company. The Authority further reviews the exporting procedure starting from the point when an offer is made or received, through the export application and end-use certification until the delivery declaration has been made. Common questions to the companies include whether they have policy documents on export controls, whether there is a person responsible for the export licences, if all items are classified by experts as required by the law and if there are special routines for handling transfers of ITT.

The Customs Agency, when present during a visit, holds the responsibility for verifying documents that may confirm that the export has followed adequate procedures, for example by checking customs declarations, invoices and bank notifications. Following ISP's visits, the Authority submits a memo to the exporting company which includes a judgment of the export procedures and suggestions for improvements.

With the enhanced procedures for issuing global licences ISP has intensified its control of internal compliance programs. The Authority finds this control to be a crucial component in order for it to allow the use of global licences.

In the last couple of years ISP has worked towards improving the supervisory function of the Authority. In 2004, the government submitted a report which included proposals for a more clear and effective public supervision.[41] ISP took inspiration from the report in its evaluation of the internal control system. Lately, the Authority has engaged in dialogues with European states, for example the United Kingdom, Denmark and Germany to share with them best practices and to learn about

---

40 ISP 2007 Annual Report to the Ministry for Foreign Affairs, p. 14.

41 Tillsyn. *Förslag om en tydligare och effektivare tillsyn*, SOU 2004:100, published on 11 October 2004.

their best practices. The revised review system for controlling the exporting industry of dual-use items is coordinated with the review system for conventional weapons. This makes sense considering ISP is responsible for the review of both dual-use items and conventional weapons.

Finally it deems necessary to mention the Swedish Export Control Society (EKF). The purpose of this association is to support export control administrators and managers of export controls within companies. The association meets on a regular basis with ISP to share the views of its members on export control regulations and licence procedures. One very hands-on function of EKF is to organize courses for companies with the aim to certify export control officers within companies.

Swedish Industry, Relations with the Swedish Parliament

The Swedish Industry

In contrast to the export of conventional weapons it is difficult to provide a clear picture of the scope of the Swedish industry for the trade of dual-use items.[42] While exporters of conventional weapons must declare the manufacture of items, this is not the case with companies that manufacture dual-use items. Hence, manufacturers of dual-use items that do not export outside the EU will not show in ISP's data. The Authority does not have knowledge of those manufacturers with the exception of those manufacturers or traders that are already under the control of the licensing authority. According to ISP's statistics, there has been an increase of licensing requests in the past five years. In 2009 the increase of applications was 60 percent compared to 2008. The items concerned by the increase were primarily controlled by the Wassenaar arrangement and the Australia Group.[43]

Swedish defence industry developed to its current size during the Cold War. Again, this may be described by the neutral position that Sweden took during this period of history, which made it crucial for the country to maintain a high defence standard of its own. Several of the operators in defence materials, including Saab (within which we these days also find Electronic Defence Systems) are also applicants of dual-use export licences. The most known Swedish dual-use operators manufacture and trade with for example telecommunication equipment (primarily encryption and heat-seeking cameras), heat exchangers, isostatic

---

42 The estimated number of Swedish manufacturers of conventional weapons is 150 of which 40 engage in export.

43 See Table 1.

presses, chemicals and separation equipment for satellites. The total business trade of the defence industry's all items and services for 2009 amounted to forty percent defence material and 60 percent civil and commercial items and services.

Foreign ownership of Swedish companies has increased over the years. At the same time Swedish companies have invested and bought affiliations abroad. In January of 2011, international media reported that Sweden had ignored US pressure to stop exports of listed dual-use items to Iran.[44] The concerned company, Colenco, is an affiliation of the Swedish owned company ÅF but the former is located in Switzerland. The responsible Swedish Authority, the Nuclear-Power Inspectorate, has confirmed that it has visited Colenco to discuss the Swedish regulations. However, due to the location of the company Swiss licensing authorities are responsible and not the Swedish. The case shows that Swedish authorities are concerned about exports even beyond their own control, at least this is the case in the Colenco example.

Parliamentary Accountability

The export of weapon material and dual-use items in Sweden has a history of being a sensitive issue. This is largely due to the Swedish position of neutrality in foreign policies. In 1984 the parliament decided to introduce an Export Council for the purpose of increasing parliamentary accountability in export policies concerning weapons and war-related materials. The Council was reshaped in 1996, which is the same year that ISP became operational. The general-director of ISP is head of the Council, which also includes delegates from all political parties that are represented in the Swedish parliament.

The general director decides which applications should be subject to examination by the Council prior to the decision made by the licensing authority. Those applications that are not reviewed by the Council must be reported separately. Since 2005 ISP has also informed the Council of authorisations provided in the sphere of dual-use items.

Final Remarks

Swedish legislation fully implements EU law and international obligations under the NPT, CWC, BTWC and CTBT. However – and as noted in the introduction of this chapter – EU Member States and member states of international organizations have a certain discretion to lay down the architecture for those systems that enforce their international

---

44 See *e.g.* article "U.S. blocked Swedish firms aiding Iran", published on 17 January 2011 by UPI.com and "U.S. cable claims Swiss linked Iran Gitmo to UBS", by Jordans, F., published on 20 January 2011 by the Associated Press.

obligations. With regards to the EU Regulation on the export control of dual-use items and technology it is clear that the EU regulation is directly binding in all EU Member States. This means, with the exception of the criminal provisions, that the regulation should not be implemented in the national legislation. All EU Member States share the same laws but carry their own responsibility to ensure that the European regulation is brought into effect in the Member State.

In broad outline the Swedish licensing system set up to control exports of dual-use items and technology may seem less effective than for example the German, Dutch and British systems whose licensing officers in a comparative perspective, allocate more resources on tracking down export offenders. As a point of departure ISP believes that Swedish exporters want to contribute to non-proliferation initiatives for which few of them are expected to intentionally violate the export laws.[45] The picture of the relatively business-friendly authority must however be seen in the light of supplementary control mechanisms. Intelligence results are regularly shared with the licensing authority and the idea is that as soon as a suspicion is identified against an exporter – either by the intelligence services or through an inspection by ISP or the Customs Agency – the Authority will increase its surveillance by intensifying its end-use controls.

---

[45] The fact that the number of preliminary licence requests has increased considerably since the introduction of sanctions against Iran in 2010 supports the suspicion that the majority of Swedish exporters are unwilling to contribute to the proliferation of WMD.

Austria
National Arms Export Control
Between Realism and Institutionalism

Heinz GÄRTNER

Professor

Introduction

Multilateral regimes (like the Wassenaar Arrangement-WA, the EU Code of Conduct and Common Positions, or the Arms Trade Treaty – ATT) are designed to control exports of conventional arms and dual-use goods and technologies to contribute to regional and international security and stability. Unlike the EU's Common Position and a possible ATT, the WA is not legally binding. All provide guidance for cooperation and compliance. The question is whether and to what degree the actors involved are interested in complying with the guidelines. To address this problem the paper applies two international relations theories, liberal institutionalism and realism, to Austria. One argument of liberal institutionalism is that international institutions and regimes have a vital catalytic role to play in promoting cooperation among states in compliance with rules and norms. In many ways this might well be the case, but the opposite is also true. The economic interests of the states and jealousy between them have long hampered the activities of various regimes that have been designed to act as a multilayered export control and non-proliferation system that had been deemed necessary by all involved.

However, it is not only liberal institutionalism that fails to explain the behaviour of states, international institutions, and regimes. For realists, it is states' interests that matter, with common norms, rules and principles mattering less, if at all. But contrary to the realist argument, states also support the general guidelines and best practices of the international institutions that have been created to avoid the destabilizing effects of the accumulation of certain categories of conventional arms and the proliferation of dangerous weapons. Austria, for example, is a strong supporter of all arms export control regimes.

The Austrian case demonstrates that neither realism nor liberal institutionalism is fully able to capture the complex relationship between the interests of individual countries and general principles and norms. The diplomatic delegations in multilateral *fora* have the difficult task of identifying the cumulative interests of the countries they represent. They must support and reject cooperation with states and other export control regimes and institutions, often at the same time.

The Realist Argument

Austria as a neutral state does not have important geopolitical interests of its own. The Austrian army imports most of its heavy equipment (tanks, fighter jets, artillery). Austria's arms exports are mainly economically driven. The realist theory does not separate the interests of the industry and the state behaviour. Nevertheless Austria has several companies that produce and export arms, weapons and dual-use goods (*e.g.* Steyr-Mannlicher, Hirtenberger). Their products include rifles, pistols, submachine guns, sports-guns, munitions, trucks, armoured vehicles, electronics. Austria ranks around the 40th place among the exporters of major conventional weapons. Austria, however, is together with the USA, Italy, Belgium among the largest small arms and light weapons SALW exporters. The major recipients of Austrian arms are in the Middle East, Asia and Africa. According to the Austrian "War Material Regulation" and the "Foreign Trade Act" Austria licences around 2000 applications for arms exports for around one billion Euros a year; less than one third are actually being exported.[1] In 2005 when Austria held the presidency of the WA Steyr-Mannlicher, it made international headlines when it sold 800 long-range sniper rifles (H-50) to Iran for the National Iranian Police Organization for the use against drug smugglers. There was a large amount of concern that the rifles would find their way into Iraq and be used against the New Iraqi Army or Coalition forces. In fact, members of the Defence Intelligence Agency (DIA) provided the Austrian Federal Ministry of Economic Affairs with documents that show Iran's support of terror organizations with weapons. Nevertheless, the Austrian government approved the sale. Before this deal Steyr-Mannlicher sold a small number of other rifles (AUG-3) to the Iranian "police and anti-drug units" although there was some resistance by the Federal Ministry of Interior to provide the licence.[2] Some observers consider this sale as a test for the bigger sniper

---

1 The Austrian Federal Ministry of the Interior and the Federal Ministry of Economic Affairs are jointly responsible for collecting data on the value of licences granted for the export of military equipment. Austria does not currently submit data on actual arms exports based on customs statistics.

2 "Die Austro-Akten von Wikileaks", *News* (Austrian weekly), No. 4, 2011.

rifle deal. Moreover, Austrian companies sold some dual-use components to Iran without the approval of the Federal Ministry of Economic Affairs, other export licences of dual-use goods have been rejected.[3] The Wikileaks[4] documents also revealed that mortars and grenades of Austrian fabrication have been found in Afghanistan. The company Hirtenberger denies to have exported them to Afghanistan. Pistols of the company Glock[5] have been legally exported to Iraq, licensed for police forces.[6]

Austria claims to have strong national legislation for its arms exports. Under Austrian law, exporting companies are obliged to inform the Federal Ministry of Interior of the nature and size of a licensed export of war material as well as the date on which it took place. The Minister of Interior decides on licence applications in consultation with the Minister for Foreign Affairs and the Minister for Defence, to make sure that no other legal provisions prohibit the export. For dual-use goods the licence of the Federal Ministry of Economic Affairs is a precondition.

The difficulty of the licensing process is demonstrated by the Libyan case. During the Libya crisis in February/March journalists[7] discovered that the Austrian company Schiebel sold four unmanned aerial vehicles (UAV) or drones to Libya with eight more to be delivered. The official purpose was to control refugees to the EU. Since theses "Camcopters" (small helicopters with cameras) also could be used for military purposes the Green Party suspected that they would be used to supervise the riots. Because of the dual-use purpose the competences for licensing were not entirely clear. The Federal Ministry for Economic Affairs responsible for the licensing of dual-use goods approved the deal. The Federal Ministry for Foreign Affairs that only has the right for a statement allegedly declined it. If the UAV would have been categorized as a military good, according to the "War Material Regulation", the Federal Ministry of Interior would have had to licence it.

Arms exports should not violate international legal obligations national law (especially Austria's neutrality) and Austrian foreign policy interests. Exports are not permitted to areas of armed conflict or tension. Some of the arms exporting states claim – consistent with the realist

---

3 "Die Austro-Akten von Wikileaks", *News* (Austrian weekly), No. 4, 2011.

4 *Der Standard* (Austrian daily), 28 July 2010.

5 "The Glock handgun is one of the best-selling pistols in the U.S.", *New York Times*, 14 January 2011.

6 When Saddam Hussein was captured in a hole in the ground in Iraq, soldiers found his Glock pistol inside. *New York Times*, 14 January 2011.

7 Among others *Der Standard* (Austrian daily), 1 March 2011.

notion – that national legislation is stronger than international norms and rules implying that the latter are superfluous or not necessary for their respective countries. Austria however, stresses that its national legislation is not stronger but consistent with international law. Austria does not make the realist argument either that the right of self-defence is stronger than arms export control norms and rules.

A draft Amendment to the "War Material Regulation" of 2011 is supposed to implement the regulations of the EU Common Position of 2008. Critics argue that it does not go beyond the EU standards or even fall behind it.[8] For example, while the Common Position speaks of "reason to believe that the technology or equipment will be diverted from its stated end-use or end-user and used for internal repression",[9] for the Amendment there has to be a "clear risk" in order to deny approval of arms exports.

The Institutionalist Argument

Conventional Weapons

According to the realist view international rules and norms are an obstacle to national arms exports. Austria, however, is a strong supporter of arms export control regimes. Austria argues that multilateral efforts to control arms exports do not necessarily contradict the interests of industries, but they are not always compatible. Austria commits itself to the EU Code of Conduct for Arms Export of June 1998. It sets certain standards as to human rights international law, internal repression and international aggression. The weapons are by and large the same as those on the list of the Wassenaar Arrangement of export control of conventional arms and dual-use goods and technologies. In its operational part, the Code requires that exports that have been denied must be notified to the EU partners. This mechanism should increase the transparency of arms export controls. In 2008 the EU adopted a Common Position on the basis of the "Code of Conduct" which is a legally binding instrument for arms exports. The Wassenaar list on conventional arms and dual-use goods and technologies becomes for EU Member States legally binding as well.

In the past Austria's arms exports lacked transparency. It has improved since the EU has adopted the Common Position. The Austrian

---

8 Amnesty International Austria and International Reconciliation Association Austria (Versöhnungsbund) to the amendment to the "War Material Regulation", 16 March 2011.

9 Council Common Position 2008/944/CFSP of 8 December 2008, Defining Common Rules Governing Control of Exports of Military Technology and Equipment, Article 1.

list is being updated in order to adapt it to the wording of the EU Common Military List. This list comprises among others, rifles, ammunition, bombs, rockets, drones and non-war material such as helmets, protection vests, software, cameras, as well as other technologies. In the past years, Austria has only submitted data for the Annual Report on the value of licences granted for the permanent exports of weapons. For the Sixth Annual Report in 2005 Austria submitted data for the first time on the value of actual exports of war material and non-war material items disaggregated by recipient country. Since then Austria also submitted data on the value of non-war material items disaggregated by EU Common Military List category.

Since the EU adopted the Common Position Austria has supported also the adoption of an international Arms Trade Treaty (ATT). It calls for a legally binding international instrument, which will draw together and consolidate states' current obligations under international law. An effective ATT should establish common international standards for authorizing international transfers of conventional arms, based on already existing commitments under international law including international human rights and humanitarian law. In the framework of the EU Common Position Austria backs the project and has organized together with The United Nations Institute for Disarmament Research (UNIDIR) a regional event for a "Wider Europe" in February 2010.

Weapons of Mass Destruction

The regulation of import, export, passage in transit of radioactive material, and transport is laid down in the Radiation Protection Act. This concerns both safety and licensing. The responsibility is shared between federal and regional (provinces) authorities. The licensing authority for the Atomic Institute in Vienna is the Federal Ministry of Science and Research conjointly with the Federal Ministry of Agriculture, Forestry, Environment and Water Management. According to Article 5 of the Radiation Protection Act the design of installations with higher potential risk has to be licensed prior to the start of the construction.[10]

UN Resolution 1540 proposes cooperative action to prevent non-state actors from acquiring any type of weapons of mass destruction (WMD). The resolution affirms the resolve of the UNSC to take appropriate and effective action against any threat to international peace and security that might be caused by the proliferation of nuclear, biological and chemical (NBC) weapons and their means of delivery.[11] Resolution

---

10 Austria, 4th National Report for the Convention on Nuclear Safety, September 2007.

11 Anthony, I. (2005) "Arms control and the Non-proliferation process", in: Sipri (ed.), *SIPRI Yearbook 2005, Armaments, Disarmament and International Security*, Stockholm: Oxford University Press.

1540 encourages UN member states to adopt effective controls, criminalize proliferation and to take cooperative action to prevent non-state actors from acquiring WMD. They are also strongly encouraged to develop and maintain appropriate and effective border-, export-, transit- and trans-shipment controls, all specifically tailored to the primary objective of preventing illicit trafficking of WMD. Most importantly, the resolution focuses not only on states as recipients of any illegal trade in WMD, but also has as its main focus non-state actors, especially terrorists, as possible buyers of such weapons and their components. States are called upon to take all actions necessary, under Chapter VII of the UN Charter to prohibit any non-state actor from manufacturing, acquiring, possessing, developing, transporting, transferring or using WMD, and their means of delivery. Although Resolution 1540 concentrates on the strengthening of non-proliferation, it is also significant because it stresses the state to non-state problems rather than state-to-state issues. The UNSC Resolution 1540 could become the centrepiece of all export control institutions and regimes, as well as a powerful instrument for countering the non-state proliferation threat. By implementing Resolution 1540 in the various existing international institutions and regimes (UN, EU, G-8, WA) and in individual states, it would be possible to achieve a closer coordination in mandates and activities, including reducing the wasteful and unnecessary duplication in reporting that currently exists, combining some staffs and more effort being put into reinforcing common efforts. The EU and the OSCE support Resolution 1540, with the United States and the European Union together stressing that they are committed to fully implementing the Resolution, including criminalizing proliferation, establishing effective export controls and protecting dangerous materials, while also providing assistance to other states that are also taking such actions.[12]

Austria has taken a range of legislative and executive measures that ensure compliance with UNSCR 1540 to prevent any development, acquisition, manufacture, possession, transport, transfer or use of nuclear, chemical or biological weapons as well as dual-use goods and their means of delivery. Austrian law penalizes any such attempt (Austrian Panel Code, Foreign Trade Act). Export control measures are carried out in compliance with the provisions of the EU Dual-Use Regulation by means of export licences. The responsible agency for administering export controls on strategic goods is the Federal Ministry for Economic Affairs. The Federal Ministry of the Interior is the licensing authority for the import, and export, and transit of war material. The brokering of

---

12 Bureau of European and Eurasian Affairs (2005), *US-EU Cooperation on the Non-proliferation of Weapons of Mass Destruction, Fact Sheet*, Washington DC, 17 February 2005.

dual-use items is subject to a licence under the Foreign Trade Decree. An advisory board with members of the Federal Ministries of Foreign Affairs, Interior and Defence should supply information on the end-users, the scope of his business and the plausibility of the stated end-use. As far as illicit trafficking is concerned Austria has been participating in the reporting system of the IAEA illicit trafficking database and its related activities.[13]

Because several multilateral international institutions and regimes have endorsed UN Resolution 1540, its concept could become a hub for the coordination of efforts to prevent non-state actors from acquiring dangerous weapons and materials. Austria, for example, is trying to become the centre and host country for the whole range of control regimes (WA, MTCR, AG, NSG and ZC).[14] However, the economic interests of member states and jealousy between them have long hampered cooperation among the various regimes that have been designed to act as the multilayered export control and non-proliferation system that all involved have agreed is necessary. With regards to arms export control institutions and regimes, these competing interests very often block each other because of the different priorities and interests of the various governments, institutions and regimes involved.

In October 2010 the Austrian Foreign Ministry for European and International Affairs and the James Martin Centre of Non-Proliferation Studies (CNS) at the Monterey Institute of International Studies established the Vienna Centre for Disarmament and Non-Proliferation. The new Centre is intended to serve as an international hub for discussions among representatives of civil society, governments, and international organizations of the most pressing nuclear disarmament and proliferation challenges.

Conclusion

On the one hand, following the realist argument, Austria and its industries have a strong interest to export conventional arms and dual-use goods. On the other hand, according to the institutionalist argument Austria's government, is keen to participate in all the multilateral arms export regimes. However, all the actors involved have different expectations in the regime and even contradictory demands. This often leads to inconsistent behaviour and rhetoric of the main actors. Some political

---

13 Permanent Mission of Austria to the United Nations, *Note to the Chairman of the Security Council Committee pursuant to resolution 1540 (2004)*, (October 2004).

14 Heinz Gärtner, *Towards a theory of arms export control*, *International Politics*, 47/2010, pp. 125-143.

scientists would call it "organized hypocrisy".[15] The arms export control regime is riddled with inconsistencies, strains and contradictions. Of course, no regime is free of these inconsistencies, yet the maintenance of "organized hypocrisy" is to some extent necessary for its survival and success. However, if the strains become too strong the regime becomes ineffective. It depends on the corporate responsibility on the part of arms exporters how much, or whether indeed at all, Austrian corporations want to curtail their business opportunities by paying attention to principles. If a responsible business community in the field of arms exports is going to be built up, a core set of rules must be consistently enforced by the companies themselves and their national governments. Austria is trying to become the centre and host country for a whole range of control regimes.

[15] Krasner, S.D. (1999), *Sovereignty: Organized Hypocrisy*, Princeton, NJ: Princeton University Press.

Portugal

Miguel SOUSA FERRO

Counsel at Sérvulo & Associados

General Introduction

In general, Portugal has consistently shown a high level of commitment to nuclear non-proliferation and arms control. It is a member of several relevant international organisations (UN, EU, Euratom, IAEA, OECD, etc.) and a Party to the most relevant international treaties (1968 Non-Proliferation Treaty; 1979 Physical Protection Convention, without the 2005 amendments; Safeguards Agreement and Additional Protocol,[1] etc.) and initiatives (Proliferation Security Initiative, Megaports Initiative, Nuclear Suppliers Group, Zangger Committee, Wassenaar Agreement, etc.).

There are no known examples of exports of home-grown goods or technologies subject to safeguards. Irradiated nuclear fuel, used in the only nuclear reactor on national territory, (the one Megawatt research reactor at the Nuclear and Technological Institute) is periodically returned to the USA (original provider). There was one recent case, reported in the media, of attempted traffic (purchase) of uranium by a founder of a religious sect, leading to a court case.[2] Another case, reported in Wikileaks, claimed an attempted sale of uranium on national territory by an "unidentified ex-Russian General now living in Portugal".[3]

---

1 Portugal's Safeguards Agreements with the IAEA was ratified in 1979, and completed by the Additional Protocol in 2001. Portugal is also a Party to the Agreement between the Non-Nuclear Weapon States Members of the EU, Euratom and the IAEA relating to the NPT (1973) and to a specific Safeguards Agreement between Portugal, the USA and the IAEA (1965). It has also ratified the OECD Security Control Convention (1957) and its Tribunal Protocol, but the safeguards mechanism established under this Treaty are suspended.

2 See: http://www.cmjornal.xl.pt/detalhe/noticias/nacional/portugal/objectivo-e-provocar-uma-explosao.

3 See: http://wikileaks.ch/cable/2008/07/08LISBON1808.html.

On the other hand, there are occasional, but very limited, exports of dual-use items (*e.g.* shipment of valves to Iran that could potentially be used in centrifuges). Only global statistics are available. There seems to be no publicly available information on Portugal's role as a transit state for dual-use items.

There is a slightly higher degree of transparency in what concerns trade in military items. A list of all the companies that have been authorised, or have requested to be authorised, to carry out industrial or trade activities relating to military goods or technologies may be consulted in the website of the Ministry of National Defence.[4]

As a EU Member State, Portugal's enforcement of rules on dual-use goods and technologies focuses primarily on the implementation of Regulation (EC) 428/2009.

As for the national legal framework, with the exception of the part relating to weapons trade, it has become drastically outdated (and is apparently under review for quite some time). It is made up of the following:

- Decree-Law No. 436/91,[5] *establishes the legal framework for the control of imports and exports of goods which may affect national strategic interests*;
- Ministerial Order No. 439/94,[6] *approves the list of goods and technologies subject to prior licensing and certification*;
- Communication No. 83/2003 of the Directorate General for Customs and Excise;
- Law No. 49/2009,[7] *regulates the conditions of access to and exercises the activities of trade and industry in the area of military goods and technologies*;
- Decree-Law No. 1/86,[8] *creates means to prevent, by the transfer of goods or services by nationals to foreign persons, possible transfers of technologies that would be detrimental to national interests*; and

4 See: http://www.mdn.gov.pt/mdn/pt/mdn/Servi%C3%A7os+Centrais+de+Suporte/DG+Armamento+e+InfraEstruturas+de+Defesa/ciaarmamento/20080822_DGAED_ComercioIndustria_EmpresasAutorizadas.htm.

5 *Official Gazette* No. 257, Series I-A, 08/11/1991.

6 *Official Gazette* No. 148, Supplement, Series I-B, 29/06/1994.

7 *Official Gazette* No. 150, Series I-A, 05/08/2009.

8 *Official Gazette* No. 1, Series I, 02/01/1986.

- General Regime of Fiscal Infractions, adopted by Law No. 15/2001,[9] last revised by Decree-Law No. 73/2010.[10]

The licensing authority for dual-use items is the Directorate General for Customs and Excise (DGAIEC), Licensing Services Division, of the Ministry of Finance.[11]

The licensing authority for military items is the Directorate General for Armament and Defence Equipment (DGAED), Import and Export Control Division, of the Ministry of National Defence.[12]

An Inter-ministerial Commission for Trade in Strategic Products had been set up, made up namely by representatives of the Ministry of National Defence (DGAED), Ministry of Foreign Affairs (Directorate-General for Foreign Policy), Ministry of Economy (Directorate-General of Companies), Ministry of Health, and Ministry of Science, Technology and Higher Education (Nuclear and Technological Institute and Universities).

It should be kept in mind that subsequent reshuffling of competences within the government has led the above quoted legal regime to be outdated in what concerns the authorities mentioned.

Furthermore, it should be noted that trade in weapons and associated equipment not classified as meant for military use is subject to a different licensing regime, run by the Public Safety Police under Law No. 5/2006.[13]

Scope of the Export Control Regime

Decree-Law No. 436/91 encompasses the "import, export, temporary export and re-export" of the items listed in Ministerial Order No. 439/94. This terminology is typical of the time when this Decree-Law was adopted and is, therefore, expectably outdated in relation to the terms of Regulation (EC) 428/2009.

Ministerial Order No. 439/94 provides a list of items (107 pages long) divided into the following categories: (i) advanced materials; (ii) treatment of materials; (iii) electronics; (iv) computers; (v) telecommunications and information security; (vi) sensors and lasers; (vii) navigation and avionics; (viii) navy; (ix) propulsion; (x) precursors of chemical

---

9 *Official Gazette* No. 130, Series I-A, 05/06/2001.

10 *Official Gazette* No. 118, Series I, 21/06/2010.

11 Contact person: dsl@dgaiec.min-financas.pt. Address: Rua Terreiro do Trigo (Edifício da Alfândega), P-1149-060 Lisbon.

12 Contact person: dgaed@dgaed.mdn.gov.pt. Address: Av. Ilha da Madeira, No. 1, P-1400-204 Lisbon.

13 *Official Gazette* No. 39, Series I-A, 23/02/2006 (as amended).

weapons and manufacturing equipment; (xi) dual-use paranuclear equipment, materials and associated technology; (xii) nuclear materials, facilities, equipments, logistic support and technologies; (xiii) missile equipments and technology; and (xiv) war material.

Category (xi) materials, *i.e.* the category specifically relating to dual-use items, is divided into eight categories: (1) industrial equipment; (2) materials; (3) equipments and components for separating uranium isotopes; (4) equipment connected to heavy water manufacturing facilities; (5) equipment for the development of implosion systems; (6) explosives and related equipment; (7) equipment and component for nuclear tests; and (8) others (*e.g.* neutron generators, radiation proof cameras…).

Category (xi) materials are divided into two categories: nuclear facilities, equipments and software, and nuclear materials. The latter are divided into: (1) natural and impoverished uranium; (2) fissionable material; (3) deuterium; (4) heavy water; and (5) nuclear-level graphite.

The obsolete national regime differs from the current EU regime on dual-use items at many levels, beyond the updates to the list of items. It does not cover brokerage. Also, it is arguable whether ITT, transit, transhipment and transfers are included, since the terminology does not expressly encompass those concepts. No catch-all clause was included.

As the regulatory framework has not yet been revised to take into account changes to EU Law, some possibilities allowed by Regulation (EC) 428/2009 are not included in the national legal framework. This is the case of general export authorisations. It is expected that the legislative review currently under way will adapt the existing procedural provisions to the above-mentioned Regulation.

It must however, be noted that, aside from procedural issues necessary to the implementation of Regulation (EC) 428/2009, the fact remains that this national legislation has been superseded by EU Regulation, and it is neither necessary nor legitimate for Member States to legislate on the same issues that have already been uniformised at the EU level.

Industrial Operator Awareness

There is no specific data available to assess industry awareness. However, the extremely limited number of licences requested each year suggest that industry awareness is low and that there may be a significant number of exports of dual-use items not reported to the authorities. In this sense, the contrast between the number of licences issued for dual-use items and for military items is particularly revealing.

That being said, recent years have seen repeated efforts by DGAIEC to raise awareness of legal obligations and of the applicable procedure. This has namely been pursued by organising events specifically tailored as outreach to companies, in parallel with training activities for customs agents. According to DGAIEC annual reports, two such activities were organised in 2008, and two others in 2009.

The authorities have also repeatedly stated their openness to provide clarifications to industry and have made an effort to broaden and improve the user-friendliness of the information available on their respective websites.[14]

Communication No. 83/2003 has officially instituted a policy of "When in doubt, ask", directed towards the industries.

National Jurisdiction

An infringement of the dual-use items regime under Portuguese jurisdiction is subject to general and specific sanctions.

Under the General Regime of Fiscal Infractions, a breach of mandatory licensing for import or export of goods or technologies may lead to a penalty of up to three years imprisonment or of a fine of up to 360 days.[15]

Specific sanctions have, however, been set up in the framework of the dual-use items licensing procedure. False statements provided in such procedures are punishable with up to two years imprisonment. Any unlawful export or re-export (or an attempt to do so) of dual-use items is punishable with imprisonment between one month and five years. A violation of the obligation to return certificates after execution or non-use is subject to a fine of up to Euros 30,000.

Depending on the infringement in question, jurisdiction for such offences will, in principle, be awarded to criminal courts or to administrative and fiscal courts.

The licensing of the import/export of military goods and technologies have also been subject to specific sanctions. The illegal research, planning, testing, assembly, manufacture, transformation, maintenance or demilitarization of military goods or technologies is punishable with

---

14 See: http://www.dgaiec.minfinancas.pt/pt/licenciamento/bens_tecnologias_duplo_uso/bens_tecnologias_duplo_uso.htm; and http://www.mdn.gov.pt/mdn/pt/mdn/Servi%C3%A7os+Centrais+de+Suporte/DG+Armamento+e+Infra-Estruturas+de+Defesa/ciaarmamento/.

15 Under Portuguese criminal law, fines are calculated by number of days. Each day currently corresponds to an amount to be set on a case-by-case basis, between Euros 5 and 500 (for natural persons) or Euros 100 and 10,000 (for legal persons).

imprisonment between four and fourteen years. Other offences, such as false statements and non-communication of mandatory information is punishable with a fine between Euros 500-70,000 (natural persons) or between Euros 1,000-200,000 (legal persons), with the possibility of additional accessory penalties (seizure of the goods and profits in question, and interdiction of exercise of management or administrative positions in companies subject to this licensing regime, for a period of ten years).

Jurisdiction for such offences is awarded by the criminal courts.

Additionally, the general regime on weapons (Law No. 5/2006) provides sanctions for the unauthorised holding and transfer of weapons not subject to special rules for the military sector. For example, under this regime, the unlawful holding, acquiring, transferring, mediating, importing or exporting of products or substances which may be used to develop, keep, store or use nuclear weapons or "dirty bombs", or transport devices is subject to imprisonment, varying between two and twelve years, depending on specific characteristics of the infringement. The criminal liability of legal persons is explicitly provided for.

Additional Elements

As can be seen from the tables below, the dual-use items licensing regime is not often implemented in Portugal, in stark contrast to the licensing of export/import of military goods and technology.

The following information has been collected from the annual reports of DGAIEC and DGAED, available in their respective websites (only until 2009, in the first case, and until 2008, in the second case).

Licences relating to dual-use goods and technologies (industrial products)	2005	2006	2007	2008	2009
Export licences	0	1	0	14	13
Import certificates	2	1	0	1	1
Delivery guarantee certificate	3	2	0	0	1

Licences relating to military goods and technologies	2005	2006	2007	2008
Definitive exports	231	290	238	259
Temporary exports	681	420	370	347
Exports not carried out	-	11	10	40
Definitive imports	619	599	521	789
Temporary imports	133	111	75	159
Imports not carried out	-	30	26	67

No information is available to the public regarding the compulsory enforcement of the dual-use items regime (*e.g.* fines for companies that do not require mandatory licences), and no examples of such enforcement are known by the author.

There are no known specific national security exceptions. Authorities have made it known that they comply with UN, EU and OSCE restrictions and embargoes.

In what concerns the licensing of the import/export of military items, DGAED has made it known that: "Only authorized companies can apply for export licences and all applications are considered and assessed on a case-by-case basis. Each application is also considered by the Ministry of Foreign Affairs, in the light of foreign policy interests, including observation of the criteria enshrined in the EU Code of Conduct on Arms Exports".[16]

Recent years have seen an increase in transparency from both competent authorities, particularly through the publication of information on official websites and the organisation of awareness-raising events. But the practical results of those efforts, in what concerns dual-use items, are clearly still insufficient.

There seems to be much room for improvement, both in what concerns the legal framework – which, in relation to dual-use items, has not been revised since 1994 – and in what concerns the enforcement of existing EU and national laws.

A first crucial step would be to bring the national legislation in line with Regulation (EC) 428/2009, as well as with country specific Regulations and relevant Security Council Resolutions adopted under Chapter VII of the United Nations Charter. It is unclear what has prevented the long ongoing legislative review process from arriving at its conclusion.

Portugal seems to be a good demonstration of the reason why the EU's intervention in this domain should be carried out through a directly applicable and enforceable Regulation. Other instruments, such as Directives or Guidelines, would lead to a very significant disparity of the control regime between Member states, which are entirely incompatible with security concerns in the context of the internal market. It also makes a case for the EU Regulation to be as precise and self-sufficient as possible.

---

16 See: http://www.mdn.gov.pt/mdn/pt/mdn/Servi%C3%A7os+Centrais+de+Suporte DG+Armamento+e+InfraEstruturas+de+Defesa/ciaarmamento/PortugueseExportControlPolicy.htm.

Czech Republic

Jakub HANDRLICA

Assistant Professor, Department of Administrative Law,
Law Faculty, Charles University in Prague

Introduction

In June 2003, an Action Plan for Non-Proliferation of Weapons of Mass Destruction (Thessaloniki Action Plan) was adopted by the governments of EU Member States. This Action Plan was complemented by the EU Strategy against Proliferation of Weapons of Mass Destruction adopted by the European Council on 12 December 2003 (EU WMD Strategy). According to Chapter III of this Strategy, the European Union must make use of all its instruments to prevent, deter, halt, and if possible eliminate proliferation programmes that cause concern at a global level. Subparagraph 30.A(4) of that Chapter specifically refers to strengthening export control policies and practices.[1]

Furthermore, the United Nations Security Council Resolution 1540, adopted on 28 April 2004, decided that *all States* shall take and enforce effective measures to establish domestic controls to prevent the proliferation of nuclear, chemical or biological weapons and their means of delivery, including by establishing appropriate controls over related materials[2] and to this end shall, among others, establish transit and brokering controls.

Consequently, the European Union reacted with a new Regulation (EC) No. 428/2009 on May 5 2009 with the aim of *setting up a Community regime for the control of exports, transfer, brokering and transit of*

---

1 See Anthony I., "The Role of the European Union in the WMD Non-proliferation", in N. Busch and D. Joyner (eds.), *Combating Weapons of Mass Destruction: The Future of International Non-proliferation Policy*, Athens, The University of Georgia Press, 2009, pp. 197-221.

2 Pursuant to this Resolution, related materials are materials, equipment and technology, covered by relevant multilateral treaties and arrangements, or included on national control lists, which could be used for the design, development, production or use of nuclear, chemical and biological weapons and their means of delivery.

dual-use items, which entered into force on 27 August 2009 (thereinafter also "the Regulation No. 428/2009").[3] In order to ensure that this Regulation is properly applied, each Member State should take measures to give the competent authorities appropriate powers in order to cope with the challenges arising from existing risks of the proliferation of nuclear, chemical or biological weapons.

This contribution constitutes a written report of my presentation held at the conference on the export control of dual-use items, which has been organized in October 2010 in Chaudfontaine (Belgium) by the European Studies Unit of the University of Liège and presents overview of the legal framework on the export control of dual-use items in the Czech Republic.

In the first part, a historical and geopolitical background of the current state of matters will be given, outlining the main milestones that had implications for the developments of dual-use regimes in former existing Czechoslovakia and its two successor countries.

The second part, will be a short overview about the most important industrial items exported from the Czech Republic and the destinations of such exports.[4]

In the third part, I will deal with the current legislation on export control of dual-use items in the Czech Republic,[5] taking the most recent Amendment No. 343/2010 Coll.[6] towards an implementation of the Regulation into consideration.

In the fourth part, I will point out major interactions between the public authorities and the private sector in the area of the export of dual-use items.

---

3 OJ L 134, 29.05.2009, pp. 1-269.

4 However, reflecting mainly the situation in the year 2009, as presented in the *2009 Annual Report of the Czech Republic's Control of Export of Military Equipment, Small Arms for Civilian Use and Dual-use Items and Technologies* as published by the Ministry of Industry and Trade. The 2010 Annual Report was not available yet when this contribution was finished.

5 This paper reflects the state of legislation in the country as of the end of January 2011.

6 In force since 7 December 2010.

Historical and Geopolitical Background: From Enemy Country to Union Membership

Czechoslovakia on the List of Dangerous Countries of the US Coordinating Committee on Multilateral Export (COCOM)

Similar to the others states belonging to the former Soviet bloc, Czechoslovakia rejected to join the European Recovery Program, known widely as the Marshall Plan, which was the primary post-World War II program of the United States for rebuilding and creating a stronger economic foundation for European countries.[7]

Instead of joining the Marshall Plan, the country strengthened its economical cooperation with the Soviet Union. From the point of view of this paper, the export of natural uranium from Czechoslovakia[8] to the Soviet Union is of major importance. While the pre-Cold War production of uranium is estimated to be around 1,000 tons, in the period from 1947 to 1992 around 110,000 tons were produced from 64 uranium deposits.[9]

The export of production of its uranium ore industry to the Soviet Union was particularly advantageous for the Czechoslovakian economy – by the end of the 1950s it represented 32.6 percent of the bulk of exports to the Soviet Union, which was compensated by the import of important commodities such as iron, oil, meat and especially cereals.[10]

Furthermore, Czechoslovakia had also a quite powerful and advanced military industry, producing aeronautical techniques, tanks and armoured carriers. The export of these items peaked in the middle of the

---

7 For further information see *e.g.*: Parrish, S. and Narinsky, M., *New evidence on the Soviet rejection of the Marshall Plan, 1947: two reports*, Washington, Woodrow Wilson International Center for Scholars, 1994, pp. 19-40 and 42-50.

8 The territory of the today's Czech Republic is actually the birthplace of industrial scale uranium mining. Uranium mining at Jáchymov (at that time called Joachimsthal and belonging to Austria – Hungary) started in the 1890s on an industrial scale, after the silver and cobalt production of the deposit declined. Uranium was first utilised to produce mainly yellow colours for glass and porcelain manufacture. After the discovery of polonium and radium (1898), the town Jáchymov became the first place in the world for commercial radium production from uranium ore. Radioactive water from the mines was also used to set up a health resort.

9 The largest deposit Příbram (vein style) produced about 50,000 tons of uranium and was mined to a depth of over 1,800 metres.

10 However, it appears that the slackness of the Soviet interest in the output of the uranium just at the end of the 1950s contributed to deepen the difficulties of the Czechoslovak economics and dislocated its central plan. For further information see: Jančík D., "Export of the Czechoslovak Uranium Ore to the Soviet Union in 1947-1959", *Acta Oeconomica Pragensia*, Vol. 15, No. 7, 2007, pp. 194-208.

1980s, when the country ranked among five of the most important exporters of military items.[11]

For the United States and its European partners, it would constitute a major danger to allow the export of sensitive items into Czechoslovakia during this period. Consequently, Czechoslovakia was introduced on the list of dangerous countries, administered by the US Coordinating Committee on Multilateral Exports (COCOM). This remained unchanged until the fall of the "*Velvet Revolution*" in the country (1989) and the fall of the "*Iron Curtain*".

Fall of the "Iron Curtain": First Major Milestone in the New History of the Legal Framework on Dual-Use Items

Similar to the other *post-Communistic* states, Czechoslovakia began to search for possibilities of industrial cooperation very soon after the fall of the "*Iron Curtain*". The industry was actually in desperate need for foreign investments and new technologies. However, technological transfer of any kind was not possible, as the country was still on the COCOM list in the very early 1990s.

The government of the United States was aware of this problem. Therefore, several important steps towards acceptance of the country's industry by the Western states were taken in the very early 1990s: in November 1990, the government agreed with acceding to the international framework of non-proliferation of chemical weapons. In the same year, export of uranium to the Soviet Union was stopped.

The first legal regulation on export control of dual-use items was issued in Czechoslovakia on 27 December 1990 as Act No. 547/1990 Coll., *on transfer of special items and technologies and on the control of this transfer.*[12] At the same time, the *Criminal Code* was amended, introducing criminal sanctions of infringement of rules on export control of these items.[13] Both legal regulations were of *federal nature*, applicable in both parts of Czechoslovakia.[14]

In the following year, Czechoslovakia – as the first of the *post-Communistic* states – enabled foreign inspection of all sites able to

---

[11] See: Cupitt R., "Export Controls: The Perspective of the Czech and Slovak Federal Republic", in Bertsch, G., Cupitt, R. and Elliott-Gower, S. (eds.), *International Cooperation on Non-proliferation Export Controls*, Michigan, Michigan University Press, 1994, p. 94.

[12] Zákon č. 547/1990 Sb., *o nakládání s některými druhy zboží a technologií a jejich kontrole.*

[13] Zákon č. 545/1990 Sb., *kterým se mění a doplňuje trestní zákon.*

[14] In the Czech Republic, this framework was had been in force until 1997, in Slovakia until 2002.

produce chemical weapons. All these efforts were considered as very important steps towards further incorporation of the country into the international export control frameworks.[15]

However, the situation was reflected quite differently in the two parts of the federation. While the industry of Czech countries was basically more differentiated and developed, there was a large region in Slovakia that depended economically on the military industry. Consequently, any kind of legal regulation restricting the trade with dual-use items was perceived quite sensitively in Slovakia. Some of the Slovak politicians made statements in *favour* of maintaining close export relations with the countries of the former Soviet Union concerning the export of military technologies. After that, the attitudes of the USA and of the Western European states towards disembarrassing the export restrictions *vis-à-vis* Czechoslovakia changed to some extent. Consequently, after the dissolution of the federation in 1992, both new countries created their own legal frameworks.[16]

The EU Membership: Second Major Milestone in the New History of the Legal Framework on Dual-Use Items

In the years after the very peaceful dissolution of Czechoslovakia, both the new established Czech Republic as well as Slovakia established their own legal frameworks. These basically reflected international commitments of both countries arising from the membership in the international groups controlling the dual-use items.[17]

In the Czech Republic, the Czechoslovak Act from the early 1990s was replaced in 1997 by a new Act No. 21/1997 Coll., *on control of export and import of items and technologies.*[18] However, the accession of the Czech Republic into the European Union created another challenge for legislation in this area. In order to implement the Council Regulation (EC) No. 1334/2000 at a national level, and as part of the

---

15 At a meeting of COCOM states held in May 23-24, 1991 in Paris, members officially approved a new industrial list of controlled technology and – on insistence of the United States – also agreed to formulate preliminary conditions for final removal of Czechoslovakia (together with Poland and Hungary) from the COCOM list of proscribed destinations. The list of conditions included creation of legal basis for export controls system in these countries, introduction of controls on their indigenous technologies and successful implementation of the first stage of the safeguard systems. Fort further details see: Cupitt R., *op. cit.*, sub 9, pp. 87-89.

16 Fort further details see: Cupitt R., *op. cit.*, sub 9, pp. 89-96.

17 Waasennar Agreement (WA), Australian Group (AG), Missile Technology Control Regime and Nuclear Suppliers Group. The Czech Republic is participating in all these international regimes.

18 Zákon č. 21/1997 Sb., *o kontrole vývozu a dovozu zboží a technologií.*

Czech Republic's entry into the Union, the Czech Government passed Act No. 594/2004 Coll., *implementing the regime of the European Communities for the control of exports of dual-use items and technologies*. This act specifically regulated the system of controls used for the exporting of dual-use items, the rights and obligations of parties transporting such items from the Czech Republic to another Member State and parties importing such items into the Czech Republic, as well as the measures that have been put in place through Council Joint Action No. 2000/401/CFSP of 22 June 2000, dealing with the *control of technical assistance related to certain military end-users*.

In response to the passing of the Council Regulation (EC) No. 428/2009, which replaced the older Council Regulation (EC) No. 1334/2000, and in order to implement this new European legislation at a national level, the Czech Government drew up an Amendment to Act No. 594/2004 Coll. – the primary objective of which was to facilitate the effectiveness of control mechanisms in the area of brokerage services and transit activities.

In November 2009, the draft of the new Amendment was circulated through the respective governmental ministries, departments, and stakeholders[19] for their review. Their suggestions made in reference to the draft were taken into consideration. The new Amendment was reviewed by the government in the first half of 2010. Afterwards, it was submitted to the Parliament, approved and published as Amendment No. 343/2010 Coll. Consequently, the Amendment entered into force on 7 December 2010.

Overview of Industries and Major Export Destinations

Most Frequently Exported Dual-Use Items and most Important Destinations

The leading importers of Czech dual-use items and technologies in 2009 were Russia (27), China (23), Iran (16) and Ukraine (8).[20] The most frequently exported types of goods this year were machinery

[19] Ministry of Industry and Trade, State Authority for Nuclear Safety, Ministry of Interior, General Directorate of Customs, Security Information Service (Counter-intelligence Service of the Czech Republic) and Office for Foreign Relations and Information (Foreign Intelligence Service of the Czech Republic). Among the industrial stakeholders, Czech Chamber of Commerce, Confederation of Industry of the Czech Republic and Defence and Security Industries Association of the Czech Republic were consulted.

[20] See Annual Report, *op. cit.*, sub 4, p. 28.

(equipment and accessories), chemicals,[21] carbon and aramid fibres, scanning electron microscopes, detection tubes and paper strips for the detection of chemical weapons, and protective gas masks.

Overview on the Quantity of Decisions Related to the Export of Dual-Use Items

In 2009, the Ministry of Industry and Trade issued a total of 158 decisions related to the export of dual-use items and technologies:[22]

- 140 permits were issued for exports to 32 countries,[23]
- 5 export permit applications were denied,
- 13 decisions were issued to suspend the proceedings (mostly due to the withdrawal of an application).

Furthermore, additional registrations were made for the use of the *general export authorisation*[24] for a total of seven countries and sixteen companies. This means that the Czech Republic currently has 36 companies that are allowed to export goods under this general export authorisation.

Current Legislation on Dual-Use Export Control in the Czech Republic

Overview of the Legal Regulations in Force as of 31 January 2011

At the beginning of this part, which presents the current legal framework for export control of dual-use items and technologies in the Czech Republic, an overview of the existing legal regulations should be presented. In the following paragraphs, presentation of the institutional

---

21 The leading export products were sodium, potassium czanides and Krasol (a hydroxyl-terminated liquid polybutadiene).

22 In order to provide idea on the relation of the quantity of the export of dual-use items and technologies *vis-à-vis* the export of the military equipments, following statistics can be presented: A total of 1,002 licences to export military equipment were issued in 2009, with a total value of CZK 10,318.8 million (Euros 390.2 million). 517 export licences were issued for exports to other EU countries, which had a total value of CZK 4,112.2 million (Euros 155.5 million). The largest number of licences was issued for exports to Slovakia (152). In terms of exports to non Member States, the greatest number of licences was issued for exports to the US (111). However, India topped the list in terms of the value of the exports, with a total value of CZK 452.2 million (Euros 17.1 million).

23 According to the data from the General Customs Directorate, there were 621 export transactions of dual-use items and technologies in total in 2009, as approved by the Ministry of Industry and Trade. See Annual Report, *op. cit.*, sub 4, p. 13.

24 As provided in the Annex II to Regulation No. 428/2009.

and procedural framework will be given, as is in force in the Czech Republic at the beginning of the year 2011.

The most important legal regulations governing the area of dual-use items and technologies are the following:

- Regulation No. 428/2009 of 5 May 2009 *setting up a Community regime for the control of exports, transfer, brokering and transit of dual-use items*, which entered into force on 27 August 2009;
- Act No. 594/2004 Coll., implementing the regime of the European Communities for the control of exports of dual-use items and technologies as amended by the Act No. 343/2010 Coll. (thereinafter only the "Act No. 594/2004 Coll. on *export control of dual-use items*"), which reflected the commitments arising from the Regulation No. 428/2009 (mainly what the brokering and transport of dual-use items concerns) and entered into force on 7 December 2010.

Consequently, the Act No. 594/2004 Coll. on the export control of dual-use items is a *general legal norm*, establishing rules on the control of exports of dual-use items, including software and technology, with the observance of international regimes, agreements and treaties binding upon the Czech Republic, and the rights and obligations of exporters of dual-use items and other persons contributing to exports. Furthermore, it also provides rules on the rights and obligations of persons transporting dual-use items from the territory of the Czech Republic to the territory of another Member State of the European Union and on control of the technical assistance related to certain military end-users.

Regulation of the Government of the Czech Republic No. 344/2010 Coll., was issued in order to provide for some more detailed instructions with regards to the Amendment of the Act No. 594/2004 Coll. and reflection of the commitments arising from the Regulation No. 428/2009 into the Czech legal order, this Regulation entered into force also on 7 December 2010.[25]

Other sector-specific regulations are laid down in a number of special acts (issued by the Parliament)[26] and decrees (issued by the competent administrative authorities).[27]

---

25 As it contained some writing errors, it was "corrected" in a form of a statement issued by the Ministry of Interior and published in the Collection of Laws under the number 371/2010 Coll.

26 *E.g.* the Act No. 18/1997 Coll. *on Peaceful Utilisation of Nuclear Energy and Ionising Radiation* (*the Atomic Act*), Act No. 19/1997 Coll., *on Certain Measures Connected with the Prohibition of Chemical Weapons*, Act No. 455/1991 Coll., *on Trade Licensing* (Trade Licensing Act), Act No. 281/2002 Coll., *on Certain*

The Act No. 594/2004 Coll., *on export control of dual-use items* does not affect the rights and obligations of exporters of dual-use items under other sector-specific legal regulations. Consequently, both the general legal framework created by the No. 594/2004 Coll. and the sector-specific legislation must be applied simultaneously. This constitutes a kind of *two-level system of control.*

Institutional Framework: Which Administrative Authorities Are Involved

The *two-levels system of control* of the authorisation proceedings is also reflected in the institutional framework of administrative authorities, involved in the proceedings. The following paragraphs provide a short overview of the authorities involved in the export control of dual-use items.

The Ministry of Industry and Trade of the Czech Republic (thereinafter only "the Ministry") as the main decision making authority in the field of export control of dual-use items and technologies

The Ministry[28] is the main administrative body controlling the export and transport of dual-use items and technologies. It is entitled to grant the authorisation for the (a) export of dual-use items and (b) the transportation thereof within the European Union from the Czech Republic. Furthermore, it shall provide and mediate information intended for exporters of dual-use items whether an authorisation will be needed for a specific kind of items or technology. The Ministry is also the main coordinator of the Czech cooperation *vis-à-vis* the institutions of the European Union, international organisations and competent authorities of the other Member States.[29]

Ministry of Foreign Affairs of the Czech Republic as a guardian of political interest of the state

While the Ministry of Industry and Trade is responsible for authorisations, other authorities assist with the process of reviewing individual export permit applications. The Ministry of Foreign Affairs[30] is required

Measures Connected with the Prohibition of Bacteriological (Biological) *and Toxin Weapons*, Act No. 148/1998 Coll., *on the Protection of Secret Information*, etc.

27 *E.g.* for the nuclear sector in the Decree of the State Authority of Nuclear Safety No. 166/2009 Coll., laying down a list of nuclear related dual-use items.

28 *Ministerstvo průmyslu a obchodu.*

29 A special Licence Department (Licenční správa) is of charge for the authorisation proceedings.

30 *Ministerstvo zahraničních věcí.*

to make sure that the authorisations that have been granted and the subsequent exports of this category of certain goods are not in violation of any political interests of the Czech Republic – and, specifically, the commitments arising out of existing international treaties and out of the country's membership in the respective international organizations. The flow of information is also reversed and the Ministry of Foreign Affairs also preventively informs the Ministry of Industry and Trade about his geopolitical concerns concerning the export of sensitive items.[31]

Ministry of Interior of the Czech Republic as a guardian of security interest of the state

The Ministry of Interior[32] is another administrative authority, issuing an opinion in the course of authorisation proceedings. The Ministry of Interior collaborates closely with the two central intelligence services, the Security Information Service[33] (which serves as the counter-intelligence service of the state) and the Office for Foreign Relations and Information[34] (which serves as the foreign intelligence service) and with the Czech police from whom the Ministry receives information relevant to the application under review. Subsequently, the Ministry analyzes this information and reviews its relevance. Only then does it prepare a statement for the Ministry of Industry and Trade.[35]

Ministry of Defence of the Czech Republic as a guardian of national defence-related interests of the state

The ability of the Czech Republic to defend itself is the result of the country's defence policy and it represents one of the principal tools for

---

31 Since 2005, the Ministry of Industry and Trade has been warning all known exporters of items that are included under Categories 8456 – 8466 of the Czech Integrated Tariff (this especially includes various types of machining tools and accessories), which irrespective of whether or not these items meet the technical criteria called out on the list of restricted goods, they can only be exported to Iran or Syria with an individual export permit that has been issued by the Ministry of Industry and Trade. As part of the international sanctions against North Korea, a permit is required in order to export a broad range of products into that country. Over time, the Ministry has had to warn 225 exporters with respect to the above. Others are being reminded of these restrictions through information, which, for the most part, is being distributed by the General Customs Directorate. See the Annual Report, *op. cit.*, sub 4, p. 28.

32 *Ministerstvo vnitra.*

33 *Bezpečnostní informačí služba.*

34 *Úřad pro zahraniční styky a informace.*

35 In order to make sure all applicants are treated equally, the Ministry of Interior has introduced an internal directive which prescribes the procedures to be followed in producing a response or statement for specific applications and when providing information to the Ministry of Industry and Trade.

promoting the country's security interests. The primary objectives of this defence policy are to protect the country's territorial cohesion and to protect its citizens and property from external threats. It is of paramount interest to the Czech Republic to defend its territory in accordance with Article 51 of the Charter of the United Nations by using both domestic forces and resources and by working in partnership with the country's NATO allies. In reviewing applications for the export and in issuing its opinion on such applications, the Ministry of Defence[36] takes into consideration the potential international impact of the given trading transaction – provided such an impact can be anticipated.

Ministry of Finance of the Czech Republic (General Customs Directorate) as a guardian of national finances and tax-related interests of the State

To facilitate proper oversight with respect to this type of trade, the Ministry of Industry and Trade provides the General Customs Directorate[37] with the requisite basic information about the licences that were issued for trade in dual-use items and technologies. In return, the Customs Directorate supplies the Ministry with data produced in the course of the activities carried out by the customs authorities in relation to the utilization of the trading licences that have been issued.

The State Office of Nuclear Safety as a Guardian of Non-Proliferation Policy

As a body of the central Government, the State Office for Nuclear Safety[38] is responsible for handling the tasks related to the Nuclear Non-Proliferation Treaty. Under the provisions of Act No. 594/2004 Coll., *on export control of dual-use items*, the Ministry of Industry and trade can only issue a permit to export nuclear materials and/or items with the approval of the State Office. As the executive and oversight body for items of a nuclear nature, the State Office is responsible for government monitoring of agents and nuclear materials and the monitoring of compliance with the requirements that exist with respect to the handling of such materials. In 2009, the State Office issued 64 statements related to the export of dual-use items of a nuclear nature. The Office also issued four decisions related to applications for the export and subsequent re-importing of dual-use items of nuclear nature.

---

36 *Ministerstvo obrany.*

37 *Generální ředitelství cel.*

38 *Státní úřad pro jadernou bezpečnost.*

Procedural framework: For which kind of exports and other related activities are authorisations needed?

The licensing process is primarily pursuant to the Act No. 594/2004 Coll., on the export control of dual-use items and is applicable to:

- The export of goods that are on the list of controlled items in the Annex I to the Regulation No. 428/2009,[39]
- The export of goods, as directly provided by the Regulation No. 428/2009,[40]
- Cases, where the Ministry of Industry and Trade makes his own decision pursuant to the Article 4 (4) of the Regulation No. 428/2009,
- Cases, when a Regulation of Government provided so with regard on the protection of human rights,
- Cases of technical assistance,[41]
- Cases of transport of dual-use items and technologies to another Member State from the Czech Republic,
- Cases of brokering services, if provided directly in the Regulation No. 428/2009,[42] or if the Ministry of Industry and Trade communicates so to the broker.

A permit to export dual-use items, which are not listed in Annex I to Regulation No. 428/2009, is also required whenever the exporter has been informed that the items in question are or may be intended (either all or just some of them) for use in connection with the development, production, handling, operation, maintenance, storage, detection, identification or dissemination of chemical, biological or nuclear weapons or other nuclear explosive devices or the development, production, maintenance or storage of missiles capable of delivering such weapons.

A permit is also required if the purchasing and/or destination country is subject to an arms embargo and the exporter has been informed that the given goods are or could be (either all or just some of them) intended for a military-type end-use or that the given goods are or could be (either all or just some of them) intended for use as parts or components of items that are included in the domestic military list and that were exported without a permit or in violation of a permit.

---

39 See Article 3 (1) of the Regulation No. 428/2009.

40 See Article 4 (1) – (3) of the Regulation No. 428/2009.

41 See Council Joint Action No. 2000/401/CFSP of 22 June 2000.

42 See Article 5 (1) of the Regulation No. 428/2009.

Sanctions

In the event of a breach of any provision of the Regulation No. 428/2009 or of the Act No. 594/2004 Coll., on export control of dual-use items, the exporter or any other person may be penalized.

Administrative sanctions are laid down in the Act No. 594/2004 Coll. in the form of financial penalty up to CZK 20 million.[43]

Furthermore, there are criminal sanctions laid down in the Act No. 40/2009 Coll., Criminal Code. Three felonies regarding the unauthorized export of dual-use items and technologies are laid down in the Code:

- Unauthorised export of dual-use items and technologies is sanctioned with imprisonment for up to eight years,[44]
- Breaching of important obligations arising from the function, which leads to export of dual-use items and technologies is sanctioned with imprisonment for up to three years,[45]
- Distortion and destruction of data is sanctioned with imprisonment for up to two years.[46]

In the current Czech Criminal Code, corporations can be sanctioned only in the regime of administrative sanctions and not in the regime of criminal sanctions. However, there are ongoing discussions towards introducing the criminal sanction also for the corporations and other legal entities.

Interactions with the Private Stakeholders

One of the key elements of the system used to control the export of dual-use items and technologies is *collaboration of the public authorities with the private sector*. Along with the governmental authorities, the exporters and, more importantly, the manufacturers involved in these activities, all become co-responsible for the efficiency of the control system.

In the Czech Republic, regular exchange of information regarding the implementation of the export control system primarily takes place in the form of consultations that are part of the communications that take place between applicants and the Ministry of Industry and Trade (as part of the application process). Exporters are able to access the information

---

43 See articles 18 and 19 of the Act No. 594/2004 Coll., *on export control of dual-use items*.

44 See Article 262 of the Act No. 40/2009 Coll., Criminal Code.

45 See Article 263 of the Act No. 40/2009 Coll., Criminal Code.

46 See Article 264 of the Act No. 40/2009 Coll., Criminal Code.

they need through the website or by attending seminars organized by the Ministry. Further, the stakeholders are to provide for their internal code of conduct with respect to the handling with dual-use items and technologies.

In 2009, the Ministry once again organized, in partnership with the Czech Trade agency, a seminar on the topic "*Dual-Use Export Controls – Current Practices and the Latest Changes*", which followed-up on similar seminars that had been organized in past years. Due to the enormous interest by the private sector in this seminar (60 attendees), the organizers put together an additional seminar that was held in January 2010 (70 attendees).

Key Messages

Traditionally, Czech Republic ranks among important European exporters of both military and nuclear dual-use items. Russia still ranks as the major destination for this kind of export.

During the last twenty years, a long journey has been done from the "enemy country" to the Union's accession in 2004. Most recently, the Czech Republic reflected the Regulation No. 428/2009 in the Amendment of existing legislation and introduced respective provisions on brokering and transport of dual-use items.

Both the international framework and European Law constitutes important pillars of the national legal framework regarding the export control of dual-use items.

As the interactions between the private sector and public authorities constitutes one of the key elements of the system used to control the export of dual-use items and technologies, measures in this area need to be strengthened in the future. Measures used in the other Member States can certainly also serve as inspiration for the Czech Republic and must be reflected in the decision making process of the Ministry of Trade and Industry.

Decision-making of the Ministry of Industry and Trade on export of dual-use items in 2008-2009

Year	Export authorisations	Destinations in total	Most important importers
2009	140	32	Russia (27), China (23), Iran (16), Ukraine (8)
2008	97	25	Russia (26), China (11), Syria (11), Iran (9)

Slovenia
Control of Export of Dual-Use Items

Vasilka SANCIN

PhD, Assistant Professor of International Law, Faculty of Law, University of Ljubljana

Introduction[1]

On the international plan Slovenia participates in relevant international export control regimes and is thus a member of the Wassenaar Arrangement (since 2004), the Nuclear Suppliers Group (since 2000), the Zangger Committee (since 2000), the Australia Group (since 2004), the Hague Code of Conduct against Ballistic Missile Proliferation (since 2004), the Proliferation Security Initiative (since 2005). Slovenia has also applied to the Missile Technology Control Regime (MTCR), but consensus among the existing thirty-four members needed to admit new members has not been reached yet.[2] Slovenia is also a party to the Convention on the Prohibition of the Development, Production, Stockpiling and Use of Chemical Weapons and on their Destruction (since 1997), the 1925 Protocol for the Prohibition of the Use of Asphyxiating, Poisonous or Other Gases, and of Bacteriological Methods of Warfare (since 2008), the Convention on the Prohibition of the Development, Production and Stockpiling of Bacteriological (Biological) and Toxin Weapons and on their Destruction (since 1992), the Treaty on the Non-Proliferation of Nuclear Weapons (since 1992), the Comprehensive Nuclear-Test-Ban Treaty (since 1999) and the International Convention for the Suppression of Acts of Nuclear Terrorism (since 2009).

---

1 This paper represents an introduction into the Slovenian context of regulation of control of export of dual-use items. Thus, it seems appropriate to address not only the particularities of this control system, but also the broader legal regime in which it operates.

2 See the Press Release from the plenary meeting of the MTCR in Buenos Aires, Argentina, 13-15 April 2011 at: http://www.mtcr.info/english/Press%20Release%20April%202011.html.

Slovenian Legal Context and Implementation of Existing Mechanisms

Relationship between International, EU and Domestic Law

To better understand implementation of obligations deriving from applicable international, EU and domestic provisions regulating the control of export of dual-use items, it is important to briefly note the relevant provisions of Slovenian Constitution.[3]

The Constitution provides that "legal acts and decisions adopted within international organisations to which Slovenia has transferred the exercise of part of its sovereign rights shall be applied in Slovenia *in accordance with the legal regulation of these organisations*"[4] (emphasis added). This article was adopted before Slovenia's accession to the EU in 2004 to provide for effective application of EU legislation and indirectly also recognizes the supremacy of EU law. Thus, in case of potential conflict between a norm of domestic law and EU law regulating the control over export of dual-use items, the latter prevails. Furthermore, this also reduces the risks of potential insufficient regulation of export control of dual-use items in Slovenia, or lack of it.

For the relationship between international and domestic law in Slovenia the Constitution provides that "laws and regulations must comply with generally accepted principles of international law and with treaties that are binding on Slovenia. Ratified and published treaties shall be applied directly".[5] This constitutional diction shall be understood only as a declaration for the adoption of treaties and their provisions into the Slovenian legal order, and not necessarily as a declaration of their *de facto* direct applicability. Direct applicability and consequently the possibility of their direct invocation by individuals before domestic courts depend on the quality of particular treaties and their provisions. Only self-executing treaties and self-executing treaty provisions can be applied directly. Therefore, the question whether a treaty or its provision is capable as such of establishing, after the ratification and publication in the *Official Gazette of the Republic of Slovenia*, rights and obligations for legal and natural persons, depends above all on how exhaustive its content is and how its provisions are formulated. If treaties or treaty provisions are non-self-executing, it is necessary to adopt internal legal

---

3 Published in the *Official Gazette of the Republic of Slovenia* (hereinafter: *Official Gazette RS*), N°s. 33/91-I, 42/97, 66/2000, 24/03, 69/04 and 68/06). The English text of the Constitution is available online at: www.us-rs.si/en/about-the-court/legal-basis/.

4 See Article 3a, paragraph 3 of the Constitution.

5 Article 8 of the Constitution.

measures (laws/regulations) to fulfill relevant treaty obligations. The term "generally accepted principles of international law" encompasses also customary international law. Moreover, this provision of the Constitution gives room for either monistic or dualistic approach in respect of the position of international law within national law of Slovenia. It is in principle based on the supremacy of international law over all domestic norms of non-constitutional character (but not over the Constitution), which has been recognized also in decisions by the Constitutional Court.

The issue of hierarchy among internal legislation and international law is further specified in Article 153, paragraph 2, of the Constitution which states that "laws must be in conformity with generally accepted principles of international law and with valid treaties ratified by the National Assembly, whereas regulations and other general legal acts must also be in conformity with other ratified treaties".

The procedural primacy of treaties is ensured also by the Foreign Affairs Act which in Article 87[6] provides that in case of conflict between provisions of a treaty, on the one hand, and provisions of a law or other regulation on the other hand, the treaty has to be applied until the competent authority reaches a decision. It is in the competence of the Constitutional Court to decide on the conformity of internal legislation (laws and other regulations) with ratified treaties and with general principles of international law. The review of the constitutionality and legality of regulations and general acts issued for the exercise of public authority also extends to the review of the conformity of laws and other regulations with ratified treaties and with the general principles of international law.

Slovenian Legislation Concerning Control of Exports of Dual-Use Items

Adoption of Domestic Legislation

Slovenian legislation in the area of control of exports of dual-use items was adopted in 2004 in order to implement the relevant EU acts, and subsequently amended in 2010. It includes the Act Regulating the Control of Exports of Dual-Use Items (previously: The Control of Exports of Dual-Use Items and Technology Act)[7] and the Decree on the Procedures for Issuing Authorisations and Certificates and on Competence of the Commission for the Control of Exports of Dual-Use Items

6 Published in the *Official Gazette RS*, N°s. 45/2001, 78/2003, 113/2003, 20/2006, 118/2007, U-I-275/05-12, 76/2008, 108/2009 and 80/2010.

7 *Official Gazette RS*, No. 37/04 in 8/10. The act was adopted on 26 March 2004 and amended in 2010.

(previously: the Decree on the Performing the Control of Exports of Dual-Use Items and Technology).

In 2008 the Ministry of the Economy prepared and published online also the Instruction Manual: dual-use items to ensure better understanding of procedures and legal norms applicable to the export of dual-use items of Slovenian companies. The Manual was amended in 2010.[8]

The Act Regulating the Control of Exports of Dual-Use Items (*hereinafter*: Dual-use Items Act) consists of 14 articles divided into four parts: General provisions (part I), Authorisation for technical assistance and the body designated for issuing authorisations (part II), The role, the powers and the duties of national authorities carrying out control (part III), Penal provisions (part IV) and Transitional and final provisions (part V).

In accordance with its general provisions, the Dual-Use Items Act regulates the measures of controlling dual-use items in the part that is not covered by the EU rules governing this field, or where Member States are authorised to further regulate this sphere in their national regulations. The measures of the control of dual-use items refer to: exports, transfer in the customs territory of the EU, transit, brokering, provision of technical assistance, and the issue of certificates related to the imports of dual-use items.[9] The Dual-Use Items Act implements the Council Regulation (EC) 428/2009 of 5 May 2009 and designates the body responsible for issuing authorisations, for the control, and the penal provisions. In line with the Council Joint Action of 22 June 2000 *Concerning the Control of Technical Assistance Related to Certain Military End-Uses* (2000/401/CFSP) it designates, for the purpose of control over the provisions of technical assistance, the body responsible for the issue of authorisations, the control, and the penal provisions.[10]

The Dual-Use Items Act defines technical assistance as "any technical support in repair, development, manufacture, assembling, testing, maintenance, or other technical services. It can take the form of instructions, training, transfer of practical or professional knowledge, or consulting". It also includes verbal forms of assistance. For the meaning of other terms used in it the Dual-Use Items Act refers to the definitions provided in Regulation 428/2009/EC.[11]

---

8 The Manual is available only in Slovenian language.

9 Article 1 of the Dual-Use Items Act.

10 Article 2 of the Dual-Use Items Act.

11 Article 3 of the Dual-Use Items Act.

Authorisation for Technical Assistance and the Body Designated for Issuing Authorisations

The authorisation for the provision of technical assistance is required for legal and natural persons, if their use is intended, or may be intended, or the provider of technical assistance is aware that it is intended for:

- Development, production, handling, operation, maintenance, storage, detection, identification or dissemination of chemical, biological or nuclear weapons or other nuclear explosive devices or the development, production, maintenance or storage of missiles capable of delivering such weapons;
- Military end-use, where the countries subject to an arms embargo decided by a common Community position or joint action adopted by the Council of the EU, or a decision of the OSCE, or an arms embargo imposed by a binding resolution of the UN Security Council.[12]

No authorisation is however required for providing technical assistance, when:

- It is carried out in a state listed in Annex II, Part 3 of Regulation 428/2009/EC;
- It concerns the provision of information "in the public domain" or related to "basic scientific research" in the meaning attributed to these two terms by international regimes, groups of countries and agreements for the control of the exports of dual-use goods, or
- It is in verbal form and not related to items to be controlled by one or several international regimes, groups of countries and agreements for the control of the exports of dual-use goods.[13]

In order to provide technical assistance requiring authorisation, the persons shall keep a register with:

- The description of technical assistance;
- The duration, and
- The final recipient.

Such registers shall be stored for at least five years from the end of the calendar year in which the person in question was providing technical assistance.[14]

---

[12] Article 3a, paragraph 1 of the Dual-Use Items Act.

[13] Article 3a, paragraph 2 of the Dual-Use Items Act.

[14] Article 3a, paragraph 3 of the Dual-Use Items Act.

The competent authorisation-issuing authority for:

- The export of dual-use items in line with Article 3(1) and Article 4(1), (2), (3) and (4) of Regulation 428/2009/EC;
- Brokering services of dual-use items in line with Article 5(1) of Regulation 428/2009/EC;
- Intra-Community transfers of dual-use items in line with Article 22(1) of Regulation 428/2009/EC;
- The provision of technical assistance in line with Article 3a(1) of the Dual-use Items Act, and
- The prohibition of transit stated in Article 6(1) of Regulation 428/2009/EC.

It is, since February 2010, the Ministry of the Economy which adopts its decision following the opinion of the Commission for the Control of Exports of Dual-Use Items (*hereinafter*: the Commission). The Government also:

- Prescribes the documentation the applicant has to submit for the issue of certificates, and
- Regulates in detail the procedure of issuing transit authorisations and prohibitions.[15]

The issuance of the Commission's opinion is thus a precondition for the issuance of authorisation; however, the Ministry of the Economy is not bound by the position expressed therein.

Before adoption of the Dual-Use Items Act there were two competent authorisation-issuing authorities, namely the Ministry of the Economy and Chemicals Office of the Republic of Slovenia. From 2001 till the second half of 2010 the competent authority within the Ministry of the Economy was the Division for Dual-Use Goods and NATO's Invitation to Tenders as a separate sector of the Directorate for Foreign Economic Relations, employing only two staff members. Due to the measures adopted to rationalize and reduce costs of the public administration in Slovenia this sector was abolished as a separate sector in 2010 and was subsumed under the Division for International Business Environment as its chapter on Control of goods and technologies of dual use. The pertinent issue of only two staff members to cover all matters in this field however remains.

15 See Article 4 of the Dual-Use Items Act.

The Role, the Powers and the Duties of National Authorities Carrying out Control

In Slovenia there are two competent bodies carrying out control of exports of dual-use items:

- The Commission for the Control of Exports of Dual-Use Items in cooperation with the Ministry of the Economy and
- The Ministry of Finance, more precisely its customs authorities.

The Commission for the Control of Exports of Dual-Use Items

The Slovenian Government established the Commission for the Control of Exports of Dual-Use Items for the purpose of coordinating and monitoring the control of exports, intra-Community transfer, brokering and transit of dual-use items, and the provisions of technical assistance. The Commission is appointed by the Slovene Government, which defined in detail its tasks and the methods of work in the Decree *on the procedures for issuing authorisations and certificates and on competence of the Commission for the control of exports of dual use items.*[16] The Commission consists of the representatives of ministries and other public administration authorities involved in the control of exports of dual-use goods in the context of their sphere of work. Each member of the Commission has one deputy. It currently has sixteen members – one representative and one deputy – from: the Ministry of the Economy, the Ministry of Foreign Affairs, the Ministry of Interior, the Ministry of Defence, the Slovenian Nuclear Safety Administration, the Chemicals Office of the Republic of Slovenia, the Customs Administration of the Republic of Slovenia and the Slovene Intelligence and Security Agency.

Notwithstanding the rules on the classified information, ministries and other public administration authorities that are members of the Commission have the right and the duty to exchange any data on the exporters and the exported dual-use goods which may be required to implement the control in accordance with the Dual-Use Items Act.[17] Furthermore, exporters, banks or other financial organisations, or any other entities which dispose of the information required for the control of exports of dual-use items, shall submit their business books, correspondence and any other information required for control to the ministry, customs authorities, and the prosecuting authorities on their request.[18] The rules referring to the exporter shall also apply to the

---

[16] Published in the *Official Gazette RS*, No. 34/2010.

[17] Article 10, paragraph 1, of the Dual-Use Items Act.

[18] Article 10, paragraph 2, of the Dual-Use Items Act.

supplier of dual-use items within the customs territory of the EU, the broker and the person providing transit or technical assistance.[19]

This Commission yearly reports to the Government and is responsible for coordinating and monitoring: the control of exports, intra-Community transfer, brokering and transit of dual-use items. It is also meant to provide technical assistance when needed. It has the right of visit and access data notwithstanding the rules on the classified information. Thus, ministries and other public administration authorities have the right and the duty to exchange any data on the exporters and the exported dual-use goods which may be required to implement the control.

International Certificates and Authorisations

The Ministry of the Economy, acting within the framework of international cooperation in the field of controlling the exports of dual-use items, on request of the importer, issues:

- The international import certificate for dual-use items (IIC), which is valid for six months, and
- The certificate on the delivery of dual-use goods (DVC-delivery verification certificate).

The conditions for issuing these certificates, the documentation to be submitted by the applicant for the issue of a certificate, and the exporter's reporting duty are determined by the Government: end-use certificate and recipient must be stated.[20]

The authorisation may be denied, annulled, modified, revoked or suspended *ex officio* or on request by the applicant (in situation of changed circumstances).

Under the Decree adopted in April 2010 the authorisations may be:

- Individual (validity up to one year) – reporting obligation: within fifteen days;
- Global (validity up to two years, on request of the exporter it can be extended for additional two years) – regulates the possibility of granting a global export authorisation – reporting obligation: twice a year (before July 15 and January 15);
- Community General Export Authorisation – reporting obligation: in thirty days after the first export and twice a year (before 15 July and 15 January).

---

19 Article 10, paragraph 3, of the Dual-Use Items Act.

20 Article 12 of the Dual-Use Items Act.

Utilized licence has to be returned to the Ministry of the Economy within fifteen days of the transaction or within fifteen days after the expiry of validity. Registers or records of exports shall be kept for five years from the end of the calendar year in which the transaction has been completed. The Ministry of the Economy may establish an electronic system for issuing licences and certificates and a secure electronic system for exchanging information between members of the Commission. These, however, have not been put in practice yet.

The procedures for issuance of authorisations and certificates are as follows:

- The application for granting the authorisation for the export of dual-use items and for the intra-EU transfers of dual-use items shall be lodged at the Ministry of the Economy on the form prescribed in Annex 1 of the Decree.
- The application for granting the authorisation for the brokering services of dual-use items shall be lodged at the Ministry of the Economy on the form prescribed in Annex 2 of the Decree.

The certificate on the end-use of the items and their consignee in the Slovenian and English language shall be enclosed with both types of applications. The end-use certificate is linked to the nature of dual-use items and the activity, and is defined in Annex 3 of the Decree. Technical documentation of the exported goods shall be enclosed with the application:

- The application for granting the authorisation for the provision of technical assistance shall contain the applicant's description of technical assistance, the duration, and the consignee, including the description of goods, the tariff number, and the designation of dual-use items under Annex 1 of Regulation 428/2009/EC the technical assistance refers to.
- The application for granting the international import certificate for dual-use items shall be lodged at the Ministry of the Economy on the form prescribed in Annex 4 of the Decree.
- The application for granting the delivery verification certificate on the delivery of dual-use items shall be lodged at the Ministry on the form prescribed in Annex 5 of the Decree.

The issue of authorisations and certificates is taxed by fees determined by tariff numbers 1, 3 and 4 of the tax fees in the Administrative Fees Act.[21]

[21] Published in the *Offical Gazette RS*, No. 42/07 (Official Consolidated Text) and 126/07.

All abovementioned authorisations may be denied annulled, modified, revoked, or suspended by the competent authorities:

- In accordance with Article 13(1) of Regulation 428/2009/EC, if it has been established that any piece of information in the application is not true, or if any circumstance, after the authorisation has already been granted, has changed so that the international commitments and responsibilities binding on the Republic of Slovenia request such action; or
- On the request of the applicant, if the circumstances which were the basis for issuing the authorisation have changed and are attributable to the exporter, broker, importer, end-user, or the person providing technical assistance.

Penal Provisions and Jurisdictional Matters

Article 13 of the Dual-Use Items Act includes provisions on offences and fines to be imposed if they are committed. It provides that legal persons, individual sole traders or individuals who perform the activities independently shall be fined for the offences from Euros 1,200 to 125,000, if they:

- Export dual-use goods without the authorisation from Article 3(1), and Article 4(1), (2), and (3) of Regulation 428/2009/EC, transfer them in the Community without the authorisation from Article 22 of Regulation 428/2009/EC, provide brokerage services referred to in Article 5(1) of Regulation 428/2009/EC, or provide technical assistance under Article 3a of this Act without authorisation;
- Fail to notify the ministry that dual-use items which they propose to export, are intended, in their entirety or in part, for any of the uses referred to in Article 4(1), (2), and (3) of Regulation 428/2009/EC, and that they were aware of this fact (Article 4(4) of Regulation 248/2009/EC);
- Perform transit for which the ministry issued a decision on the prohibition of transit (Article 6(1) of Regulation 428/2009/EC);
- Fail to keep detailed registers or records of their exports and brokering services (Article 20(1) and (2) of Regulation 428/2009/EC), and a register on the provision of technical assistance (Article 3a (3) of this Act);
- Fail to submit, on request of the competent authority, detailed registers or records of their export, transfer and brokering services (Article 20(3) of Regulation 428/2009/EC), and the information on providing technical assistance (Article 10(3) of this Act).

The responsible person of the legal person who commits any of these offences shall also be fined from Euros 120 to 4,100. A private individual shall be fined from Euros 120 to 1,200 for committing an offence.

The Penal Code of the Republic of Slovenia includes a provision[22] dealing with imports and *exports* of radioactive substances and provides that "whoever imports into the country or *exports* from it nuclear or other hazardous radioactive substances or waste contrary to regulations, shall be sentenced to imprisonment for not more than five years" (*emphasis added*). If the offence is committed in a criminal organization established to carry out such acts, the offender shall be sentenced to imprisonment of one to ten years.

Jurisdiction to supervise the export of dual-use items at borders belongs to the Customs Administration of the Republic of Slovenia, while the jurisdiction to decide disputes in this regard appertains to the regular courts and the Constitutional Court of the Republic of Slovenia.[23]

Statistics

According to the data gathered from individuals employed by the competent authorities there were approximately 100 to 120 authorisations issued per year in the period of 2008-2010 (90 percent exports and 10 percent transfers), while one was denied.

There existed no provisions on brokering and prohibition of transits before 2010 and the authorities registered no cases of violations of these provisions in 2010.

Annual exports of dual-use items represent approximately Euros 80 million or 0.05 percent of all exports.

In the period between 1 January 2009 and 1 September 2010 customs authorities carried out:

- 384 controls during customs procedures,
- Thirty-eight inspections, and
- Two searches.

---

22 Article 334 of the Penal Code, published in the *Official Gazette RS*, No. 55/2008, 66/2008 and 39/2009.

23 The Constitutional court's Case No. P-26/09 (16 December 2009) dealt with a jurisdictional dispute regarding determination of the competent authority. It decided that due to the fact that in accordance with the transitional provision of Article 59 (3) of the Act Amending the Minor Offences Act, Article 14 of the Act Regulating the Export of Dual-Use Goods, which did not allow accelerated proceedings, ceased to apply, and due to the fact that the circumstances determined in Article 52 (2) do not exist, as a result of which accelerated proceedings would not be allowed, the General Customs Directorate has jurisdiction to decide minor offence proceedings.

In the same period they identified seven offences by legal persons and the penalties imposed were fines or reminders.

Conclusion

The Government is currently preparing amendments to the Act Regulating the Control of Exports of Dual-Use Items and the Decree on *the procedures for issuing authorisations and certificates and on competence of the Commission for the control of exports of dual use items*, which are to be adopted by the end of 2011. This indicates the Government is prompt in adopting necessary amendments to align domestic legislation also with the developments within the EU. In any case, there is a safety clause in the Constitution, which would give precedence to the EU legislation even in cases of conflicting domestic provisions.

In the opinion of the competent bodies in Slovenia authorities controlling export of dual-use items generally do not encounter greater challenges in conducting their work, while improvements are required for control of intangible transfers of technology. However, the concern was expressed that only approximately 3 percent of all exports are checked due to the random selection of individual exports to be checked, which is caused by insufficient human resources of the customs administration.

In order to familiarize the industry with the relevant legal framework and procedures for the export of dual-use items the Ministry of the Economy twice a year organises an informative seminar, while customs authorities carry our peer visits to individual companies.

The author of this report however doubts the need of absolute secrecy professed by the Ministry of the Economy with regard to the concrete examples of industries in Slovenia involved in the export of dual-use items, contrary to what seems to be the practice in some other EU Member States. This lack of transparency of governmental control mechanisms' work also deprives non-state actors, in particular non-governmental organisations and individual experts on the topic, to be a part of an additional informal layer of surveillance over the persons (legal or natural) involved in the export of dual-use items.

Bulgaria
Administration of Export Controls

Velislava ZHIVKOVA

International Relations, Section Head,
State Enterprise Radioactive Waste Bulgaria

Introduction

The Bulgarian policy in the field of export control and non-proliferation is subject to commitments under multilateral export control agreements concerning the international sanctions or restrictions under the UN, EU and OSCE. Bulgaria is a party to all multilateral treaties and conventions in this field and actively participates in the multilateral export control regimes – the Australia Group, the Wassenaar Arrangement, the Nuclear Suppliers Group, the Missile Technologies Control Regime and the Zangger Committee – and strictly applies the rules and requirements of these regimes.

The foundations of the export control system in Bulgaria date from the period 1995-1996 with the adoption of the Law on Control of Foreign Trade in Arms and Goods and technologies with possible dual-use (1995) and its Rules for Implementation (1996). In 2002 these documents were amended as the changes introduced were crucial for the realization of the main foreign policy priorities of Bulgaria related to the membership of Bulgaria in NATO and the EU.

Scope and Structure of the Export Control Regime

Control applied both within the frameworks of international organizations and regimes, and at a national level covers certain categories of conventional weapons, related equipment and their means of production as well as a wide range dual-use items and technologies which may be used both for civilian purposes and for the development, production and proliferation of weapons of mass destruction (WMD).

The current legislation maintains the two-level structure of the national export control regimes. Practically, the control of export, import, transit, transfer and transportation, as well as on arms brokering and dual-use items and technologies, is performed at two levels:

– First level of control: Interdepartmental Council for issues regarding the Military Industrial Complex and the Mobilization Readiness of the Country to the Council of Ministers. At this level of control the reliability and stability of natural and legal persons registered under the Trade Act who apply for a licence is assessed.

– Second Level of control: Interdepartmental Commission for Export Control and Non-Proliferation of WMD. At this level of control a supervision of the parameters of the individual transaction prior to the permission of this transaction is performed, taking into account the reality/validity of the presented documents (including verifications through diplomatic channels), the end-user and uses involving other parties in the transaction (freight forwarders, brokers, carriers), the presence/absence of legal and political commitments on bilateral and multilateral basis, the provisions of Common Position 2008/944/CFSP *setting common rules on arms exports*, as well as additional circumstances that may arise in the course of evaluation of each case.

According to Article 71 of ADUITECA,[1] the Interdepartmental Council, the Interministerial Commission, the Minister of Economy, Energy and Tourism, the Minister of Foreign Affairs, the Chair of State Agency for National Security, the Director of National Customs Agency of the Ministry of Finance and their official representatives exercise control over the implementation of this Act.

Legal framework, Authorisation and Enforcement procedures

Legal Framework

After the legal foundations had been laid down in the period 1995-1996 and several further amendments had been introduced, pursuant to the recommendations of the European Commission and in accordance with best practices in this area, the Bulgarian export control legislation was updated in late 2006. In the context of the EU accession on January 1, 2007 in February 2007 a new law – *Arms and Dual-Use Items and Technologies Export Control Act (ADUITEC)*[2] – and its implementing

[1] Promulgated, State Gazette No. 11/2.02.2007, amended, SG No. 109, 20 December 2007, effective 1 January 2008, amended and supplemented, SG No. 36, 4 April 2008, amended, SG No. 82, 16 October 2009, effective 16 October 2009, amended and supplemented, SG No. 13, 16 February 2010.

[2] Promulgated, State Gazette No. 11/2.02.2007, amended, SG No. 109, 20 December 2007, effective 1 January 2008, amended and supplemented, SG No. 36, 4 April

regulations were adopted. The Act reflects the provisions of Council Regulation EU No. 1334/2000, as well as those of the EU Common Position of 2003 for the control of brokering activities. This Act was supplemented by the *Regulation for Implementation of the Law on Export Control of Arms and Dual-Use Items and Technologies.*[3]

In 2009 the law was updated, as the new Council Regulation No. 428/2009, replacing Regulation No. 1334/2000 was incorporated. The latest amendment in the Act is from 16 February, 2010, and aims at a timely implementation of Regulation (EC) 428/2009 *establishing a Community regime of export controls, transfer, brokering and transit of dual-use items and technology.*[4]

The Bulgarian Government adopted and published a list of countries and organizations towards which the Republic of Bulgaria applies prohibitions or restrictions on the sale and supply of arms and related equipments in accordance with United Nations Security Council (UNSC) resolutions and decisions of the EU and the OSCE. The List is constantly being amended; the last amendment is from September 2010.

The last List of Arms and a List of Dual-use Items and Technologies for import was adopted with a Decree (CoM) No. 216 of 30 September 2010.

A *Draft Military Items and Dual-Use Items and Technology Export Control Act*[5] was accepted from the Council of Ministers at the end of 2010. The draft law lays down rules and procedures with respect to products related to defence, which transpose the relevant provisions of Directive 2009/43/EO, taking into account the commitments of the Republic of Bulgaria under international treaties, conventions and regimes in the area of export control and non-proliferation of weapons of mass destruction.[6]

2008, amended, SG No. 82, 16 October 2009, effective 16 October 2009, amended and supplemented, SG No. 13, 16 February 2010.

See: http://exportcontrol.bg/docs/Arms_and_DualUse_Items_and_Technologies_Export_Control_Act.pdf.

3 Adopted by Decree (CoM) No. 72 of 3 April 2007, published in SG, ed. 32 of 17 April 2007, as amended, ed. 39 of 15 May 2007.

4 *Security Policy of the Republic of Bulgaria – Non-proliferation, Disarmament and Arms control*, Ministry of Foreign Affairs website: http://www.mfa.bg/bg/pages/menu/22.

5 Available at: http://www.mee.government.bg/ind/doc_arms/ZAKONOPROEKT_S_OTRAZ_19.11.pdf.

6 Report from Traycho Traikov, Minister of Economy, Energy and Tourism to the Council of Ministers of the Republic of Bulgaria in regards to a project of a Decision of the Council of Ministers for approval of a Draft Military Items and Dual-Use

The Act for the implementation of Council Regulation No. 1236/2005 *concerning trade in certain goods which could be used for capital punishment, torture or other forms of cruel, inhuman or degrading treatment or punishment* was adopted on 16 October 2009.

Authorisation Procedures

Exports, Imports, Transit and Transfers of Arms and Arms Brokerage

According to the current ADUITECA from 16 February 2010, in order to import arms to Bulgaria, one is required to hold:

– A general or limited authorisation for export, import and transfer of arms, issued by the Interdepartmental Council on the Issues of the Military-Industrial Complex and the Mobilization Preparedness of the Country with the Council of Ministers;

– A licence for import of arms, issued by the Interministerial Commission for Export Control and Non-Proliferation of the Weapons of Mass Destruction with the Minister of Economy and Energy.

In order to export arms from Bulgaria, one is required to hold:

– A general or limited authorisation for export, import and transfer of arms, issued by the Interdepartmental Council for the Defence Industry with the Council of Ministers;

– A licence for the export of arms, issued by the Interministerial Commission.

Exporters of arms "shall submit to the Interministerial Commission a delivery verification certificate or its equivalent, including quantity, type, respective identification (serial number, certificate, specification) and the end-user in the transaction, issued by a national competent authority of the country of the end-user and verifying the delivery, but no later than three months after the date of its arrival in the country of the end-user".

To perform *arms transit* through the territory of Bulgaria, one is required to hold a licence for transit of arms, issued by the Interministerial Commission. The transit licence for arms shall indicate the route of passage through the territory of the Republic of Bulgaria and the scheduled date of passage.

To perform *arms transfers* from Bulgaria, one is required to hold:

– A general or limited authorisation for export, import and transfer of arms, issued by the Interdepartmental Council;

Items and Technology Export Control Act. Available at the website of the Ministry of Economy, Energy and Tourism: http://www.mee.government.bg/ind/arms.html.

– A transfer licence for arms, issued by the Interministerial Commission. The authorisation for export, import and transfer of arms may be general or limited with respect of the positions according to the list of arms and/or in terms of the country of the end-user or the exporter. The limited authorisation is issued for no more than three-thirds of the categories of the List of Arms and/or for no more than 5 countries, against which no restrictive measures have been imposed.

To perform *arms brokering*, one is required to hold:

– A registration for brokering, issued by the Interdepartmental Council;

– A licence for brokering transaction with arms, issued by the Interministerial Commission.

Only individuals and legal persons registered under the provisions of the Commercial Act and registered for brokering by the Interdepartmental Council pursuant to the Law on Export Control on Arms and Dual-Use Items and Technologies may carry out arms brokering. The registration to carry out arms brokering is done by the Interdepartmental Council for the period of three years.

Table 1: Export, import, transfer and transit of weapons, 2009

Activity	Number of Authorisations	Value (Euros)
Export and Transfer (mainly to USA, India, Germany and Algeria; 1, 2, 3, 11)	432	145,003,244
Import and Transfer (mainly from Czech Republic, Germany, Ukraine and Serbia)	294	71,801,455
Transit	14	No information available
Total Authorisations Denied	8	No information available

Source: Annual Report of the Interdepartmental Commission for 2009.

Exports, Transfer, Transit and Imports of Dual-Use Items and Brokering with Them

In case that the items you intend to *export* are listed in Annex I of Regulation 428/2009 one has to register with the Interministerial Commission for export.

Once the registration has been processed, one will be given a certificate for registration, valid for three years, and after it expires every following registration shall be for the same period of time. Once one has been registered for export and transfer and holds a certificate for registration, one may file an application for an export authorisation of dual-use items and technologies. Four types of export authorisations are available:

- Individual export authorisation – valid for up to one year, subject to one extension of up to six months. It is issued for a given country by one delivery or by partial deliveries pursuant to trade relations between the exporter and the foreign country party.
- Global export authorisation – valid for up to two years, subject to one extension of up to one year. It is issued for export of a given type or category of dual-use items, stated in Annex I, except for the items, mentioned in part 2 of Annex II of Regulation 428/2009, which is valid for export to one or more countries of dual-use items, stated in part 1 of Annex IV of Regulation 428/2009.
- General export authorisation – it is published by the Interministerial Commission – valid for up to two years, subject to a one time extension for up to one year. The general export authorisation is issued for export of dual-use items of Annex I, except for the items, mentioned in part 2 of Annex IV of Regulation 428/2009. The general export authorisation is published by the Interministerial Commission.
- General export authorisation of the Community.

Exemptions, as set forth in the Arms and Dual-Use Items and Technologies Export Control Act, which also require an export authorisation should be considered.

Table 2: Export of dual-use Items, 2009

Activity	Number of Authorisations	Value (Euros)
Export	19	7,206,021
Realized export	24 (incl. 5 from 2008)	No information available
General Export Licence from the Community No. EU001	(4 companies – 35 exports)	987,367
According to "catch-all" clause, Export	3	2,171,720
Total licences denied	2	No information available

Source: Annual Report of the Interdepartmental Commission for 2009.

Transfer of dual-use items and technologies may be performed by all persons, without being necessary to be registered under the provisions of the Companies Act. Subject to control is the outgoing transfer of dual-use items and technologies. Dual-use items and technologies that are under control at transfer and for which a transfer authorisation is required, are enlisted in Annex IV of Regulation 1167/2008. To be able to make a transfer, one has to register with the Interministerial Commission. Once the registration has been processed, one will be given a certificate for registration valid for 3 years, and after it expires every following registration shall be for the same period of time.

Table 3: Transfer of dual-use Items, 2009

Activity	Number of Authorisations	Value (Euros)
Licences for transfer Granted	5	2,808,272
Licence for transfer Granted realized	6 (incl. 1 from 2008)	2,876,204
Total licences denied	0	0

Source: Annual Report of the Interdepartmental Commission for 2009.

Transit authorisations for dual-use items are issued by the Interdepartmental Commission for each specific case under a procedure specified in the Regulation in the application of this act. The authorisation issued shall have a validity term of up to one year and this may be extended once for a six-month term.[7]

To *import* dual-use items and technologies one does not have to be registered under the provisions of the Companies Act. Only the import has to be registered. The import is registered by the Ministry of Economy and Energy. Dual-use items and technologies that are registered at import are stated in the List of dual-use items and technologies, subject to control at import – Decree (CoM) No. 213, 2 September 2008. The import will be registered within seven days and one will be given an import certificate which is valid for one year and may be extended once for the period of six months.

Table 4: Import of dual-use Items, 2009

Activity	Number of licences Granted	Value (Euros)
Licence for import	32	116,757,141
Licence for realized import	34 (incl. 2 from 2008)	107,585,644
Total licences denied	0	0

Source: Annual Report of the Interdepartmental Commission for 2009.

To carry out *brokerage* with dual-use items and technologies, one must have a registration for brokerage, issued by the Interdepartmental Council. Brokerage with dual-use items and technologies may be carried only by individuals and legal persons, registered under the provisions of the Companies Act and registered for brokerage by the Interdepartmental Council. This registration is for the period of three years.

---

7 *ADUITECA* from 2010, Article 53c(3).

Authorisation Procedures According to the Draft Military Items and Dual-use Items and Technology Export Control Act[8]

This draft of a Law envisages the abolition of the licensing regime for the transfer of products related to defence within the Community as it is replaced by a registration procedure. According to Directive 2009/43/EO, a certification procedure for recipients of products related to defence from other Member States, with which the certified recipients will be able to benefit from the simplified procedure of inclusion in the general authorisations for transfer, published by the Member States of the suppliers. The reliability of the certified Recipients will be assessed based on a number of criteria spelled out in the draft Act. The Interdepartmental Council is the body which will carry out the certification.

The draft law introduces individual, global and general permits for the transfer of products related to defence from the territory of the Republic of Bulgaria to other Member States, and provides for the removal of the permit regime for transfer in certain specific cases listed by the Directive and its replacement with registration. The introduction of new types of permits will allow for the inclusion of more recipients of specific categories of products related to defence in one or more Member States. The publication of a general authorisation for the transfer and the issuing of a global authorisation for transfer of products related to defence from the territory of Bulgaria allows for multiple transfers and the elimination of procedures applications for authorisation of individual transactions. In order to facilitate the procedures for the issuing of permits for export and import, the draft law provides in certain cases and under certain conditions for the issuance of global permits for exports and imports, as well as for the application of registration regimes instead of permit regimes. The Minister of Economy, Energy and Tourism is the body which registers import, export or transfer.

The scope of control of brokering of products related to defence is extended, in terms of the category of persons who may carry out such activities and therefore be subject to control of their activities by the competent authorities which is supplemented with: Bulgarian citizens, nationals of other Member States and citizens of the European Economic Zone which are residents of the Republic of Bulgaria, as well as third-country nationals who are authorized for permanent residence in Bulgaria.

---

8 Report from Traycho Traikov, Minister of Economy, Energy and Tourism to the Council of Ministers regarding a Project of a Decision of the Council of Ministers for approval of a draft Military Items and Dual-use Items and Technology Export Control Act.

The proposed changes will lead to the harmonization of the national legislation with the one of the European Union and to the creation of more favourable business conditions through obsolescence, streamlining and optimizing of most of the current administrative procedures, and will bring additional clarity regarding the rules for the implementation of control measures for activities with products related to defence and dual-use items.

National Jurisdiction: Enforcement Procedures

According to Article 76 ADUITECA (from 16 February 2010) persons who engage in exports, imports, transfers, brokerage, transport and/or transit of arms without the respective licence, registration or authorisation shall be sanctioned with:

– A fine of BGN 5,000 (approximately Euros 2,500) to BGN 50,000 (approximately Euros 25,000) for natural persons and officials of commercial companies in case the committed act does not constitute a crime;

– A property sanction amounting from BGN 25,000 (approximately Euros 12,500) to BGN 250, 000 (approximately Euros 125,000) for legal persons and sole proprietors;

– A fine or a property sanction amounting from BGN 50,000 (approximately Euros 25,000) to BGN 500,000 (approximately Euros 250,000) for an established repeated infringement.

According to Article 77 ADUITECA (from 16 February 2010) persons who engage in exports, imports, transfers, transit and/or brokerage of dual-use items without the respective registration, authorisation or import certificate shall be sanctioned with:

– A fine of BGN 5,000 (approximately Euros 2,500) to BGN 50,000 (approximately Euros 25,000) for natural persons and officials of commercial companies in case the committed act does not constitute a crime;

– A property sanction amounting from BGN 25,000 (approximately Euros 12,500) to BGN 250,000 (approximately Euros 125,000) for legal persons and sole proprietors;

– A fine or a property sanction amounting from BGN 50,000 (approximately Euros 25,000) to BGN 500,000 (approximately Euros 250,000) for an established repeated infringement.

Article 78 ADUITECA (from 16 February 2010) stipulates that persons who engage in activities in contravention to the scope and the terms of an issued authorisation or import certificate fail to present documents, data, information and reports or obstruct and/or refuse access of an official exercising controls under this act shall be sanctioned with:

– A fine of BGN 1,000 (approximately Euros 500) to BGN 10,000 (approximately Euros 5,000) for natural persons and officials of commercial companies in case the committed act does not constitute a crime;

– A property sanction amounting from BGN 5,000 (approximately Euros 2,500) to BGN 50,000 (approximately Euros 250,000) for legal persons and sole proprietors;

– A fine or a property sanction amounting from BGN 10,000 (approximately Euros 5,000) to BGN 100,000 (approximately Euros 50,000) for an established repeated infringement.

According to Article 79 ADUITECA (from 16 February 2010) persons who fail to comply with their obligations under articles 69 and 70 shall be sanctioned with:

– A fine of BGN 2,000 (approximately Euros 1,000) to BGN 20,000 (approximately Euros 10,000) for natural persons and officials of commercial companies in case the committed act does not constitute a crime;

– A property sanction amounting from BGN 10,000 (approximately Euros 5,000) to BGN 100,000 (approximately Euros 50,000) for legal persons and sole proprietors;

– A fine or a property sanction amounting from BGN 20,000 (approximately Euros 10,000) to BGN 200,000 (approximately Euros 100,000) for an established repeated infringement.

Officials appointed by the regulatory body shall draw up acts for ascertainment of violations. The penalty shall be issued by the regulatory body which has ascertained the infringement, or by its authorized official. The ascertainment of violations, issuance, appeal and enforcement of penal provisions shall be made under the Law on Administrative Offences and Penalties.[9]

Conclusions

The Bulgarian Government is aiming at maintaining a contemporary export control system in accordance with the up-to-date European and international standards in this field. Especially with the adoption of the *Draft Military Items and Dual-use Items and Technology Export Control Act* at the legislation level this aim will be to a great extent achieved as the national legal framework will be in compliance with the European

9 As amended in *Official Gazette*, No. 10 of 1 February 2011.

regulations in this area. Nevertheless, enforcement and inter-departmental cooperation has to be strengthened further to provide an even better compliance with the legislative requirements. Electronic communication between ministries and institutions needs to be further boosted in order to achieve improvement in the exchange of information. In terms of industry awareness, however, there is much to be done. Outreach activity with industry including dialogue between political spheres and industrial operators must become more regular in order to encourage companies to implement Culture of compliance and establish internal compliance programmes (ICP).

Croatia

Ivana MICIC

Researcher, Stockholm International Peace Research Institute

Introduction

The Republic of Croatia has been active in its goal to contribute to the non-proliferation of weapons of mass destruction (WMD). Realising this goal comprised the implementation of international obligations and the strengthening of its capacities through establishing and enforcing legislation and procedures on the national level. Since gaining independence in 1991 Republic of Croatia has made significant progress in relatively short time in its non-proliferation efforts, especially taking into consideration the political (post-war) situation, and the fact that at the time Croatia was subject to sanctions,[1] did not attach much importance to non-proliferation issues and had no legal basis for dual-use export controls. The creation of a new export control system was driven by a number of factors, the most important of which was the political decisions to demonstrate that Croatia is a responsible member of the international community and willingness to become a EU Member State. In this context, the demands associated with EU membership – and the need to align national export controls with relevant sections of the *acquis communautaire*[2] – also played a key role. Croatia aspires to become a EU Member State and is hoping to reach that goal by 2012.[3]

1 The United Nations arms embargo against it was lifted in 1995 UN Resolution 1021 (1995) (http://www.un.org/Docs/scres/1995/scres95.htm) and the EU one in 2000 Council Common Position of 20 November 2000 amending Common Position 96/184/CFSP concerning arms exports to the former Yugoslavia (2000/722/CFSP) (http://eurlex.europa.eu/LexUriServ/LexUriServ.do?uri=OJ:L:2000:292:0001:0001:EN:PDF).

2 In order to become a Member State, countries have to accept the *acquis* of the EU. *Acquis* evolves and include among other legislation and decisions adopted, joint actions, common positions, declarations, the case law of the Court of Justice, and capacity to implement them. See: http://ec.europa.eu/enlargement/enlargement_process/accession_process/how_does_a_country_join_the_eu/negotiations_croatia_turkey/index_en.htm.

3 The date of entry is still uncertain.

In order to achieve EU membership, Croatia must align its national laws and regulations with the *acquis*. In this context, Croatia introduced dual-use export controls in 2005, modelled after the EU Dual-Use Regulation[4] and has adopted EU standards such as the Council Joint Action 2000/401/CFSP (of 22 June 2000) *concerning the control of technical assistance related to certain military end-uses*[5] and the Council Common Position 2003/468/CFSP (of 23 June 2003) *on the control of arms brokering*.[6]

Croatia has become an active member of the international non-proliferation community, not only by becoming a member or a signatory country of international non-proliferation agreements and regimes but also in hosting international non-proliferation-related events.[7] Indeed, in 2011 Croatia participates in the following international export control regimes: the Australia Group (AG), the Nuclear Supplier Group (NSG) and the Wassenaar Arrangement (WA), and as well as in the Zangger Committee (ZC).[8] It also applied for membership in the Missile Technology Control Regime (MTCR). Croatia is a party to and member of the main non-proliferation conventions and agreements: the Biological and Toxin Weapons Convention (BTWC), the Chemical Weapons Convention (CWC), the Comprehensive Test-Ban Treaty (CTBT), the Hague Code of Conduct against Ballistic Missile Proliferation (HCOC) and the Nuclear Non-Proliferation Treaty (NPT). It also endorsed the Proliferation Security Initiative (PSI) and the Global Initiative to Combat Nuclear Terrorism (GICNT).

This chapter will describe the Croatian export control system during its process of the EU adhesion. Unless otherwise stated, it will focus on the strategic trade of dual-use items,[9] including export, brokering, and transit/transhipment controls.

---

4 The EU responded to the UNSC Resolution 1540 requirement of transit, transhipment and brokering controls for dual-use items through a revision of the Dual-Use regulation 1334/2000, and adoption of new, "Recast Regulation" – Council Regulation (EC) 428/2009 which came into force in August 2009.

5 See: http://www.consilium.europa.eu/uedocs/cmsUpload/l_15920000630en02160217.pdf.

6 See: http://eurlex.europa.eu/pri/en/oj/dat/2003/l_156/l_15620030625en00790080.pdf.

7 See below: Regional and International Co-operation subchapter.

8 WA and NSG since 2005, ZC since 2006 and AG since 2007.

9 In Croatia, the export of arms and military goods is regulated by a different law: the Act on Export and Import of Military and Non-Military Lethal Goods – an English version can be found on the website: http://kontroaizvoza.mingorp.hr.

Dual-Use Export Control System

Legal Framework

Modelled after the EC Dual-Use Regulation, Croatia adopted the Act on Export of Dual-Use Goods in 2004, which came into force on 1 January 2005. Prior to this point Croatia did not have any legislation in place on these issues. The law was revised and amended in 2008 by adding criminal penalties, control of technical assistance, brokering and transit of dual-use items in order to meet the standards set by UN Security Council Resolution 1540 of 2004.[10]

The EU 428/2009 Recast Regulation was adopted one year after the revised Croatian Act on Export of Dual-Use Goods adopted in 2008. However, the amended Croatian law is in line with the Recast Regulation. One reason for this is the participation of Croatia in EU projects in the field of dual-use export control since 2005.[11] Thanks to this early involvement, Croatian officials drafting the amendments received support from EU legal advisors who were aware of the discussions held on the EU level. Croatia decided to integrate changes and pass the law before the adoption of the Recast Regulation, considering that the remaining discussion at the time was not applicable to non-member States.

As EU membership draws near, Croatia is revising the law again. This time, Croatia plans to include amendments that will come into force as soon as they become a EU member. The new revised law will enable the direct implementation of the EC 428/2009 Regulation in Croatia with additional national provisions/adds-on as foreseen by the EU Regulation.

Alongside the primary law, Croatia adopted secondary pieces of legislation; one for updating control lists[12] which are the same as the EU's; and others on application procedures, such as the Ordinance on Application Form for the Issuance of Export Licence for Dual-Use Items and for Providing Brokering Services and Technical Assistance[13]

---

10 See: http://www.un.org/Docs/sc/unsc_resolutions04.html.

11 The first Pilot Project 04 was implemented by Stockholm International Peace Research Institute (SIPRI) see: www.sipri.org; followed by Pilot Project 05, 06 and Long Term Project – and now EU Programme "EU cooperation in dual-use goods" implemented by the Federal Office of Economics and Export Control (BAFA) see: http://www.eu-outreach.info.

12 Regulation on the List of Dual-Use Items published and updated in *Croatian official journals*: 184/2004, 62/2007, 57/2008, 63/2009 and 3/2010.

13 Published in *Croatian Official Journal* 34/2010, an English version can be found on the website: http://kontrolaizvoza.mingorp.hr.

and the Ordinance on Application Form for the Issuance of Import Certificate for Dual-use Items.[14]

Licensing System

The Croatian Ministry of the Economy, Labour and Entrepreneurship (MELE) is the Authority responsible for issuing licences. In contrast to the EU, Croatia issues only individual and global export licences.[15] General licences per EU standards[16] are not yet applicable in Croatia. The decision to issue or deny an export licence is taken upon the proposal of an Interagency Commission. This Interagency Commission has permanent members from the Ministry of Foreign Affairs and European Integration (MFAEI), Ministry of Interior (MoI), Ministry of Defence (MoD), Customs Administration and MELE, all of whom give their opinion and are involved in the decision making process. However, when needed, representatives from other institutions such as the State Office for Radiological and Nuclear Safety (SORNS), the Ministry of Health and Social Security, the Ministry of the Sea, Transport and Infrastructure (MSTI), the Ministry of Agriculture, Fisheries and Rural Development, the Croatian Chamber of Commerce and the Security and Intelligence Agency (SIA) are also consulted. The interagency cooperation is facilitated by the Tracker system[17] launched in 2009. Tracker is a US-designed information technology tool that links different institutions including the permanent members of the Interagency Commission, and the SORNS, the MISTI and SIA. MELE issues licences through the Tracker System.

MELE describes the evolution of what constitutes the decisive question in issuing or denying a licence. "During the Cold-War period the decisive question was based on national security: 'Is this export going to have negative consequences on the national security of my country? Nowadays the emphasis is not specifically related to national security but to non-proliferation of WMD and even international terrorism: now the main questions are related to the *end-use*: 'Who is the recipient of this export? And what is the purpose of this export?'".[18]

---

14 Published in *Croatian Official Journals* 166/2004 and 123/2007, an English version can be found on the website: http://kontrolaizvoza.mingorp.hr.

15 An individual licence grants permission to an exporter to export a specific item to a specific end-user. A global licence grants permission to an exporter to export more than one type of item to one or more identified end-users (both the items and end-users are stipulated in the licence).

16 Community General Export Authorisation (CGEA).

17 The Tracker system (see: www.trackernet.org) was donated by the US Export Control and Related Border Security Program (EXBS) see: http://exportcontrol.org/.

18 See: http://icp.mingorp.hr.

The assessment criteria for licensing decision are stated in the initial 2005 law. According to the law, a licence will be denied if the export would:

> Threaten the fulfilment of the international obligations of Croatia and the security and defence interests of Croatia or is contrary to its national security strategy; be contrary to the international political and economic interest of Croatia; would enable the out-break and continuation of armed conflict in the country of end-use of goods or the use of the goods for encouraging of riots in the country of end-use of goods. Furthermore, MELE shall refuse the export licence application if the goods are not in accordance with the information stated in the licence, and if upon the request of the Ministry the exporter or the manufacturer does not allow inspection of the goods or and records related to these goods (…).[19]

In 2008, it added an amendment stating "the licence would be denied if the export is contrary to the principles of the European Union Code of Conduct for Arms Exports".[20] Additionally, Croatia has put in place a catch-all[21] mechanism based on the EU model.

Croatia granted 94 export licences for dual-use goods in 2009 and 78 in 2010. Until now there has not been any requests for issuing brokering or/and transit licences.[22]

To date, MELE has not denied any export licences. One of the reasons is that MELE is consulted by companies who have doubts about the export of their items. Consequently the companies generally either withdraw the licence applications or decide not to submit one.

Croatia has brought its export control system in line with the EU's to the extent legally possible. This also applies to the EU Regulation's Annexes, apart from the specific issues which are only applicable to the EU Member States (*e.g.* Annex II and IV and some particular boxes in Annex III).[23]

In 2006 during the EU screening process,[24] Croatia was assessed "to a large extent aligned with the *acquis*" but suggested that "Croatia needs

19 Article 10 of the Act on Export of Dual-Use Items. See: http://kontrolaizvoza.mingorp.hr.

20 Now Council Common Position 2008/944/CFSP of 8 December 2008 *defining common rules governing control of exports of military technology and equipment*, *Official Journal of the European Union*, L335, 13 December 2008.

21 Article 5 of the Act on Export of Dual-Use Items. See: http://kontrolaizvoza.mingorp.hr.

22 Interview Croatian officials.

23 See Council Regulation (EC) No. 428/2009 of 5 May 2009.

24 The Commission has launched the analytical examination, commonly called screening, forms the first phase of accession negotiations. See: http://ec.europa.

to adapt its legislation to the EC rules regarding the *possibility for exporters to change the end-user*".[25] This was a misunderstanding of the legal provision, as the exporter has five days *to inform* MELE in case of the change of the end-user. Furthermore, there is a mechanism of revoking or cancelling a licence in case any of the data has changed, such as the end-user (without notifying the Authority for an approval or issuing of a new licence due to change).[26]

The role of individual officials in the development of Croatian export controls has been important. Since the start of the establishment of the dual-use export control system in MELE, the officials in charge of the two responsible departments[27] have stayed the same and have been active in the development and enhancement of the system. While the procedures and laws are in line with the EU *acquis*, the EU screening process has suggested some improvements regarding personnel (the need of more personnel) and the institutional structure (concerns regarding two departments dealing with dual-use export controls was raised). Like in any administration, a change of personnel may affect the system; particularly significant may be a change if all experience and institutional knowledge is held by only two persons. Since these recommendations were made, MELE has employed additional staff.[28] Even though the system is managed by two different departments, today the cooperation between the two proves to be efficient.

The Dual-Use Industry

Croatia is not a significant producer of dual-use goods. However, its geographic location makes it a potentially important transit state. The majority of firms operating in Croatia that produce dual-use items are multinational companies that are already familiar and compliant with

---

eu/enlargement/enlargement_process/accession_process/how_does_a_country_join_the_eu/negotiations_croatia_turkey/index_en.htm and http://ec.europa.eu/enlargement/pdf/croatia/screening_reports/screening_report_30_hr_internet_en.pdf.

25 See: http://ec.europa.eu/enlargement/pdf/croatia/screening_reports/screening_report_30_hr_internet_en.pdf.

26 Article 14 of the Act on Export of Dual-Use Items. See: http://kontrolaizvoza.mingorp.hr.

27 Trade Policy and International Relations Directorate (Export Control Department) and Directorate for Trade and Internal Market (Department for Weapons and Licences).

28 For now four (in a process of filling two places) officials are foreseen to work at Trade Policy and International Relations Directorate (Export Control Department) and five people are fully employed at Directorate for Trade and Internal Market (Department for Weapons and Licences).

export control requirements.[29] However, due to the complexity and nature of dual-use items, companies might be subject to export controls without being aware that their items are to be controlled. For that reason, MELE annually organises industry outreach events to explain their export control obligations to exporting companies operating in Croatia. In 2009 MELE also produced a handbook for companies[30] and reaches out to industry directly and/or through the Chamber of Commerce. MELE has created a specific "export control" webpage on the MELE website with regularly updated information to facilitate visibility of export control-related information and to provide support for industries.[31]

On the ministry's webpage, it is possible for companies to find guidelines for implementation of a model internal compliance programme (ICP)[32] so that it may successfully conform to Croatia's export control law. The programme has been described by the Croatian government as a "new Internet tool that helps Croatian companies to conduct their business in compliance with International and Croatian standards of export control of strategic goods".[33] The model ICP was introduced by MELE in 2010 and has been implemented on a voluntary basis except for companies, which are applying for a global export licence.

Internal Compliance Programme (ICP)

MELE introduced the model ICP following the philosophy: "We want to increase exports to the fullest extent, but also to ensure legal compliance with all regulations and standards of export controls of the global community".[34]

On the webpage guidelines MELE as a first step explains the importance of export control and of the implementation of ICP for industry. It further highlights the change of dynamic from the previous period, when state-owned entities were responsible for exports and when the responsibility on exporters was minimal, to what MELE defines as the "21st-century model which is based on a partnership and shared responsibility of both state and industry".[35] MELE highlights that

---

29 The biggest exporter of dual-use items (telecommunication equipment) is Ericsson Nikola Tesla.

30 Supported by the "EU Cooperation in Export Control Programme", see below: http://www.eu-outreach.info.

31 *Id.*

32 Donated by US EXBS, see: http://exportcontrol.org/.

33 See: http://icp.mingorp.hr.

34 *Id.*

35 *Id.*

the state's duty is to optimise legitimate trade based on national regulations, while requesting from industries further analysis of the end-users.

As a second step, MELE provides guidance and explanations concerning industry's responsibility in export controls and also highlights the negative consequences for industry of unintentional illegal export, such as the damage to the company if it were discovered that its products had contributed to the proliferation of WMD. Not only would such an incident receive international news coverage that could damage the industry's reputation, but it could also call into question the effectiveness of the Croatian export control system. The ICP website outlines the enforcement of procedures available to Croatian authorities to prevent companies from unintentionally contributing to the spread of WMD. The state can impose a penalty in case of an unintentional export, and having an ICP can be a significant mitigating circumstance when the state determines the penalties.[36] ICP is not compulsory for foreign trade. However, given the benefits it confers to both the state and industry, it is recommended.

Thirdly, MELE provides some of the following examples of export activities which should have in place an ICP in order to ensure that dual-use items do not fall into the wrong hands:

> Companies producing or distributing goods or weapons which could be used in the manufacture of weapons of mass destruction or the missiles that carry these weapons; companies engaged in the production or distribution of dual-use goods; if a company sells products or services of a foreign partner without the knowledge of his intentions regarding the use of the product; delivery of the product outside the country without prior determination of the technical specifications and checking if the export licence is required; transfer of some defence equipment to one embassy, agency or Authority of a foreign government.[37]

As a fourth step, MELE is clarifying all the administrative elements of an ICP which includes guidelines for the establishment of an ICP within a company and a development of a specific manual for industry. Indeed, links to documents can be found on the webpage that help the company to adapt the ICP manual step-by-step. The ICP manual covers issues such as statement of company policy, appointment of employees, record-keeping, training, notification, classification of products and technology, the risk of diversion, processing orders and internal audit.[38] In addition to the manual, the implementation tools are developed in

---

36 *Id.*

37 See: http://icp.mingorp.hr.

38 *Id.*

order to help industry to comply with Croatian export control regulations. The ICP website also lists all references that industry can check, such as national law and procedures for export of dual-use and military items, the EU Regulation, and a list of parties that have been refused the right to export (the "Denied Persons List") established by the Bureau of Industry and Security of the US Department of Commerce.[39]

MELE attaches high importance to its relations with industry and the major role that industry plays in export controls while acknowledging its own responsibility of informing industry of its obligations. As mentioned above, MELE organises a yearly outreach to industry awareness raising event on the export controls obligations and the relating law, and uses this opportunity to inform participants about any changes that have occurred during the previous year. Since launching the ICP, MELE has also been organising workshops on the implementation of the ICP in different regions of Croatia in order to reach out to a greater number of industries and to raise awareness on export controls.

Enforcement (Including Penalties)

The Croatian Customs Administration is responsible for enforcing Croatia's dual-use exports regulations and, by law, it is the agency that "shall conduct the control of the dual-use items export and shall perform conformity assessment of the goods with the export licence".[40] The Customs Administration is a permanent member of the Interagency Commission and works in close cooperation with MELE as well as with the police, border police, intelligence agencies, the foreign office and the prosecutor's office.[41] Since 2008, the Customs Administration's Customs Training Centre has been conducting activities in the field of strengthening administrative capacity by training customs officials through seminars with the main goal being to raise awareness on export controls, including the legal framework, export procedures, investigation procedures, recognition of dual-use items, risk analysis and profiles, and WMD related issues.

The Croatian government has added criminal penalties in a revised 2008 law for breaches of export control law to the administrative penalties already foreseen in the 2005 law. To this effect Article 18a was added which provides the possibility to give sentences of imprisonment

---

39 See: http://www.bis.doc.gov/dpl/thedeniallist.asp.

40 Croatian Act on Amendments to the Act on Export of Dual-Use Items, see: http://kontrolaizvoza.mingorp.hr.

41 See: Presentation "Customs Mobile Teams by Dominik Kozary", Customs Administration, Republic of Croatia, http://exportcontrol.org/.

ranging from six months to five years[42] to any person who breaches export control regulations.

Regional and International Co-operation

Over the last five years, Croatia has become active in the international non-proliferation *fora* and has participated in and organised a number of events regarding this issue. MELE officials have worked with various donors on the issue which has contributed to the development of the dual-use export control system and capacity of absorption by the Croatian government in establishing the system.

The EU was one of the donors which assisted Croatia and it has been one of the first countries to participate in the EU Pilot Project 04, which at the time was implemented by SIPRI.[43] Croatia has remained a partner country of the follow-up Pilot Projects 05 and 06; and Long Term Project (LTP) EU Programme "EU Cooperation in Export Control", implemented by the German Federal Office of Economics and Export Control (BAFA).[44] The country's geographical proximity to the EU and its status as a likely new Member State in the near future – which means that Croatia will soon implement and enforce EU dual-use export controls – has made among other, Croatia a long term partner in the EU Project. Participation in the EU projects has allowed Croatian officials to establish contact with EU colleagues and those from the South-East Europe region, exchange experiences, participate in the various conferences in the EU, and obtain support and assistance in the various seminars and activities; and bring its law in accordance with the EU *acquis*. Another active donor in Croatia is the United States Export Control and Border Security (EXBS) programme which has contributed actively to the development of Tracker and the ICP and the organisation of various export controls-related seminars and workshops. Croatia has also organised seminars in coordination with EU and EXBS programmes, for better cooperation and to avoid duplication of work.

Croatia hosted two significant events on non-proliferation in 2008: the PSI Adriatic Shield 08 Exercise and Ninth International Export Control Conference.[45] With the support of NATO, Croatia organized in 2009 a workshop on developing the National Strategy against Proliferation of Weapons of Mass Destruction. For the purpose of further improving the system for the control of the non-proliferation of WMD, Croatia has decided to start a project for the preparation of the National

42 See: http://kontrolaizvoza.mingorp.hr/default.aspx?id=144.

43 See: http://www.sipri.org/research/disarmament/expcon/ec_activities/eu_projects.

44 See: http://www.eu-outreach.info.

45 See: www.exportcontrol.org.

Strategy against Proliferation of WMD. The ultimate goal is to prepare and adopt the Strategy by the end of 2011 and to make this strategy a model according to which other countries in similar geopolitical environments might prepare their own national strategies.[46]

Together with Romania and NATO/EAPC, in June 2008 Croatia organised a workshop for the countries in the region on the topic of implementing UN Security Council Resolution 1540 in the Regional Arms Control Verification and Implementation Assistance Centre (RACVIAC). Additionally, in 2010 the UN organised a workshop on the "Implementation of United Nations Security Council Resolution 1540 (2004)" in Croatia for the South-East European Cooperation Process (SEECP) countries.[47]

Croatian officials' experience is more and more sought after, not only on the international level but also by donors to share their experience on the regional level. For example, EXBS requested Croatian officials to be speakers in Kosovo to explain the Croatian export control system, and they were requested by SEESAC (the South Eastern and Eastern Europe Clearinghouse for the Control of Small Arms and Light Weapons) to present their expertise on the conventional arms export control side in the FYR of Macedonia.[48] Through the EU Cooperation in Dual-Use Goods Programme, Croatian officials share experience and their challenges in developing and implementing their dual-use export control system with their colleagues from the region. It is important that Croatian officials have a peer-to-peer approach for successful cooperation on the regional level.

Conclusion

The willingness to contribute to non-proliferation coupled with the aspiration of becoming a EU Member State were the driving forces for the Croatian Government, in particular for MELE in establishing a dual-use export control system. Croatia has come a long way in the last twenty years since its independence and has reached major milestones in export controls since establishing its own national system six years ago. While building the new governmental structures and adapting to the market economy, an export control system was one task among many others that had to be taken on. Despite that, Croatia became a model

---

46 Croatian Ministry of Foreign Affairs see: www.mvpei.hr.

47 Republic of Albania, Bosnia and Herzegovina, the Republic of Bulgaria, the Republic of Croatia, the Hellenic Republic, the former Yugoslav Republic of Macedonia, the Republic of Moldova, Montenegro, Romania, the Republic of Serbia, the Republic of Slovenia, and the Republic of Turkey.

48 Interview of Croatian officials.

example for establishing an export control system (and to its relation to industry) in such a short period of time. The access to various international donors and the respective assistance/cooperation programmes as well as the efforts of officials involved and their intention to establish Croatia as a serious and reliable partner on the international level were also important for this success. The driving force behind the process has been the political decision to push for EU membership and the resulting need to align with EU rules and regulations. These factors combined contributed to a relatively rapid establishment of an export control system. Croatia has now brought its systems in line with the EU standards, with some remaining differences not applicable to non-EU members. As stated above, MELE is preparing Croatia's adhesion to the EU and already working on a system that is fully harmonised once Croatia becomes a Member State.

Croatia is perceived as a success story. Nevertheless, a lot of challenges lie ahead during the enforcement phase. Indeed, the system is relatively new and may be tested especially with EU membership. The enhancement of the system will not stop with adhesion to the EU; it might even put more pressure on Croatia. Actually, EU membership will put Croatia's system to the test as it will have to enforce export controls for items produced in other EU Member States and exiting the common customs area *via* Croatia. Additional enforcement capacities and reinforcement of the system will be required as the implementation progresses and new challenges arrive. And last but not least, strategic trade control systems require constant adjustment due to the very nature of the trade they are seeking to control, both ever developing trade patterns of legal business transactions and procurement methods for illegal WMD programmes. Croatia is demonstrating that it takes these challenges seriously and is continuing to be active in the enhancement of its dual-use export control system.

Notes on Contributors

Sara Depauw studied Political and Social Sciences (International Politics) at the University of Antwerp and holds a European Master's Degree in Human Rights and Democratisation (EIUC). In May 2006 she joined the Flemish Peace Institute – a research institute that forms part of the Flemish parliament – where she conducts research and prepares policy advises. Within the research programme on 'arms trade and arms production' she concentrates on the (sub)national, European and international juridical framework of external trade in strategic goods.

Professor Doctor Heinz Gärtner is Professor at the Austrian Institute for International Affairs (OIIP) in Vienna, Austria and lecturer at the University of Vienna. He also acts as a Special Adviser to the Austrian Ministry of Defence. He was academic member of the Austrian delegation of the Wassenaar arms export control arrangement in the framework of the Austrian presidency (2005). He supervised several large projects on NATO, and comprehensive security, and arms control. Heinz Gärtner received the Bruno Kreisky (legendary former Austrian Chancellor) Award for most outstanding Political Books.

Elisa Giangrasso has a Bachelor Degree in International Relations (2006) and a Master degree in EU Governance and International Politics (2009), both obtained at the Faculty of Political Sciences of Catania University (Italy). During her academic curriculum she dealt with several topics concerning security, carrying out researches on the development of a nuclear non-proliferation (NNP) policy at international and European levels. In particular my final thesis, written under Professor Michel's supervision, was focused on the analysis of EU nuclear non-proliferation policy and its role in the Iranian case, through the lenses of different theoretical approaches on EU integration process.

Doctor Jakub Handrlica is Assistant Professor at the Department of Administrative Law and Science, Law Faculty, Charles University in Prague. He is member of the International Nuclear Law Association, Czech Nuclear Association and of the Energy Law Research Forum. He deals primary with Nuclear Law in his research.

Doctor Odette Jankowitsch-Prevor is a distinguished expert in general nuclear law, radiation protection and safety and security legislation, including non-proliferation and international anti-terrorism norms. Being an IAEA consultant she acts as government advisor and provides lectures at national and regional training seminars. Moreover

Mrs Jankowitsch-Prevor is a lecturer at International School for Nuclear law and ESARDA. In addition to prominent career in IAEA, she held several UN posts in UNIDO and UNESCO.

Irena Kołakowska is a Licensing Officer in the Ministry of Foreign Affairs of the Republic of Poland since 2008. Responsible for assessment of license applications her main domain is the risk analysis. She also covers the Wassenaar Arrangement on Export Controls for Conventional Arms and Dual-Use Goods and Technologies. She also carried out outreach seminars for defence industry. Graduated from Warsaw University, Faculty of International Relations.

Professor Doctor Quentin Michel is Professor in European Studies at the Department of Political Science, University of Liège. He has worked as an "Expert National Détaché" for the EU Commission (DG Trade Unit E4 Dual-Use Export Control). In addition, he also regularly assumes expertise related to export control regime for national, European and international organisations and fora. Since 2009, he edits and makes available online an analysis of *The European Union Export Control Regime: Comment of the legislation article by article*, which he updates regularly, for the benefit of scientists, industries, lawyers and political actors.

Ivana Micic is a Researcher with the Stockholm International Peace Research Institute's (SIPRI) Arms Control and Non-proliferation Programme. In addition to research work on trade controls and non-proliferation issues, she has designed and implemented a range of capacity-building activities – at the regional and national levels – to strengthen trade control systems in South Eastern Europe. In 2008-2009 she worked on the implementation of SIPRI's project on strengthening capacities to investigate and prosecute export control violations in South Eastern Europe. Prior to joining SIPRI in 2007 she undertook research on security sector reform and on South East European border controls. She contributed to the SIPRI Yearbook since 2010.

Sylvain Paile is a Researcher at the European Studies Unit of the University of Liège. He holds Master degrees in International and European Public Law as well as Political Science and his researches focus on the European security and defence, notably through the aspects covered by the regulations of the sensitive items' trade. He graduated also from the International School of Nuclear Law (University of Montpellier 1 – OECD/NEA) in 2010 and is a member of the International Nuclear Law Association.

Doctor Vasilka Sancin is an Assistant Professor of International Law at the Faculty of Law, University of Ljubljana and an expert adviser to the Ministry of Foreign Affairs on issues of international law. Among others, she is a member of the Nuclear weapons, non-proliferation & contemporary international law Committee of the International Law Association and of the International Nuclear Law Association.

Miguel Sousa Ferro is counsel at Sérvulo & Associados (Lisbon) and a doctoral candidate at the University of Lisbon Law School. He obtained his law degree at the same Law School, holds a Masters in European Studies from the College of Europe (Bruges) and the Diploma in International Nuclear Law from the University of Montpellier. He has published on several issues of Nuclear Law, Competition Law and European Law.

Doctor Laszlo Stefan has worked for a number of years in export controls at the Export Control Section of the Authority of Defence Industry and Export Controls in Hungary. He has studied Philosophy and obtained a Master's Degree at the University of Vienna (2005), and a degree in Law and State Sciences at the Catholic University of Pázmány Péter in Budapest (2001). Later he acquired a post-graduate Diploma on European Law and Diplomacy (2002).

Claudia Topp is a Franco-German jurist specialized in Public international law. She began her career as a lecturer at the University of Toulouse I. Afterwards, she had positions within the legal direction of Siemens SAS in Paris and she was company lawyer and director of the Public Relations and Marketing department in the legal editing house Lexxion in Berlin. She has worked for the last five years within the framework of export control in Germany and she is preparing her doctoral thesis in this field.

Maryna Tsukanova is a Researcher at the European Studies Unit of the University of Liège. She holds Master degrees in Computer Science and in Political Science. Her main fields of research cover strategic trade matters as well as international export control regimes. She collaborates with the Joint Research Centre of the European Commission (JRC) for issues related to the use of trade data for export controls and participates in the EU Outreach Projects.

Anna Wetter is a PhD candidate at the Law Faculty at Uppsala University, studying European criminal law through the case study of the EU's regulation for exports of dual-use goods. Before joining the PhD program, Wetter was employed by the Stockholm International Peace Research Institute (SIPRI) for a period of four years, during which she was working on a European Commission funded project on the EU's regime for controlling exports of dual-use products.

Velislava Zhivkova holds an LLM in International and Comparative Nuclear Law and Policy from the University of Dundee (UK) a postgraduate diploma in International Nuclear Law from the University of

Montpellier I, France and a Bachelor degree in Nuclear Technologies and Nuclear Power Engineering from the University of Sofia, Bulgaria. She is currently working with the State Enterprise for Radioactive Waste in Bulgaria, where she is participating in the fulfilling of State's obligations under the International Export Control Regimes related to nuclear materials.

Non-Proliferation

Cette collection a pour principal objectif de traiter les différents aspects de la problématique des risques associés aux activités humaines. Parmi celles-ci, le développement scientifique, technologique et économique s'impose de plus en plus comme un moteur fondamental du changement social. Dans cette perspective, le concept de risque se révèle un outil pertinent d'analyse des processus de transformation sociale. À titre d'exemple, les recherches en génie génétique, de même que l'utilisation civile de technologie militaire, soulèvent inévitablement des questions d'éthique, de santé publique, d'environnement et de gestion des politiques publiques. Il est dès lors souhaitable d'envisager la problématique des risques à la lumière d'une approche multidisciplinaire qui mobilise tant la communauté scientifique que le monde politique et économique, voire même la société civile. Cette collection intègre des monographies et des ouvrages collectifs, principalement en langue française ou anglaise.

Series Editor

Quentin Michel and Sébastien Brunet

Published Books

N° 5 – Quentin MICHEL (ed.), *Sensitive Trade. The Perspective of European States*, 2011

N° 4 – Quentin MICHEL (ed.), *Terrorisme. Regards croisés / Terrorism. Cross Analysis*, 2005

N° 3 – Sébastien BRUNET, Anne BERGMANS, Anne BERTRAND & Patrick BIREN (dir.), *L'expertise en questions. Domestiquer l'incertitude dans la société du risque*, 2002

N° 2 – Pierre HUPET (dir.), *Risque et systèmes complexes. Les enjeux de la communication*, 2001

N° 1 – CD-Rom, Quentin MICHEL, *Articles nucléaires et articles à double usage : régulation du commerce au sein de l'Union européenne. Doctrine, jurisprudence et législation*, 2001

MIX
Papier | Fördert gute Waldnutzung
FSC® C083411

Kolibri 360 GmbH
Ferdinand-Jühlke-Straße 7
99095 Erfurt, Deutschland
produktsicherheit@kolibri360.de